UPCOMING CHANGES

PROPHECY & PRAGMATISM
FOR THE LATE NINETIES

UPCOMING CHANGES

PROPHECY & PRAGMATISM
FOR THE LATE NINETIES

A Michael Book
by Joya Pope

EMERALD WAVE
Fayetteville, AR

UPCOMING CHANGES:

PROPHECY AND PRAGMATISM

FOR THE LATE NINETIES

Copyright © 1995
Joya Pope

Printed and bound in the United States of America.
Cover design and title pages by Karen Briggs Smelser.
ISBN 0-942531-38-8

$13.95

EMERALD WAVE
FAYETTEVILLE ARKANSAS

To all the healers, seen and unseen —
most especially to Duane.

C O N T E N T S

ACKNOWLEDGMENTS

Thanks first go to Michael for unwavering support throughout this project and for being an incredible and credible source of information and synthesis.

There are many people to thank for their support with this project. Tim Vaslett's kind, interested, and persevering help with channeling questions and focus was absolutely invaluable. He encouraged me to open up many new areas of dialogue and discovery.

Janice Kegler first helped me clarify what the scope of this book was to be. Lia Marie Danks prompted me to begin the book, beautifully and smoothly as is her way, this about two minutes after I'd moved to Arkansas from California! My many conversations with Dan Vega whose profound sense of oneness with the Earth, its creatures and its potential for change helped me stay clear-eyed and strong of heart while immersed in certain parts of this book. Ultimately because of him, I asked Michael better questions about environmental change and gained inner understanding and peace sooner than I might have otherwise.

Big thanks must go to Addie Adamson for patiently reading and helping with language in so many stages of this book and to Carrie Trinka, for her diligence, detail orientation, and valuable suggestions. Donna Henschell offered fruitful commentary and exceedingly kind and loving support. Thanks also to Roger Henry for transcribing tapes which were rarely easy to transcribe and for quickly re-typing certain chapters when computer glitches made them inaccessible. I very much appreciate Karen Smelser's grace, beauty, and energy, and her talent in bringing ideas into full graphic life.

Duane Hall again found himself without his pal and social partner as I disappeared into my Mac, but he gently kept me in good shape and good spirits nevertheless — though he too wished books weren't such bizarrely dominating, all-encompassing time-consuming projects!

FOREWORD

After experiencing and experimenting with many of the spiritual disciplines and growth offerings that became abundantly available in the late 60s and 70s, I learned to channel. For a few years, I channeled my higher-self and some other wonderful beings who tended towards statements like, "Trust. Don't worry, we are with you." While this always felt extremely soothing on an energetic level, which I liked, I did not usually quit worrying about whatever it was I was worrying about. While I was bringing in loving support, I obviously wasn't receiving the level of information or a philosophical point of view which could help me grapple with the actual circumstances of my day-to-day life. Before long, channeling fell into disuse.

Then in 1984, I was introduced directly to Michael by JP Van Hulle. Before long, I asked for and began receiving communication from Michael. With a strong desire for clear, specific, intellectually valid information and this amazing new source, channeling now felt worthwhile and exciting. By 1987 I was completing my first book on Michael's material about human personality and behavior, and my work had become writing, teaching, and channeling, exclusively.

Convinced more recently of the need for a realistic look at some of the prospects for the next ten years, I once again started spending days and months with Michael and my Mac. In writing and in the private readings I do, my greatest personal satisfaction seems to come from being able to present a perspective which helps people breathe easier because life, warts and all, suddenly makes better sense — intellctually and emotionally. I hope the observations and ideas presented here will serve as useful steering for you and assist in keeping our world stable and us inspired throughout this period of change.

Jolting anyone out of a pleasant sleep or life of comfort with words about fast change and possibilities of danger was not my idea of a good time. In fact, I abhorred the idea, though I finally became convinced mid-stream that apathy was worse than stirring up fears. I was being internally pushed to write, or believe me, I'd have been out adventuring in my new part of the country much more often. I did receive, quite to my surprise, some strong prodding from Michael when my proportion of fooling around was high compared to the time I was spending on this book.

We are turning here, on a dime. You can position yourself consciously or unconsciously. Conscious is usually better. How we all choose to view change and manage it, whether growing and transforming, sputtering with anger and fear, or withdrawing into ourselves and shutting down, becomes the passageway not only to our individual futures, but also to our collective future as well, and another major reason for this book.

Joya Pope
April 1995

A note on English usage:

Most Michael channeling became direct, that is, oral, years ago. At that point the English started sounding more natural than the Ouija-board formality of the earliest Michael books, the *Messages from Michael* series by Chelsea Quinn Yarbro.

Spoken communication, channeling included, doesn't often make for an ideal page. Speaking and writing are very different forms of communication. What you have in your hands is the result of my work with the reams of material channeled for this book. It is a collaborative effort, written in Michael's voice.

I had best make a few points here about pronoun usage. Michael, as you may know, is not an individual, but the group consciousness of just over a thousand souls who have completed all earth lifetimes and are now teaching from another plane of existence, two steps away from this, the physical plane. In conversation, I refer to the group energy that is "Michael" as "he" (and not "they"), because that is what makes sense in English. Michael, however, refers to himself as "we", which is how the text reads because it is in "his" voice.

Instead of using only male pronouns to refer to humans of both sexes, or the cumbersome he/she, him/her, etc., one or the other, male or female, is used here interchangeably.

And when old words die out on the tongue,
new melodies break forth from the heart;
and where the old tracks are lost,
new country is revealed with its wonders.
—Rabindranath Tagore, Gitanjali

May you live in interesting times.
—Chinese curse

ONE

Interesting Times
Old Patterns, Coming Patterns

There will be no day or days then when a New
World Order comes into being. Step by step
and here and there it will arrive, and, even
as it comes into being it will develop fresh
perspectives, discover unsuspected problems,
and go on to new adventures.
—H.G. Wells

God is day and night, winter and summer,
war and peace, surfeit and hunger.
—Heraclitus

A PARADOX
The future is ever-changing. All you do changes it. Your actions change your personal future and eventually mass events too.
Yet, people are fairly predictable, and out of this comes the ability to prophesy.

Earth is at a crux point, with many futures available. None involve pleasantly coasting along or living as unconsciously as in the present. The Earth can't take it. But how beauteous or how austere Earth becomes is yours to choose. That choice ever so greatly will affect your future and your future lives. The image of a peaceful world with a healed natural environment is a good philosophical start. Practically applying the principles that would allow the world to prosper in such a way is the next vital step.

NEW VISION

This is a great time and a precarious time. Transitions often pit all that will be against all that was in a narrow bottleneck, where everything heats up for a while. In this narrow passage, the world's ways are quickly changing; the old story is being rewritten, the tune updated.

Thank your higher selves for having you in a body, roaming through these milepost decades of human evolutionary history (though at nearly six billion, the whole gang of available souls is pretty much collected). You all desired to monitor and experience the widespread twists, shifts, and whorls of this complex and consequential era. You may also be incarnate in order to aid world transformation, to accelerate, or perhaps ease, these late-century developments, to protect your future as you create it.

Tales of great social and political change are in your newspapers and your faces daily. The crash of the Berlin wall was the first loud clue to the immensity of what was to come. Dictators, medals, statues and all, have nearly vanished. Worldwide economic boycotts of South Africa peacefully broke the apartheid system, and found the country transitioning into black rule with surprising grace and steadiness. Mozambique, badly broken by South Africa and western powers, has hired the Transcendental Meditation folks to help it heal and rebuild. Eastern Europe won enough freedom to hang itself or fly, and is busily doing both. Britain is finally released North Ireland to decide its own future. Bottom-of-the-barrel peasants in Chiapas, Mexico startlingly and elegantly let the world know of their despair with government policies. They were not crushed, but negotiated with. The Russian people haven't worked through the current disarray, but they courageously felled a coup by the old boys. Anita Hill gave American women the focus to fell other old boy systems. Incest, child, and spousal abuse popped out of the back room and on to media discussion tables. More and more people are refusing to be denied their basic rights. Los Angeles erupted after the judicial system (once again) ignored racially-oriented police violence. Amnesty International is no longer half-gagged, but enjoys new potency.

Western Europe is negotiating away on thousands of differences, aiming to open borders to unite countries that have perennially irked and warred with one another. All grow stronger and richer with this cooperation. Suddenly there is scant public tolerance for financial corruption in high places; politicians worldwide fumble in bright view, making ethics a newly interesting subject. Italy shook off its do-nothing cynicism and has been busily rooting out multi-layered governmental and Mafia corruption. The unprincipled, monetarily entrenched healthcare system in the U.S. is receiving some of the critical attention it deserves.

Along with this good news comes a crushing amount of violent behavior. Social violence continues to escalate in the U.S., Latin America, Russia, and even Japan. Political violence is on the rise in numerous places all over the world. And as dictatorships fall, previously suppressed ethnic disputes are rising to the surface and being played out violently.

Any period of great metamorphosis tends to cause formidable economic problems; financial systems march easily with stability, but not with change. The long-rich United States sometimes stumbles, its deficit-spending economy problematic, but then Western Europe, Japan, and even the Gulf States are having money issues too. The impetuous spending of the 80s now seems excessive, even downright dangerous to Congressmen as well as to millions of former shopping addicts.

So what about Peace and a Golden New Age, you say? Well, you will savor hints of both, but for now the transition phase itself will continue grabbing your attention in a fairly satisfying way. Reality is going to look pretty fascinating — and remain pretty fluid. Certainly you have a challenging interval here with an adamant, sometimes ferocious, backlash mulishly attempting to stop change with nary a smile towards the young future. Still this is a period bound to thrill most of our readers to their very cores because of the major value changes which will ultimately deliver needed relief to all life on the planet. The 90s will bring to an abrupt end many old ways of thinking and see the emergence of many new approaches to collective life on Earth. Already you are living in a quickly shifting borderland between one age and another. The five mid-decade years will see chaos, disintegration and breakdown, but new honesty, creativity, and social innovation will open many new doors. The reluctance of society to confront certain issues will weaken by necessity.

It is specifically new vision and novel trailblazing that will keep these years from feeling like the Depression era's gray survival mode. Cultural transformation happens in sputtering fits and starts. While the 90s may feel like bumps and grinds, surging forward only to lapse into sudden amnesia or regression into crazed backlashes, the alterations will be positive and pervasive. Since the whole surface of life everywhere will have an unsteady quality, the steadier your vision, the better. The more you are able to inspire others with a sense of possibilities, the better. Humans will be letting go of much, but building fresher, more workable societies and giving the Earth a chance to heal.

Common rights and community rights are on the verge of taking on new importance. The current primacy of individual rights and freedoms, which allow each person to do whatever he or she wants (a concept widely valued in Western civilization but mocked by Muslims and hardly comprehended by Asians), will come under increasing scrutiny as society frays. Individuals will be called on to be more responsible to the whole, more socially responsible. People will be asking very basic questions: How do you stop the downward spiral of the natural world? What can be done to restrain human numbers? How can you get all children nourished and educated, and adults productive and happy? What kinds of governmental or social systems support, motivate, and bring out higher potentials in people? What is affordable? What saves the Earth? How can I help? Even the question of how to transition out of petroleum use is put on the discussion table.

CHICKEN OR THE EGG?

Mass consciousness is in the process of changing significantly. Major inner changes are always reflected in the physical world. The first and primary shift is a shift in individual consciousness; from that all else follows. Humanity right now is experiencing one of the most momentous and interesting transitions in collective consciousness that it will ever make. These shifts in perception are already deeply changing the way societies collectively think, feel, and act.

The future can best be spoken of in terms of probabilities. People create it and people have a certain degree of free will to change it. Collectively humans create policies, modify events, and the future — though at this point in time the Earth can hardly be called an inactive participant. From our perspective, it still appears unlikely that this decade, or the next few, will be as apocalyptic as Nostradamus, Edgar Cayce, or many others have predicted. Consciousness has moved along a little better than expected.

Nevertheless, the planet is due for an increasing degree of foundation rattling, provoked by humanity's chaos as well as by volcanic and earthquake activity, harsher weather patterns, subsequent economic downturns, food shortages, insect surges, and new health concerns. While this may appear more Gray 90s than Gay, in retrospect the decade will stir fondness because people will have discovered more fulfilling ways of living, both individually

13

and within their local and world communities.

We want to speak to you in fair detail about the nature of this consciousness change, as well as how it may manifest in the world. We'll discuss the many ways in which the Earth itself is pushing these changes along. And we wish to speak to you about developing a perspective and a personal spirituality that is neither magical thinking — burying a saint's statue head down in the yard until your favor is granted — nor a blind faith that exiles your intellect, and responsibility, to the back forty — the Space Brothers are coming to ascend "us" from this mess. Peace means being centered, serene during the storm, not taking yourself, guns, dogs, and dehydrated foods to some survivalist's haven only to be perpetually on guard.

Many of the coming years will be exciting; all will be challenging. The more centered you can remain, the more creative you will be and the more happy to be alive — and then, you will be doing your part to bring about a peaceful shift.

T W O

Mass Consciousness
The Shifts of the 90s

The 1990s sure aren't like the 1980s.
—Donald Trump

We must indeed all hang together,
or, most assuredly, we shall all hang separately.
—Ben Franklin

A WORD ABOUT CONSCIOUSNESS
Consciousness is all. Everything begins here, inseparable from everything else. Should you feel stuck, helpless and convinced that nothing you can do will ever make a difference, then you aren't likely to change your diet for the better, learn to meditate, prepare for new work — or plug the cracks around the door that the wind sings through. Conversely, should you believe that what you think and do makes a difference, you are immediately empowered, more lively and upbeat and, no surprise, the quality of your life improves. Though what's on the move in mass consciousness doesn't fit neatly into this helpless/empowered dichotomy, the example does demonstrate one simple way consciousness works and why it's important.

Consciousness flows to you from your soul or essence, and also comes from the past life experience and wisdom you carry within. It filters through the personality traits you have chosen to work with this lifetime. (Some people are born upbeat, others cynical; some may look at life with such caution that they hardly dare move, while others are impulsive or aggressive.) Your consciousness is affected by the mind-set of others, most especially your parents — and the mentors and gurus you later choose. It is affected by your society's values. And it is affected by the new quality of light and energy coming to the planet to support these current changes.

Some lifetimes are slow, full of little but dull repetition; others flow comfortably; still others move with ground-shaking quickness, continually packing in major experience and growth. Sometimes a person, or society, is able to breeze along, easily stretching to adjust as circumstances change. Other times, change drags a person or country with it, kicking and complaining. The human personality is almost always happier with a little foreshadowing, allowing it to anticipate and prepare.

CHANGING GEARS AFTER 2500 YEARS

The 90s will birth about as much change in the way people think and act and as much consciousness growth as the last four decades put together. Given the last four decades, this is bound to strain the imagination. The pace of the twentieth century is still increasing, pushing people and their social systems to grow quickly and then be ready to move again. Political systems will be pressed to catch up.

Consciousness, whether individual or collective, tends to have a life of its own. For instance, the hyper-materialism of the 80s will likely cause those years to remain known as the "Greed Decade". Crave, buy, charge, steal. Show off those material goods. Enjoy your toys. These values permeated life just a decade ago. Apparently the U.S. and a good part of the Western world needed one last gagging look at me-first materialism before something new could truly emerge.

The 90s are not about greed; you realize that already. Awareness is growing that present systems — political, environmental, educational, economic, and social — are out-of-date and not handling increasing levels of people and problems. Many are breaking down of their own accord, some through their own corruption. The times are ripe for a primary rearrangement of human priorities. Getting rid of so much that is old may mean "Detox Decade" will be the label that eventually sticks on the 90s.

The five mid-decade years especially will see incredibly fast movement, a monumental shift really, in the way humans live, act, and interact. Shifts of this magnitude don't happen often or at random on a planet; there is a predictable pattern we can share with you, a sequence to epochal change of this nature (though having a sequence does not necessarily prevent chaos in-process).

Planet Earth is thrashing about in this its third major planetary consciousness shift. This particular shift is always the most intriguing and difficult juncture of all on any planet, full of the most hopeful potentials, and packed with chaos and resistance.[1] In order to throw some light on current change, it would be helpful first to briefly focus on each of the prior shifts in global consciousness.

CONSCIOUSNESS SHIFT #1

Earth's first major transition occurred back in what is prehistory to you now when large numbers of your ancestors began moving out of simple survival situations (and survival consciousness) with nomadic, hunting and gathering, or early agricultural lifestyles. Enough among them had mastered the natural world that they began collecting together, to share the ideas that ultimately allowed more complex and interesting societies to de-

---

[1] Every planet with sentient, conscious beings on it goes (grows) through the same patterns, even though the creatures are very different from humans — peaceful, non-tool-users for instance.

velop. They found that human existence could be made more dependable when people cooperated and concentrated on putting more order into their manner of living. Leaders were indispensable in creating change like this, but many ordinary people must always be involved or little happens.

Consciousness is always reflected in life. As people moved towards more interaction and collaboration and towards a set of agreed on behaviors they gave birth to great agrarian civilizations of the Neolithic period. This movement away from loose bands and clans to more complicated communities was the first widespread social rearrangement in human cultural evolution. It provoked monumental changes in the way most people lived. And it was first and foremost a consciousness shift.

These early societies developed with the belief that if existence were carefully organized and everyone followed well-defined rules, life could be good for all. You controlled yourself, others if necessary, and the environment to the degree possible, with the hope and belief that life would then flow smoothly. And, in fact, people did begin to enjoy the security that a more regimented existence could give. Codes of laws were issued, dictionaries and encyclopedias compiled, calendars became accurate, sundials came into being, and many, many holidays and feast days were celebrated.

Prior to this shift, the job description for most men included hunting or fishing, protection and construction, while women generally gathered seasonal foods, grew some foodstuffs, managed cooking, child-care, and crafted baskets, pots, and clothing as needed. Now, with life becoming more organized, labor became more specialized. Societies developed to the point that people were able to become apprentices — and masters — in certain arenas, perhaps as a priestess, healer, or midwife, or as an irrigation or agricultural specialist, animal expert, builder, or clay, metal or leather, worker.

A predominantly Goddess-oriented spirituality arose: God was a woman in all the places where these breakthroughs in social and material technology were made. The feminine principle tends naturally towards identity with life and nature, and, in fact, both were revered. The power of the Goddess was to give goodness to life, to nurture and love, not to punish or exact obedience. Quite different from the Gods of the next consciousness period, the ones with whom you are so familiar.

Because mere survival was no longer the prime issue, people became increasingly community centered, lives became more assured and, as you may have noticed from the art of the period, more celebratory. Times were so comfortable and truly civilized that most people were able to live without protective walls surrounding their communities and cities. Throughout Europe, India, Mesopotamia, and Arabia in this period, village sites were most often chosen for beauty, good water, soil and pasture, not for their defensive value. The people of this era enjoyed the abundance they had brought to life, creating things of beauty and technologies of production, not destruction. When metals started being worked, they became decorative objects, religious items or tools, not usually swords or spears. Sounds rather like an implausible fairy tale now, doesn't it? Hold on, there's more.

As can still be seen from extant grave and housing sites, people shared without much hierarchy; women were perhaps a little more "on top", though in most places they didn't subjugate others, including men; nor did a class of priests, rulers, police, or army exist to corner the wealth or labor of these citizens. For thousands of years, many human societies were able to live with little social inequality or violence, in a manner quite different from the norm of the last 2500 years.

The overall regard for rules, laws, and cooperative effort were the new, compelling consciousness elements that pervaded these several thousand years and made quite a turnabout from the survival consciousness of the previous period. In turn, these early societies were so radically different from what followed them that it became difficult, even just a few generations out, to believe what was said about life in the "golden times."

"All good things were theirs. In peaceful ease they kept their lands with good abundance, rich in flocks and dear to the immortals." This from Hesiod, a Greek poet, describes what many of his time had heard rumored of a "golden race". Hesiod was in fact referring to these societies, which were by his time of 700 B.C.E. mostly gone, their cities demolished, the people scattered bands of migrants. Gods and spears were taking over from the Goddess.

It was nigh impossible for the anthropologists of the nineteenth and twentieth centuries to look at the physical evidence they'd dug up with unjaded eyes and free minds. To them, these unfortified societies looked weak and defenseless. The lack of hierarchy was seen as primitive; they couldn't imagine that it might be a blessing. The seeming importance given to women was too incomprehensible a notion to draw much of their attention. It is unusually difficult to think outside your cultural norms. Few manage.

"Let's cooperate, pay attention to rules and make our communities work for everybody." This was the type of consciousness that generally held sway on the Earth from about 10,000 B.C E. until these communities were fractured in the period leading up to the time of the three infinite souls, Lao-Tse, Buddha, and Christ. Infinite souls manifest in times of transition and great need to nurture and support change, but also to aid stability. The lengthy and uneven transition period between the two eras contained especial violence in the the time leading up to the birth of these great souls.

These consciousness periods we are describing to you are not monolithic, with every community, state, or country evenly exhibiting these civilized, collaborative qualities. Always some societies and some individuals will be off doing their own things on different time schedules, ahead or behind, but out of sync with the flow of mainstream thinking. (Many of you who are old souls now have personal experience of this in almost every lifetime!) Some areas were able to remain safe and peaceful longer, connected to the values of the past. Other societies forged ahead into the new experience very early.

CONSCIOUSNESS SHIFT #2

What changed? What was it that caused the violence that pushed these societies to the brink and eventually eclipsed them? Consciousness, of course, and from it people's actions. Change welled up from within in some societies, like Egypt, which shifted very early to a primarily male-dominated, hierarchical form of government which included slavery.[2] In other societies, change came riding in with outside forces. Can you pull up those memories of invading hordes of barbarians surging down from the North, the nightmare that wouldn't go away? Their Gods were swords and blood and action. No reverence for stable social organization, for mystical or religious experience; in fact, not much reverence for life. Barbarians, Huns, Goths, and Vandals terrified pastoral people and their peaceful communities, destroying the pleasant fabric of millions of lives.

Power was what they worshiped. They used their knowledge of metallurgy to make daggers, spears, and swords. Warlike, destructive, and growing in numbers and ferocity, they invaded in waves, knocking out countless settled communities in Old Europe and the Middle East, creating great masses of refugees for well over one thousand years.

But it wasn't just these ruthless souls from the North exhibiting newer, aggressive behaviors. People everywhere were starting to change. The high regard many had previously held for cooperative orderly behavior began to feel spiritless, impotent, chumpy. An individualistic urge to dominate anything perceived to be weaker took hold early within some people, cultures, and countries and later in others.

Phoenicians funneled their people's new sense of independence into exploration, colonies, and trade. The Mayans built

---

2 Atlantis was a highly structured, highly technological society that existed as an enclave in a fairly primitive world. Its actions caused its own demise about 14,000 years ago.

great cities, feudalized the countryside, and enslaved people they "won" in wars. A great empire was formed in India, and the caste system set in place. The Jews, after being roughly expelled from Egypt, nabbed Jerusalem for themselves, causing horrendous carnage along the way. Sparta made a life philosophy out of its warrior-like ways, and pridefully experimented with chemical warfare. The Assyrians launched into the wars which ultimately ruined it. Women lost their civil rights everywhere. The Persians and Greeks gleefully fought everybody. Alexander the Great terrorized continents in his bloody quest to conquer the known world. Rough and powerful Rome proved lethal, not only to the soulful Etruscans.

As chronic warfare, invasions and dislocations became par for this period, the old partnership ways of thinking went. People started thinking individualistically and egotistically, no longer of the whole. This was the era of fortress and wall building, now necessary to keep out new enemies. Attunement with nature disappeared, replaced by fierce, dominating behaviors which worked not only to the detriment of cowering majorities but to the detriment of the natural world. The new consciousness counseled: Fight for your own advantage in every situation. The weak deserve contempt. Winner take all and power to him. "Him," because, typically, people in women's bodies weren't so easily able to take direct advantage of this shift in values.[3]

As outrageously unpleasant and bloody as all this was, it was not a wrong turn for history. Rather, the shift was a normal part of a larger growth experience that had many positive points as well as the misery of the negatives. This third period always sees a move away from cooperative community structure to pushy, combative, individualistic, me-first ways of being. Humans grow through participating in these behaviors, gradually becoming more assured, energetic, confident, in-control beings. They are

[3] Riane Eisler's book, *The Chalice & The Blade*, beautifully describes both the Neolithic period and Goddess worship as well as the crushing of those agrarian communities. Michael says she has somewhat over-idealized the era, but that it is an excellent antidote to what male historians and anthropologists have traditionally done and to the history you have grown up with.

not compassionate or charitable, though, because impressing their will on the world suddenly takes precedence over anybody's hurt feelings or hard times. The individual ability to assert wins out over common values and rights for the community at large.

On any planet with sentient, self-aware life (there are many), the sentient beings must first work through physical survival issues in their environment, and then work on social order and the attempt to assure predictability. Once this cooperative community phase is accomplished, the urge grows to push the limits and discover what happens. On the positive side, it is a move into a fearless kind of thinking which encourages and supports individuation, daring exploration, and intellectual innovation. It usually conveniently includes the drive and courage to persevere and overcome obstacles.

As you can see, the Earth is currently reeling from exactly these narrowly focused, egocentric behaviors. On planets which are as actively aggressive as Earth, a mere twenty percent, this consciousness stage is bound to be brutal, and ultimately thrust the very survival of the planet into question. The poisons of warfare as well as other unthinking assaults on resources can destroy any planet's ability to carry life.

CONSCIOUSNESS SHIFT #3

The transition gathering steam in the 90s will move people amazingly far from the individualistic explorations of the past and towards a world where partnership, compassion, and conscience will once again flourish. Communication, creativity, kindness, intimacy, friendly neighborhoods, emotional aches and pains, worries and considerations of all kinds will be coming play.

Being on top, like having the most toys, ultimately leaves a bewildering, lonely spot, which starts calling attention to itself. This is Earth now, with the voice getting louder and louder; materialism doesn't feel so satisfying. Looking only to one's own or to one's country's advantage doesn't have the same cachet as before. Many people will be busily redefining who is part of their "big family" and who is not, with the thrust of consciousness being towards making the "family" as inclusive as possible. Can it include angry rap singers, those whose health is uninsured, those who desire abortion, impoverished underclasses, immigrants, Castro, Russians, Haitians, Serbs?

This new consciousness has been filtering in more noticeably and affecting many groups of people since the 20s. In the 60s, it became more loud and compelling. After 1987 (yes, Harmonic Convergence) it was set firmly in place. What the 90s are bringing is a short, intense transition into the new era. An extraordinary factor in the present shift is its speed. This new perceptivity is coming on strong, strong enough to penetrate many societies all around the world during this decade. This is a turnabout time, a time when many far-reaching changes will be set in place.

Some change will come as a crash course, chaotic and harsh, as it did to Eastern Europe. The disassembling U.S.S.R. had its excitement and elation also, but faces many problems, problems which could be whipped up into ethnic hatred and miserable wars or settled with communication, compromise, and a perspective which keeps the whole in mind. With these countries, you have been seeing changes at breakneck speeds. People everywhere will become impassioned, pushing their societies towards better forms of governance, equitable solutions to money, health care, education, and towards principled handling of natural resources. On the opposite and reactive hand, some will be equally and adamantly pushing for a return to the fundamentals of an idealized, simpler past.

Change means life isn't stable, and we are talking about monumental changes rolling through the decade. A person's mind may understand the value of change and theoretically adjust, perhaps even being glad for it, but the body itself and the personality are bound to regret any loss of reliability or predictability. Our interest in putting out an overview is that it will tend to anchor people, to help make the seeming turnabouts less distressing.

We aim to take away some of the shock, and by pointing towards the macro picture and the vast improvement in the way life will be lived and shared, we expect to be able to help minds and spirits stay positive. Awareness and flexibility are especially useful in a fast current.

NEW CONSCIOUSNESS

With this new consciousness approaching center stage, the world will eventually see greater environmental respect, more liberal and pragmatic politics, individual responsibility and community needs being highlighted, personal and business ethics coming under strong scrutiny, and an educational system which promotes left and right brain thinking. A continuing, pervasive examination of relationships in all their permutations, glorious and inglorious, is inevitable.

If this consciousness shift had even a hundred years to gradually root in it might still feel wrenching. However, we are talking about ten or twenty years for a major change of focus in almost every aspect of life; change that will affect everyone on deeply personal everyday levels.

The chain of factors causing such a quick shift are an overpopulated, ecologically overspent, in-debt world, with flagrant corruption everywhere. Add: increasingly strong and erratic weather; continued drops in per-capita food production; increased volcanic activity and debris; three powerfully devastating earthquakes in economically prominent areas. Your globe will be reeling. The good news is that people will then be catalyzed into using their creativity and hearts and into acting more locally, collectively, and helpfully towards each other, simply because those are the only behaviors that have any chance of making life better.

These major shifts in consciousness are tremendously exciting times in any planet's history. Many, many, many of you wanted to be around for the experience. Underlying these changes, though, is an Earth that must decrease human populations in order to heal and cleanse. It is not possible for all humans to remain and to keep breeding — even at less than the current exponential rates. Earth's population will be reduced by twenty percent or more by 2000. More on that later, but you are right, it is not going to be easy; there is much human grieving to do over the loss of roughly one billion people.

Reincarnation Update
The Soul Age Concepts

For certain is death for the born
And certain is birth for the dead;
Therefore over the inevitable
Thou shouldst not grieve.
—Bhagavad Gita

If a man does not keep pace with his companions,
perhaps it is because he hears a different drummer.
Let him step to the music which he hears,
however measured or far away.
—Henry David Thoreau

PEOPLE TRANSITIONS

Before moving on to the economic, social and Earth changes expected during the coming years, it would be appropriate to focus on the concepts of soul development because the soul age process so strongly underpins coming world changes.

Reincarnation, the view that the human soul takes many bodies in its search for experience and enlightenment, weaves itself in and out through the soul age concepts. If reincarnation does not make easy intellectual sense to you, or annoys because of a Judeo-

Christian upbringing, you can, if you wish, simply let yourself be aware that people do in fact seem to exist at different levels of development and capability, for whatever reasons. And, you can notice the ways in which different cultures, or perhaps different communities in your area, are affected by the developmental levels of people making them up, differences which can't be well accounted for by education alone, or income, or even religion.

In a body, it is quite natural to think of chronological age as being something of a guide to how "mature" a person is. It certainly is true that experiencing life over many decades is likely to increase the ability to handle it better. A forty year old is less inclined to fly off the handle than someone half that age, the major factor being longer perspective. Also, it is a rare forty year old who would even consider going back to being twenty, were it possible; the wisdom the years give is too strongly valued to exchange for that fresh, young body.

However, there is a disparity among people which is easy to notice, right? Not all forty year olds are balanced characters. Some children are more mature and capable, whether age two or age sixteen, than their peers. Occasionally teenagers are much more together than their own parents. Why is it that some find life easier to handle than others who may have many more years of experience under their belts?

In a cosmic, metaphysical sense, people's souls develop over a period of time, over the corpses of many bodies. In the Western world, people generally don't think about living many lifetimes; even less do they have any concept that completing many lifetimes creates a greater level of wisdom than when life first started.[1] But this is what actually happens: the soul develops and matures over many dozens of lifetimes of experience. Just as with body age, the older your soul gets the more capable you tend to become on the Earth. That extra experience creates more ability to act decisively with wisdom: you learn and earn your

---

[1] Reincarnation originally played a minor part in Christian theory. It was deleted as a political gambit in the fourth century at Constantinople.

enlightenment by coping with life.

Part and parcel of the "being physical" game, even for the experienced soul, is coming into a body, each time innocently, with
conscious memories of what has gone before fading rapidly after
birth. It may even take decades to figure what you "planned" to
accomplish with your life. Nevertheless, your body, personality,
psychology, abilities and talents, your degree of flexibility or
rigidity as well as the richness or the flatness of your thinking are
all influenced absolutely and powerfully by the number of lifetimes you've had and the growth and insights you have gained
through all that experience. These traits and competencies come
in with your essence and energy field, not through your body's
cellular structure. (Energy field patterns, though, do have a
strong effect on a body, right down into the cells.)

HUMANS, WHALES, DOLPHINS

People make up the planet. Actually it is more correct to say
people make up your part of the planet. Humans are the sentient,
self-reflective species on the land and the subject of this book.
Dolphins and whales, the sentient, self-reflective species of the
oceans, follow exactly the same soul growth patterns — without
the technology or written language of humans. Interestingly, humans generally aren't considered as sentient by cetaceans, but as
slow (read: non-telepathic!) dense thinkers, who neither play nor
create at high levels. Though there are rumors to the contrary,
cetaceans widely believe that humans are so violent that they
could not possibly be sentient.

The basic feel of the planet, or your community, depends on
who is present, how fresh, how scared, how plucky, how feeling,
how wise. As we view it, the focus is on survival issues in your
earliest group of lifetimes; then you work on developing order
and some predictability. After that you spend lifetimes chasing
power and developing keen instincts. Next come the tasks of
communicating, sharing, and developing compassion. Finally,
you search for a personal spiritual philosophy which can make

sense of this rough-and-tumble old planet.

At the present time on Earth, the average person, the person who creates and reflects mainstream, is coming out of his "experimenting with power" phase after having completed many lifetimes devoted to cultivating individualistic, materialistic and even quite aggressive behaviors. Joe Average has been seeking his own advantage for long enough that he finally wrapped it up and is now stepping forward, wondering if there isn't something more. Life on the material plane seems a little flat. Being on top, even the excitement of lusting for more and getting it, ultimately leaves a bewildering, lonely spot, which has started calling increasing attention to itself. For many people, this internal voice is now growing louder and louder and more insistent. Fill me up with something new, not more power and more stuff, it says. This is the hinge point at which many, many people find themselves now, and helps create the period of fast change the Earth has embarked on.

SOUL SEASONS

As alluded to, there are five rather distinct levels or stages the soul goes through in its lengthy maturation process. Before your very first incarnation, each of you signed up for the whole game. The only way out is through, i.e. by completing the entire process.[2]

These five levels bring to mind the image of chronological body age, which is why we label them as we do. The first developmental level we call *infant*, and it occurs in the earliest group of lifetimes. Like an actual infant, the person tends to feel very new and awkward in the body. Life is not known and seems fairly scary and complicated. When, after many lifetimes, you know on an inner level that you have gained sufficient control over survival issues, you move along to the next growth stage and start exploring more of your world. The *baby* level is akin to being a

---

[2] There are always system-breakers, but Michael says jumping out of the system tends to happen because of the compounded stuckness of lifetimes, not quick enlightenment.

toddler; you have gained more confidence, but are not yet independent and, despite some bluster, you cling tightly to the code of conduct fed to you by your parents and society. When lifetimes of rules and dogma are experienced so that order is internalized, an individual then pushes off into the next level, *young*. Now, you hit your worldly stride, use your will, get things done, explore, make money and impact the physical universe. When that's experienced and feels complete, you move on to the emotional issues of life.

Having had a great deal of past experience, the *mature* level person tends to be able to manage most areas of life well, and gradually learns not to hide from feelings and how to handle the myriad aspects of the emotional life. Enter the last stage, *old*, and you grow less enthralled by either emotional excitement and pleasure or worldly success. Instead, your quest is to find inner clarity about the purpose of life and inner peace in the midst of life. You'll search for a means of expression which is true to your heart, soul and self, that serves others or the Earth in a way that interests you.

To expect a baby soul to handle life like a mature soul is similar to expecting a ten year old to master psychology and become a therapist! You are pushing the process. Infant or baby souls will not respond flexibly in the way an old soul can, nor will they necessarily act logically or reasonably according to a young soul's definition. It is for these reasons, and an army of others, that the soul ages have an interesting time trusting and understanding and living with each other.

Each soul stage is augmented by all previous experience, but proceeds off on its own trajectory. No level is any better or worse than any other — in fact, each level has virtues while it also creates its own brand of trouble, both for itself and for others. Each of these five major levels of human unfoldment commonly takes twenty to forty lifetimes to complete, depending primarily on whether a given essence or soul likes moving at a speedy clip or at a relaxed, more leisurely pace. Those who enjoy tear-

ing up the road often lead fairly disheveled physical plane existences; those who prefer life at a slower, more thorough pace tend
to keep the material plane scene nicely together, but are prone to
becoming stodgy and mired — unlike the fast movers. Which is
better? Neither, it simply depends on who is doing it and what
kind of Earth experiences a soul wants to create. The world is a
more interesting place because fast, slow, and middle-of-the-
road exist.

THE INFANT SOUL

Infant lifetimes are the most rudimentary, with an individual's learning predominantly centered around physical survival. A
Person bumps right into all the written and unwritten rules of society. Not knowing what is expected, or how to fit in, makes for
confusion and occasional resentment. The infant soul intellectual
center is not yet fully opened. Confidence is lacking because its
not easy to comprehend what makes anything tick or what consequences an action will provoke. Often sacrifices will be made to
buy off demons or get the favors of spirits. Because so much is
unknown, infant souls live with a great deal of fear. But, still so
fresh from the Tao, from God, they often retain a sense magical
connection and mystical oneness with nature.

Only a very small percentage of infant souls choose to be
born into complex Western societies, instead reasonably preferring simpler lives in more elementary cultures, with no check-
books to balance, no electric bills to remember or pay, and no
moral necessity to appear regularly each morning at 7:55 am to
punch in on the old time clock.

Earth is currently accepting its last few groups of new infant
souls. This closure to new souls happens on most planets with
sentient life and allows the average soul age of the planet to move
forward more rapidly since it is no longer being continually
weighted by the entry of new souls.[3]

---

[3] 5% infant in the U.S. and slightly less in industrialized Europe. Many undeveloped nations have 25–40% infant souls.

THE BABY

As you graduate yourself to toddler level, you fervently hope you are done with leaky huts and rudimentary living. This soul age is ready to acquire some polish — and, in fact, would feel proud about never being late to punch that time clock. The underlying goal of this phase of existence is to develop and maintain order, internal and external, to the extent possible. This was the soul age that grouped together in Neolithic times and invented the great and peaceful agrarian civilizations previously discussed.

Nowadays, the baby soul often chooses to be born into an authoritarian society or will migrate toward a fundamental religion or structured job in order to learn, and to begin to obey, the one "right" set of rules for socially acceptable behavior. A person in this good-citizen stage is happiest with you if you also obey the same rules, exactly to the letter, please. So, keep that lawn mowed and get to church on Sunday morning! The many baby souls in the U.S. are especially happy when ensconced in the clean, conservative, still stable, small- to medium-sized towns of middle America.[4]

THE YOUNG SOUL

The adventuresome young soul pulls away from the cautious group-think of the baby period. This soul age does not want rules restricting behavior and will often earn the right to be the rule-makers. Church now tends to be used as a place to network, not as a place to find "the rules" or a philosophy to perfect one's behavior. Young souls want to be the quickest and the best and tend to be dauntless, brimming with determination to mold life to their specifications.

The strong, innate urge of the young soul period is to fulfill your ego by putting your imprint on the world. The motto now:

---

[4] 20% in the U.S. The percentages vary widely in European countries, with baby souls generally making up the most traditional and conservative segments of any population. Societies with large traditional elements, like Germany, Spain, Portugal and Greece, have more, say 30-40%, and England, Holland, France, Sweden, 20% or less. Japan currently has about 35%.

Might makes right. No matter whether the might is subtly implied power or blatant physical bullying; whatever gets the job done will be utilized and admired.[5]   Because young soul energy flows easily after externals, they often climb towards the top of whatever field they choose. Smart and hard-working, they have given the U.S. its competitive edge, its hi-tech marvels, and its recent roost at the top of the power heap.[6]

Prior to the mid-70s, young souls ruled a large majority of all countries. Presently, most industrialized countries have mature souls heading government, but young souls and their military friends still hold sway over nearly all developing countries, busily issuing fiats and edicts to control life in their domain. No, the responsibility does not make them anxious: It is the experience of power they are after. Making their part of the world particularly cornucopic does not enter the equation.

This stage does not deal easily with emotion, or respectfully with the rights and feelings of others. Thus in dealing with physical plane reality, the young soul is able to be practical to a level difficult for the older soul to grasp. This heavy concentration of focus on the material plane develops stamina, backbone, courage, acumen, and leadership ability — handy traits for anyone on a very physical planet like Earth. Good traits for you old souls to remember.

THE MATURE SOUL

When the mature set of lifetimes begins, the drive towards outward success is mellowed by a new, often compelling desire to give personal, intimate relationships more time and importance. Inner creativity, feelings, and people now begin to matter. Cultivating a sense of connection with all life becomes the new consciousness quest. If you have a church, you use your churchgo-

---

5 This helps explain the comment of one U.S. Senator who said the recent Russian coup attempt failed because its leaders lacked the "courage" to kill Gorbachev and Yeltsin.

6 32% young world wide and in the U.S., where that percentage will continue to shrink. Japan, a smart new competitor has 40% young, with more on the way.

ing to help you perfect your behavior, and sometimes to give you solace through difficult periods. You develop sensitivity and can feel the full force of your actions on the world — impacts which rarely bothered the young soul at all. You may feel so deeply connected with all life that it becomes too painful to drop bombs, subjugate others, hunt for sport, wear fur, or kill an insect. Abuse the child or kick the cat, your conscience will toss up guilt to prod you into examining your behaviors.

Both the world and the U.S. have expanding mature soul populations, with numbers greater than any other soul age. Mature soul mentality now spills over to affect all the rest of society, exhibiting something of the famous hundredth monkey effect whereby consciousness changes slowly at first and then suddenly, like lightning, as more and more monkeys — or humans — start displaying new behaviors.

OLD, WISE, OR TIRED?

The last stage of earthly development, the old-soul phase, fixes a person's attention on the search for meaning and on finding a way to come into acceptance and enjoyment of life as it is. The growth lessons of this stage prompt you to begin to detach from emotional drama and intensity and de-emphasize material needs. The resultant philosophical detachment is often the basis for a rather keen sense of humor about life.

While old souls with all those lifetimes under their belts may be rich and wise internally, they aren't much valued in a materialistic, action-oriented world. Furthermore, the inclination towards laziness is strong: the old soul has done it all before. The old soul grows up late, rarely managing until age thirty-five to coherently pull their many facets together. This is embarrassing and humbling, especially because those young souls are internally integrated and raring to go at age twenty-one. Figuring out how you want to express yourself in a world you're not particularly in tune with takes time also. By concentrating less attention on the material plane, you are less likely to be well off financially, and thus incur another loss of status. For all these reasons, the old soul tends to have problems with self-esteem in the world. Many become awkwardly self-deprecating. But despite these difficulties, the well-integrated old soul who has done her homework, has quick access to the very broadest of perspectives and an ability to stay centered and objective when others can't.

Many old souls grow sloppy and disrespectful in their dealings with the physical plane, which, or course, tends to make life less comfortable and less enjoyable. The idea is to be able to handle the material plane with ease, to put sufficient attention on it so that life flows smoothly, allowing you to pursue spiritual and philosophical interests. It is rare indeed to graduate yourself from the incarnation cycle before you can handle life with grace and find sustained enjoyment and pleasure in physical existence.

HOW SOUL AGE FLAVORS A NATION

You can see right off how having an abundance of any one of these soul age groupings in a country will deeply affect what goes on within its borders — and often outside those borders as well. Furthermore, as soul age mixtures change according to new births, deaths, and immigration, a nation will change to reflect what is happening with its citizens. Many times countries will grow in a logical progression, just like a person, from infant to baby to young. That kind of growth tends to make the nation feel more stable and comfortable as it changes. But interestingly and confusingly, a country can also be strongly young or mature and then fall back a notch or two to baby, if that is who decides to start being born there. Several Arab nations are in this situation currently, having more baby souls and fewer young, mature, and old souls now than they did in the recent past. India and Persia were once favored old soul enclaves, but no more.

Previously, we highlighted some of the more agreeable societies that have been created by baby souls coming together in large groups, but they have also created the not-so-kind. Baby souls have instigated hundreds of holy wars to proselytize and force change on others; with regularity, they have lynched, burned, and tortured those with differing views. They have created and lived with extreme xenophobia, especially in the East, and everywhere practiced bigotry against any other color and stripe of human. Noisy intolerance of differences among people is the major social shortcoming of baby souls.

When young souls incarnate, their aim is to gain experience with power and control, for their underlying purpose is to see what impacts they can physically create. Feudalism, which often worked out to be a harsher system than slavery, was a political form tailor-made to give handfuls of young souls the exposure and exciting educations they desired. In fact, the hierarchical styles of governance of the last 2500 years or so were enjoyed and perpetuated by the young soul, who usually managed to get himself born into the "right" family in the first place in order to insure his piece of the action. Without a favorable birth, a man would pick up the nearest available power tool, perhaps a sword to fight his way in, perhaps an education, a skill, or a wife with a rich father. A woman traditionally needed to select a man to seek power through him, an interesting and thwarting twist for the young soul woman to solve.

Colonialism, yet another young soul invention, gave whole countries a chance to exploit wide areas of the world. Turkey, Russia, China, India, Britain, France, Spain, Portugal, Belgium, and The Netherlands all built themselves empires by subjecting militarily and technologically weaker nations to their whims and wills. The New World especially offered unprecedented opportunity — guns, horses, plus blankets loaded with the smallpox virus produced easy victories against native populations. Some colonists pushed to bring their one true religion to the "savages" at the edges of the world, while others focused on bringing order, education, European language and culture, but the bottomline impetus was the plunder of New World resources.

Huge standing armies, another young soul fantasy come true, could roll over neighboring territory with enough manpower to scare everything else off. History is full of the names of these military minds with expansionistic dreams. Napoleon said he cared nothing for the lives of millions — neither did Hannibal, Alexander the Great, Attila the Hun, Genghis Khan, Tamerlane, Hitler, Stalin, or Pol Pot. Mature souls often fight with their neighbors over bitter, old issues, but they tend to lose stomach for the degree of violence required to keep whole empires under control.

Dictatorship, typically an egotistical, strong-armed way to rule, is easier to accomplish when the masses still look to authority to tell them what to do. Baby and infant souls are innately suspicious of independent thinking; rulers who train them to comply and obey don't need huge military machines to maintain the peace. Tyranny is more difficult to pull off against a countryside full of young souls — as Britain found out in Massachusetts a couple hundred years ago.

Mature souls may choose lifetimes under oppressive political systems and use the emotional intensity as a growth experience. Sometimes they suffer; sometimes they rebel. Old souls are generally so completely fed up with despots and disheartening political systems that they plan their lifetimes carefully to avoid both. Occasionally they get stuck too: Political realities aren't all that predictable and life sometimes doesn't come close to matching your astral plan. Talk to all those old souls in Russia about that!

YOUNG SOUL CREATIONS, PAST & PRESENT

The Roman Empire straddled the baby/young borderland, both in its distribution of soul ages and also in its period of power. Think of those sturdy, grounded guys out tromping around, clashing with the common folk, raping and pillaging as they went, always pushing forward, grabbing territory as they went. To new territories they proudly brought their brand of civilization and infrastructure. As the empire grew ever more colossal, clever new ways to keep it all running smoothly were concocted. The Roman experience wasn't simply about bleeding the outlying territories of money and resources, but about the pleasure and challenge of creating order and structure in the hinterlands, a sometime baby soul passion but of great interest to the young soul expansionist also.

For the last 2500 years, the largest, most influential soul age group has been this gang of young souls. Their numbers, which kept increasing as people evolved and populations increased, obviously had much to do with how bloody a read history now is. Happily for our readers, this is what the world is turning from.

Individuals sitting atop the power heap will almost always fight to protect personal privileges, but when masses of young souls incarnate into poverty stricken areas, something in society always must give. When eighteenth century Europe began burgeoning with young souls, it became imperative to find an arena for their new energy and sense of themselves. Enter North America! Because it was primarily the energetic, enterprising individual who managed to beat his way to the shores of North America in the first place, the young nation became with the aid of these disenfranchised masses, a country with a pervasive young soul flavor. Young souls will jump faster than anyone to grab an opportunity to forge a better life, even if it means doing something so wrenching as leaving behind everything which is familiar.

These adventurous souls created a new kind of country, one based on the freedom of the individual (well, actually the white male) to excel, grow, do business, and bear arms as he wished. Rustling the country away from its original caretakers with strong-arm tactics and double-dealing was predictable behavior for any gang of young souls. Notice, though, that the actions and tactics taken against the Indian nations were hugely more acceptable then than they would be at the present moment. With the approach of the Columbus quincentenary, the media focused the issue by giving Native Americans and others air time. Much of the reflexive thinking that had for centuries bestowed mega-hero status on Columbus subsided.

UPCOMING CHANGES

One underlying reason why the U.S. became so powerful and successful was simply its young soul willingness to exploit resources, work hard, and keep a clever eye open for better, more efficient means of production. The country which rushed to fulfill its "manifest destiny" had no qualms about taking from nature or from less developed nations for profit — so long as those nations weren't (exactly) colonies, an understandably sticky subject for the new and expanding nation.

That the country was strong and could do what it wanted was cause for relief and celebration, not self-examination or guilt. Though the U.S. controlled as much of the world as it could, the means and verbiage were more subtle than the colonial control methods of previous centuries; still, there was little worry over the propriety of displaying military might to protect investments abroad. For the young soul, a potent military is imperative because it enhances status and gives muscle to all interactions with the rest of the world. When President Reagan projected his dark side onto the Soviets and ordered up piles of weapons (picking the pockets of the middle class to do it and saddling the future with a $2,500,000,000,000 debt), many were pleased with the results.

Traditionally the U.S. had two feet on the young soul side of the military equation; now, one foot is tentatively moving onto mature soul turf. Today, the huge U.S. military force and defense budget are widely seen as a potentially fatal drain upon the country. People are also sensing that fighting has its drawbacks, even for the "winners." Citizens who feel comfortable about allowing the military to corral nearly half the country's wealth each year are rarer and rarer. New solutions are begging to be found, though the timing is not yet quite ripe for the leaders to appear; the citizenry must first be solidly behind changes of this nature because backlash potential is high. The military is touchy about losing power.

These days, when a country has a gang of young souls (as do many Pacific Rim countries, the Arab Gulf States, Luxembourg, and Monaco), putting a bunch of fellows in military outfits and telling them to grab what they can won't open doors very easily. One might manage to expand a border or even soak up a country or two, but no more empires lie waiting to be formed with these tactics. That is why Saddam Hussein looked like such a dinosaur. It is brighter and more discerning to find another niche, a non-military niche, which Japan, Hong Kong, Thailand, Singapore, South Korea, Luxembourg, Monaco, and the Cayman Islands have done quite nicely.

Technologies applied to war are always useful on the path toward domination. Arrows, swords and guns, ships, tanks, telescopes, satellites, and bigger and better bombs all have been able to give one country or another an edge over others. Japan, after clear and humiliating defeat, saw the future wasn't war and quickly and dexterously retrenched and rebuilt, discovering in the process that technology applied to everyday things could be a means to riches and world power.

When technology blooms in a young soul country, it is often without much common sense or morality around it. It just goes where it goes, no holds barred, with often interesting results. Imagine being in a vegetative coma (nearly one million U.S. citizens), kept alive by a machine that insists on breathing for you, for five or ten years?[7] Or imagine being a scientist, sizing up the potentials of a sticky, volatile substance called napalm. Young souls are likely to be the ones to push ahead with something as tricky as nuclear weapons or genetic manipulation, experimenting like crazy with little concern for downline problems. If it can be done, like the atom bomb, the young soul wants to do it. (The young souls involved with the Manhattan Project had few of the moral repercussions that their mature soul co-workers did.) Those ecologically disastrous thirty-mile-long drift nets the Japanese persisted on "fishing" with, because they were so efficient (deadly), are another example of shortsighted technology,

---

7 You may not be spending much of your time in your body, but neither are you as free as you might be.

this time one that essentially sterilized the oceans and made tomorrow's catch ever more elusive.

GETTING YOURS IN A CHANGING WORLD

Young souls believe in getting theirs now, while they can and before someone else does. If they think at all about causing problems downstream, they tell themselves the people of the future will be clever and technologically advanced enough to figure out how to handle any difficulty that could arise. Their blindness to the need to shepherd and conserve resources is slightly disingenuous, as evidenced by their own greed to get at those resources, now, before anyone else — and before those resources are gone for good.

The U.S. was founded with guaranteed freedoms and an egalitarian spirit so that the hard-working and ambitious, no longer just the aristocrats, could potentially create a good life. Everyone (well, at least those white males) was to get a fair shot at riches and political power. This made for a lot of competition, which was considered an excellent stimulant. Unlike traditional Europe or Asia or present day Africa and South America, you could theoretically be born anywhere and with the required smarts, gumption and stamina aim for whatever heights your soul desired.

Currently, significant numbers of young souls are being born into the lower classes in several Latin American countries — Brazil for one — where they rarely find a door to success they can pry open. In Latin countries, the children of the poor ordinarily scrape and suffer along, going nowhere. But, because young souls have a low tolerance for indentured servitude and lack of opportunity, they are migrating in hordes to Brazil's larger cities where, because jobs are not actually available, they are creating a major crime wave, driving the rich crazy. These poverty-stricken, ambition-charged souls are also pressing into the Amazon region to farm and mine. There they must contend with rich ranchers fighting a brutal fight to maintain their feudalistic control over the area and new environmentally provoked policies making it illegal to burn the forest, typically their only route to land acquisition.

Like the three hundred ragtag Ottoman nomads who long ago rode into Constantinople seeking their fortunes (and seeded a huge empire which spread over seven centuries and Europe, Asia, and Africa), young souls are adventurers who will nearly always take action to force the issue of their own success. This action may be as innocuous as making sure you get the grades and loans for college or as revolutionary (and violent) as forcing your own society to open its doors and rethink its ancient class policies.

When a young soul elite is running a country and has most of the wealth cornered, it instinctively tends to prevent the poor from being educated or even too well nourished; conscious or unconscious, the idea is to maintain tight control, easily. Feeding the poor, educating them or letting them have a shred of hope, clout or self-respect feels dangerous because soon these unwashed masses could be agitating for a bigger piece of society's pie. Cruelly exploiting other humans as fodder for your own wealth and comfort is part of the young soul experience, and part of what is changing for many as the world moves along.

The new consciousness permeating the globe says people count; it is not okay to treat any of them as subhuman dirt beneath your fingernails. (In fact, animals are already in the process of receiving more rights too.) Young souls needing to experiment with power, dominance and control-laden leadership will still manage to find their experiences, but within smaller and smaller arenas and with less easy acknowledgment of their prowess and power.

NATIONAL PERSONALITIES

Societies shift and evolve over time. Major social change depends considerably on ordinary people and which soul ages are getting themselves born where. If the U.S. were suddenly to gain a larger contingent of baby souls (instead of the influx of mature souls), the nation would leap towards a conformist, conservative, Christian near-theocracy with increased isolation from the business of the globe. Baby souls are more interested in running a tight, homogeneous ship than in freedom of thinking or being or money. They want everyone to be responsible; after all, that is the behavior they are beginning to cultivate. The right to bear arms would likely remain, but certainly not lively freedom of speech. It is their alarmed and noisy backlash that is temporarily pulling the U.S. to the right. Freedom needs to be examined occasionally so that it gives people what they want, as individuals and in their society. This backlash will certainly set mature souls thinking about how much anti-social behavior they want to accept from either the poor or from the far right!

Germany, once the militaristic young soul country that provoked two world wars, is now thirty-five percent each baby and mature, with only twenty percent young remaining. Reunification didn't pose the traditional threat since both baby and mature souls tend to be family and community oriented. Power politics now holds little interest. In fact, so many Germans found U.S. maneuvering in the Gulf war embarrassing or reprehensible that they refused to pitch in with the funding other rich nations managed. Not surprisingly, the jobless, angry youths of Eastern Germany, with their Nazi emblems, social hatred and violence, are generally young souls with no easy entree to society's power and money. They get fierce, scary and powerful in the only way they see to do it.

India and Persia once were gentle, philosophical, old soul-influenced societies. Now, India is mostly baby, though moving at full gallop towards a materialistic young soul phase and majority. India's rich and powerful higher caste elites cast a cold eye on the squalor, malnourishment and misery the masses must live with. Outbreaks of scary, contagious diseases like cholera and plague will force concern for sanitation and public health. Compassion, not a strong suit for young souls, will be lacking for awhile. As Persia transmuted into Iran with the Khomeini revolution, most of its young and mature souls managed to escape, taking with them a goodly amount of the country's wealth and technical expertise.[8]

The Dutch, notoriously cruel colonists in their country's young soul phase, are now primarily mature and old, utterly liberal yet perfectly practical in their politics and social policies. For centuries the young mayors, ranchers, and businessmen of Latin America, i.e. the richest ten percent, easily held tight reins on the impoverished baby and infant soul masses. Now, as mentioned, they are experiencing a real threat to their rule from the sizable numbers of young souls born destitute into landless families and jobless communities. The upper crust is being pressed to find ways to accommodate the newly noisy poor.

In the postwar years, England moved away from its colonial, young soul past. Because its largest grouping of people are now mid-mature, yesterday's strong urge to dominate the world is mostly just a memory, having been replaced by ideas of social justice and fairness for all classes, except for the Irish, who aren't willing to be sitting targets.

Ethnic hostility is bound to increase and be a point of pain and growth for many in today's world. Mature souls rarely blow up their planets — as young souls are prone to do, given the technology — but are inclined towards drama and wrenching fights with each other until their newly formed compassion is stretched to include even those annoying neighbors. Discord like this is not about an appetite to control the world, but is more akin to the intense power struggles and frictions which often occur within families and long-term relationships.

After World War II Russia changed even more radically than Merry Old England. It moved away from it's previous heavy concentrations of baby souls (dominated by a young aristocracy) to become a primarily mature soul country with large contingents of old souls. These incarnating mature and old souls were aware that Russia was about to undertake an interesting, large-

---

[8] Iran is now approximately 30% infant and 50% baby.

scale social experiment in which everyone was to give and take according to ability and need. Faced with yet another group of ambitious young souls who quickly co-opted the revolution, grabbed control of the new power structure, and ruled as a police state for private gain, the many mature and old souls saw the opportunities for social innovation dry up. Often the best they could do was stay quiet, be cautious and survive. Mikhail Gorbachev, a late mature soul, had the rather daunting life task of putting those mature soul social experiments back on track. Although he unhinged the authoritarian system and unglued political and intellectual suppression, chaos is the experiment of the moment.

As the planet ages, the people on the planet also grow and develop. Leaders are indispensable, but people flavor their communities and it is their personal stage of development that is the major factor controlling the evolution their societies will make or not make. With mature souls coming into more eminence, the qualities of life they naturally create will come more to the forefront of everyone's existence. There will be more caring interactions with people, animals, and nature, and extra pandemonium and hair-raising emotional disputes.

WORLD OF THE FUTURE
Right now after twenty plus centuries of young soul rule, 700 out of every 1000 people are illiterate, they can't negotiate their own written languages. It is worse for women, nearly 800 out of that 1000. Half the humans on the planet will be hungry tonight and more tomorrow night. In this group of 1000, a mere 60 people control half the money.

Mature souls won't be able to put up with statistics — and existences — like these for long because they truly understand all humans to be connected. Impoverishment this gross cries for attention, though given the population overloads, these numbers are nearly impossible to "fix." Nevertheless, living from the heart is part of what is emerging. Feelings of connectedness to all humanity and concern about fairness are part of the new ethos. Managing population growth so that people aren't born as throwaways, and in turn don't eat up the environment, becomes all important. Letting anyone starve or freeze or go without medical care or education or security in old age is anathema, when the underlying conviction is that all people should be taken care of — well, at least all of "us". The news is that the "us" you care about keeps stretching and expanding. The issue that ups the ante excruciatingly is that as vastly overpopulated as the world is there are gigantic problems about who can get provided with what.

Mature souls, as we have noted, don't always pull off living openly from their hearts and sometimes end up overwhelmed by emotionality. (Watch those soap operas.) Whether lessons are caused by personal or political drama, their lives are aimed towards eventually being able to accept all people into their hearts. When mature souls fight instead, they may feel invigorated for awhile, but soon fighting wears on them and it becomes all too evident that another solution must be found. (The numerous TV talk shows that encourage guests to whine and yell at each other over relationship woes help push the awareness that endless bickering doesn't work.) Even victory, if it has meant stomping on others, doesn't feel clearly wonderful. The mature soul has many difficulties on the road to interdependence and cooperation, but that clearly is the chosen destination. And the new collective destination.

In the 90s, people will experience sweetness and rude shock over how deep interdependence actually runs. Borders have never been more porous, and not just to drugs or smuggled goods and people, but to ideas and plagues, the other fellow's toxic debris and monetary and social irresponsibility. What one nation decides clearly ripples out to affect all. It always did, but now effects are heightened. The iron fact of environmental interconnectedness will cause the foot-dragging U.S. and Japan to come under increasingly adamant world pressure to amend the practices which contribute to acid rain, dying oceans, dying forests, and ozone depletion. Before too many more years pass, the entire world will see the necessity of hashing out the issues surrounding fossil fuel use. The unsustainable consumption of industrialized countries, and the equally unsustainable quantum leap of populations in most of the developing world, will be scrutinized with the imperative of somehow applying the brakes.

MATURE SOUL INFLUENCE IN THE U.S.

Mature souls in the U.S. have always been around, but never before with such high percentages. Collectively in the past they often formed the vocal minorities which took aim at societal injustice, like the abolitionists agitating for those who had few rights. To a huge degree, they have been the creative phalanx; the constitution designers and signers, the writers, philosophers, critics and satirists, the scientists, and the actors, artists, dancers, singers and musicians who gave the U.S. vibrancy and wealth.

The lively spirits who made the 1920s roar were a highly noticeable group of mature souls. Given the right environment, this soul age will celebrate life to the maximum, which they did outlandishly. The 20s became party time, wild time, free-thinking time, a few years to roll noisily over the straitlaced prohibitions of baby souls — giving them a few good shocks was part of the fun. Then came the years of the Great Depression, sobering enough to to put a lid on exuberant public displays of this new energy. Though wilder aspects of mature soul energy were submerged by the hard times of the 30s and 40s, social compassion was higher than ever and many political and social safeguards were put in place.

President John Kennedy's murder, which drowned out youthful hopes of creating social change within "approved" channels, fired up the next wild outbreak, that of the 60s. The new, larger flock of mature souls was no longer willing to put up with dull gray, suited-up, three-piece, half-dead, nice 50s' housewife kind of lives. Once again, there was insistence on personal freedom, fun, emotional intensity, enhanced by experimentation with drugs. Again the backlash materialized, though this time the form was different. Civil rights leaders were snuffed out, the war in southeast Asia grew and lingered, and the economy of the 70s slipped badly — but none of this was enough to ruin the gumption or crush the values of this emerging consciousness.

Though the gray world reasserted itself, this time much of what hippies and yippies were about integrated itself right into the greater society's value system. Life stayed a little looser. Peace and love and self-gratification continue to hold infinitely greater appeal for the majority than another Vietnam. Anti-Gulf war demonstrators carried flags — instead of burning them — because they considered themselves to be a valid part of the culture, not outsiders as before.

In the U.S., mature souls are once again beginning to assert themselves in increasingly prevailing ways. They are working avidly to bring the still-powerful young soul corporate world to some common sense around the environment and ordinary citizens to some crisper thinking regarding throwaway consumption and environmental contamination. The issue of animal rights now has much emotional energy behind it. Hunger and homelessness, welfare and hopelessness, and the way teenage pregnancy glues a person to poverty are drawing strong attention. So is a healthcare system which lengthens life span with high-tech gadgetry and high expense, but does little to promote positive health. Half of all Americans visit an alternative healthcare practitioner each year, enough to begin to break the monopolistic grip of medical doctors. The educational system and the basic neglect of children in the U.S. will soon come into strong focus, along with the deafening stream of violence from television and movies which has skewed children's values. Mature souls will keep finding aspects of life that need fixing and then heave their collective weight towards establishing those changes. They want flexibility in their societies, one reason for the loud new call for democracy worldwide. A soul comes to see flexibility as valuable personally and socially only in the mature development phase.

Mature souls are willing to dunk some individual freedoms for the good of all. Young souls don't think in terms of the common good or their responsibility to it. The slant in the U.S. has been towards having immense personal freedom, with little responsibility imposed upon it. Freedom with no social responsibility has created nihilism in the ghetto, the stockpiling of weapons by militias, and corruption at the top. The wings of freedom shouldn't need to support hurtful individualistic actions.

Baby souls are the traditionalists who generally act as deadweight against fast forward movement. They may grumpily allow themselves to be prodded along, or ferociously battle change. In the early 90s, a number of rather gloriously failed conservative leaders (Jerry Falwell, Jim and Tammy-Faye Bakker, Oral Roberts, Jimmy Swaggart) helped drain moral authority from the right. So did the notoriously hate-filled 92 Republican convention which ultimately caused many righteous old sticklers to lose their seats in Washington and in state capitols. Yet, 94 saw younger replacements back in full force. The debate over responsibility is far from complete.

Baby souls think they alone know the true meaning of responsibility, as they know what is good and who is bad. You can hear their new representatives kicking up a storm in the likes of Rush Limbaugh, who (irresponsibly) hesitates not at all to bend facts any which way to suit his point of the moment. Humans have a weakness for scapegoats; baby souls are particularly susceptible to putting blame and evil "out there." That there aren't any bugaboo communists around to hate leaves a big gap, but having a President in the White House intent on making "scary" social reforms gave an easy focus to conservative worry and anger over the basic change patterns now flowing in the world, ready or not. All the fury and nastiness aimed daily at Clinton has created definite problems for him, low popularity at the polls and ego embarrassment being a small part of it. Working in the negative energetic climate created by professionally whipped up hatred, caused a severe shock to his system and drained his creative energies. While this atmosphere of projected malice might actually give a young soul head of state more energy to work with, anyone with an opened feeling nature would find these assaults unbalancing and exceedingly difficult to handle.

Despite all this fury, the political issues now easily controlled by baby souls are few. Their territory is slipping, which is one reason they fight so hard. The issues looming largest on the baby soul agenda in the U.S. include taking the teeth out of the federal government, maintaining gun rights, abolishing abortion and welfare rights and governmental support for the arts, preventing full civil rights for homosexuals, and a new, many-pronged struggle which is attempting to ensure that all children receive a conservative education, i.e. one that does not contradict the Bible or open them psychologically to seemingly dangerous new age ideas about inner-self and inner-wisdom.

Clinton dropped the ball on government reform. It was easy enough to do, even for a policy wonk like himself, deeply intrigued by the structure and direction of government. The unconscious, liberal, mature soul tendency is to keep adding more protections and more help for more people, while being too weak, kind-hearted, or fuzzy of mind to clean up what no longer makes good sense. It is the Republicans now spearheading a move to downsize and reform government. They have much popular support behind them. Baby and young souls especially are so angry at governmental waste, miles of regulations, sclerotic bureaucrats, shuffling politicians and welfare recipients that they are itching to destroy the old wherever they can — at least until it adversely affects them personally. Newt Gingrich's grenade lobbing is bound to have many positive effects: The threat of destruction often encourages fresh thinking, which needs to happen in most every capital on the globe.

EARTH NOW!
Only in the last several years have mature souls bulged the

bell curve in their direction. Worldwide, as in the U.S., mature souls now account for thirty-four percent of the population and young souls thirty-two percent. A single percentage point or so would not make such a tremendous difference were it not for the current of consciousness swerving so dynamically towards a mature soul world, a world where individual people count. For many right now, the effect is like getting magnetized by the future, sucked into it, ready or not. It is this action, this crazy momentum which triggers confusion, fear and the digging in of heels by conservatives and traditionalists longing to go back to old values, old ways, often some panacea which never actually existed. This fundamentalist conservatism is particularly powerful in the U.S. and in India, where it is noisy and must be always taken into account; in the Middle East, where it is dangerously divisive; and in Russia and areas of Eastern Europe, where many are eager for a strong hand to settle life down.

Look at the positive events of the last few years; the previously unthinkable is happening in nearly every corner of the world. The European Community countries, which have bickered, been suspicious and jealous of each other for centuries, carefully started cutting red tape between their borders, heading towards a similarity of laws and easy travel for people and goods. This difficult-to-achieve cooperation makes Europe incalculably richer. When the moment arrived that Eastern Europeans no longer had to put up with tyranny, they seized it and shook off their handful of dictators; even wretched Albania's citizens are occasionally stirring. Twenty or more areas in the old Soviet Union have declared themselves to be sovereign states desirous of self-determination. It is clear to most of them that they had best cooperate and compromise with each other — or risk chaos and devastation. (Occasionally, though, the fight looks too satisfying to resist; lessons then pile upon lessons.) Nepal's revered, but knavish and corrupt monarchy was attacked, again and again, until it agreed finally to make sufficient democratic reforms to satisfy the many daring agitators. Dismantling apartheid is obviously fiendishly difficult, but South Africa is plunging ahead with relief and elation, having admitted finally that it must be done. Though Haiti will be on shaky ground for some time, it managed, with U.S. support, to throw off several layers of heartless strongmen.

Though not all uprisings or elections are successful — China, Burma, Cambodia, Kashmir, Mexico, Yugoslavia, and more than a few African fiascoes come to mind — citizens are suddenly less willing to put up with the same old plagued existences. People all over the planet are managing to change the societies in which they live and to focus world attention on others where change is being stalled.

In the U.S., the mature soul viewpoint has enough critical mass that the military, for example, did not jump all over Saddam Hussein, first blush — nor did most Americans think it should have. It waited for diplomacy first. The mature soul forte in crisis solution is talk, talk, and more talk, with everyone putting all feelings and concerns on the table, until solutions all can live with are found. This stubborn warrior proved intractable: A bullying young soul on a power trip may only understand a powerful fist punching back — military shock therapy. Even though flexing military muscle is going out of style, it will still be the only way some leaders hear no. In Saddam's case, it may yet take a bigger blow than the first Gulf episode proved to be.

Though George Bush managed to attach some tenuous glory to himself after the Persian Gulf War, many were left with an acrid after-taste and the glory proved short-lived. People are focused on economic and social issues and won't be distracted by the call to patriotism or the possibility of greater world domination. (Saddam, after all, seemed more the buffoon than the antichrist.) Let's take care of our own values and educations and environment and businesses. Life at home must work and work well. That's mature soul thinking.

THE SOUL AGES

Age	Person	Culture
Infant	Awkward, New Unsophisticated Unclear about Consequences Undeveloped Conscience	Simple Lives Nomadic, Tribal Connected with Nature Few Artifacts
Baby	Develops & Follows Rules Respects Leaders & Experts Conventional Rigid, Intolerant	Invented Civilization Family Centered Stable Communities Patriotic, Jingoistic
Young	Ambitious, Competitive Capable, Hardworking Efficient, Non-Emotional Self-Seeking, Shortsighted	Military Might, Wars Technological Wizardry Rich, Materialistic Conquers Nature
Mature	Creative Emotionally Open Desires Meaning & Beauty Soap Opera Drama	Cooperative, Egalitarian Creativity High Nature is Conserved Ethnic Fighting
Old	Relaxed Individualists Spiritual, Philosophical Focused Inward & Upward Lazy, Loose with Rules	Liberal, Non-Judgmental Solves Problems Uniquely Lives with Nature Infrastructure Shabby

FOUR

Off the Beaten Track
Men and Women

A not so modest proposal for safer streets:
What this country needs is a federal law
forbidding men to go out on the streets
unless they are accompanied by a woman.
—Judy MacLean

It is now possible for a flight attendant to
get a pilot pregnant.
—Richard Ferris, President, United Airlines

POWER BATTLE

In the young soul power battle between the sexes, men won. That doesn't mean they won every skirmish, or found peace at home, but they held life's stronger cards. The quality and scope of most lifetimes depended greatly on the sex of the body you chose. You received very different types of experience with each sex, adding to your development and to the richness and complexity of your human résumé. In a male body you were virtually guaranteed not only more muscle but also more privilege, both of which counted abundantly in a young soul world. Thus power, the quintessential young soul pleasure, was easier to obtain with a male body, due both to its greater strength and to the way most societies were structured.

It only figures that a young soul world would spark inequality between the sexes. One sex was bound to gain authority over the other. In fact, men and women have been out of harmony since Greek times, and robustly out of harmony since the Roman era. The epochs before that had some cultures which honored men and women equally, and some others in which either men or women prevailed. The pendulum on Earth swings slowly back and forth between male and female domination, with shorter periods of peace and equality at the end zones of one sex's domination of the other. In about one thousand years when the planet grows into its old soul phase, men and women will gradually give up their power struggles with each other.[1]

IMPULSIVE AND IMPASSIONED

Mature souls will create male and female interactions expressive of mature soul dynamics. Men and women will be looking at each other with more interest, desire, emotional intensity, and sexual longing, while simultaneously yearning for peace and balance. Mature souls value stable family life, yet they want to feel alive, vital and challenged to grow. Sounds confusing, right? Add to that the tug-of-war women feel between their thirst to take advantage of fresh, exciting opportunities for power in the world and the mature soul hunger for high romance and fulfillment through relationship.

The thrust of the late 90s will create a flourishing climate for male/female intimacy. With so many economic, environmental and spiritual challenges, men and women are pushed into handling the outside world rather than concentrating on personal conflicts. When focused on problematic events, couples tend to pull

---

1 As a planet moves into its later stages of development and begins to be dominated by mature and old souls, life always speeds up, growth time is compressed, everyone is pulled forward more quickly. That is why the baby soul era took three to four times as long as the young soul era, and why the young soul era took three times as long as the mature soul era will.

together, forget surface irritations and bond ever more deeply as they handle outer issues.

Individuals develop inner strength in hard times; couples often develop a deep, abiding mutual trust. Normal mature soul dramatics — petty bickering, simmering jealousies, bouts of insecurity, affairs born of boredom — are suddenly relegated to the back burner. When enough difficult external events are set in motion, your own soap opera will seem extraneous.

As people move into their heart centers and away from their power centers, the desire for vital relationships will be strong. Given the new consciousness climate, fewer men will be blind to women's issues. Mature soul men are more likely to be concerned with making life fair for everyone than in sticking to their advantages. As men pull back from domination, they leave more room for a relational and emotional life. Societal support for the emotional evolution of men will be strong — you can already see this occurring. The value of women will soon move up another notch simply because the average female is much more knowledgeable about the emotional, intuitive world than the average male. Because of the way the two sexes are influenced by hormones, women will continue to have an easier expertise in the inner world and men, easier expertise in the outer.

Boundaries between the sexes are breaking down and will continue to do so over the next two decades. Those fifty and sixty year olds with heavily-fortified opinions about what is appropriate behavior for a woman or a man are increasingly seen as old-fashioned and out-of-touch. Parents who try to imprint their children with locked-in, constricted sexual stereotypes will have a tough time because neither society nor the media will support them. In most Western societies, younger people who attempt to live narrowly defined sex roles will be viewed by their peers as inept and stunted. In the near future, there will be few legal or social partitions between what a woman or a man can do. Baby souls don't change easily; many will cling ferociously to the old ways, but they are being propelled along by change like everyone else.

Mature soul energetics have already supported men in opening their hearts and feeling natures, and allowed them to be more tender fathers and kinder participants in life. Some men, to humankind's surprise, found they exulted in staying home and not being out in the world with traditional male occupations. In the last decade, Western men have made tremendous leaps toward knowing themselves; they have been identifying and expressing feelings and integrating their active, intellectual sides with their inner perceptivity. Men will continue to unchain themselves from the flat, one-sided productivity society seemed to demand of them.

Much of this current male growth was predicated on women stepping into their own power. In finding their voices, women allowed men to soften; men lost their excuse, or their need, to be strong all the time. While men were originally very uneasy, very much threatened by the fortitude with which women were insisting on power, many are now adjusted and able to enjoy the advantages of the new situation. The younger the man and the older the soul, the easier the adjustment tended to be.

WARRIOR WOMEN

How did it happen that the lot of women changed so quickly? It relates to good astral planning and fortunate political timing. Pushing the female sex ahead looked like an interesting task which would turn lives upside down and give variety to the man/woman experience. And, it was time for the pendulum to swing.

Starting early in the century, handfuls of interested souls (the shock troops) put themselves in female bodies on the front lines, determinedly pushing to make women and society aware of the severe limitations placed on the female sex. Laws changed and thinking began to change, but it wasn't until the 70s that the critical mass necessary to make major societal shifts was incarnate and stirring. Large numbers of women in their teens, twenties and thirties were suddenly unwilling to put up with the same old lives or lies. They started to stand up for themselves, and were willing to punch the guys, or the system, in the nose when handed can't-do lines. This can-do mass of young, mature and old soul women managed to get their feet in new doors (and up telephone poles and down in submarines), creating myriad new openings for their sex's fuller participation in life.

Many, many, of these women were warriors, the role that is feisty, strong of body and most inclined to fight for principles.[2] Warriors often tend to choose and savor the physicality of male lifetimes — and suddenly here they were, women with agendas. Traditionally the U.S. has had almost thirty percent warriors, predominantly male. This was very good for business and for keeping the country perking along in an efficient, organized fashion. With a very high proportion of these warriors choosing women's bodies over the last few decades, this role became a very significant portion of the under thirty-five female population.

Putting sturdy warrior women on the front lines was good tactical thinking on the part of the astral committees planning this historical change — and it worked. (Astral plans don't always manifest perfectly. All the mature and old souls who excitedly incarnated into Russia in the 30s and 40s in order to create an equitable society weren't so lucky; most of them ended up with severely restricted lifetimes.) But these contemporary warrior women are doing fine, gaining more power every year while redefining the way society thinks a woman should look (more muscles), act and think (more independent).

In the next twenty years, opportunities for women will continue to enlarge. Girls born in the 80s and 90s will barely realize how major were the changes or how difficult the struggle that made the openings they step through as a normal part of exis-

---

2 Michael's systematic way of looking at people identifies seven "roles", warrior being one. Whatever role you are, you keep it in every life, getting good and comfortable with it. Each role has favorite behaviors and particular ways it gives to all the other roles. Warriors are orga - nized types who enjoy the challenges and pleasures of the physical plane. Refer to *The World According to Michael* or other Michael books [see back pages] for complete explanations.

tence. Boys won't be any more aware of how greatly the world changed to allow for the fuller expression of their feeling natures. When flowing right along with a major consciousness change, what is new becomes normal with amazing speed.

It is difficult for a person from a Western country to comprehend that even now only small pockets of humanity believe women are equal beings. Many, many cultures still view women as a kind of sub-species with few rights. But, with the exception of isolated enclaves of the more recalcitrant, most cultures on the planet will soon come to the realization that women are in fact human and have rights, possibly even equal rights, to the pleasures and responsibilities of the world. For the majority of the population now, that is only a suspect notion — like the idea circulating among dolphins and whales that humans may be sentient, ensouled beings, and not simply technologically dangerous, unthinking primitives.

However, as we've mentioned, the mature soul consciousness shift is strong and compelling. The manner in which the powerful Western world "allows" its women to act — in and out of films — starts to affect men, women, and cultures worldwide. Stephen Spielberg and George Lucas began to create heroines with smarts, courage, and formidable independent streaks. Madonna's message is coming in loud and clear: Women can be strong, successful, and have fun without "paying for it". But, don't hold your breath waiting for Rambo to take a dive at the third world box office!

The recent surge toward fundamentalism in the Middle East is seriously eroding whatever rights or claim to decent treatment women had. For one, it is a backlash reaction against the enhanced status of women in the West. Some of this insistence on keeping women in their place, though, comes from essence level needs to keep old male/female dichotomies available for experience now — and to keep the drama open for future lifetimes too. However, these choices keep women down and further isolate and marginalize Middle Eastern countries, amplifying already volatile situations.

GOD THE FATHER STEPS DOWN

As long as a patriarchal religion is the spiritual viewpoint of choice, inequality between the sexes will persist. In people's minds, God being one sex makes the other sex inferior. Though some Christian churches are expanding the role of women and their attitude toward them, not one has added Goddess worship. It is a rarity for established religions to recast themselves and lead people forward; few are free to change with evolving societal needs. Worldwide, religions are stuck, mired down with outdated beliefs and assumptions. People need new institutions as well as new spiritual leaders.

Around the turn of the century, we see it likely that four or five infinite souls will begin to make themselves known and, as they are prone to do, greatly affect the world.[3] These great and loving beings will be both male and female and their skin colors will embrace different corners of the world. All will have essentially the same message — love each other, respect each other, honor nature. These luminous souls will very greatly affect the way religion is practiced, making it more nature oriented and less patriarchal and more inclusive. Much religion actually promotes separation, judgment, fear and even hatred. Infinite souls always work to overcome these human tendencies. A humbled world edging into the mature soul era is more likely to listen. Having two or three female infinite souls of varying races will give a towering lift to the way everyone views women and boost women's lives everywhere.

---

[3] Each infinite soul is actually a group of souls so large and all-encompassing that it is just a breath away from the Tao, from God. Infinite souls are always very affecting, and come typically in times of great change and need. The most recent infinite souls have been Christ, Buddha, Lao Tse, Krishna, and Quetzalcoatl, all of whom helped smooth the world's transition into young soul consciousness. The world has previously seen many infinite souls in female bodies, whose names now linger as old Goddess names like Astarte and Bridget.

NEW TO POWER?

When any group has been kept from power for a long period and then gains some, it is likely to act up. A lot of the nastiness employed by women in the 70s (like infighting among blacks in South Africa or among various ethnic groups in the old Soviet bloc) is the result of being disenfranchised for so long. The newly empowered act like adolescents for a while, work it out, and then come to a new level of maturity and responsibility. Change is always roughest when first launched. It may be necessary to be noisy, cranky, and disobedient to get attention. Nevertheless, the mature soul will begin to see clearly that people are one. At that point, the necessity of finding compassion and getting along becomes obvious. People will begin to view others, including the opposite sex, as interesting variations of the human fabric, as opposed to the us–versus–them consciousness scenario of the young soul.

WHO'S GOT THE RULES?

As parity between the sexes increases, customary patterns of behavior fall into meaninglessness, which can create disorder and mayhem. How is it all supposed to be? Who's on first? What's a homer, anyhow? Ruts, grooves, and supposed self-evident truths won't hold you in place, and new truths have little chance of turning into reliable dogma because everything changes too often. That's part of the fun and a good part of the trouble.

The average person on the planet has now had dozens of past lives and many female and male bodies. Even without conscious recall, this extensive backlog of experience with both body types affects a person's thinking. American or Saudi, a mature or old soul is innately less comfortable with sexism (or racism), though social imprinting always takes some getting over. Eventually it starts to seem crazy to limit what anybody can do or feel by the type of genitals (or skin) possessed. This extensive backlog of past life experience serves to loosen up the thinking that would limit the behavior, achievements and status of women (or people of color).

If you have lived but ten or twenty lifetimes, you are going to remain strongly identified with your body and your society of the moment. But when, like many early mature souls, you have lived eighty or a hundred lifetimes, that identification gradually loosens and lightens. A part of you knows that you are not your body, that social rules always change, and that a person can be quite feminine, yet competently run a business, or be strongly male, and cry, dance, and nurture others. In mature soul times, the rules of appropriate behavior get pretty marshy. This makes for conflict, high emotional intensity, as well as occasional backlashes from segments of society which need clear definitions and limits, not bounding change. Anti-abortion stances and other combat against women's rights will continue to exist, keeping life between the sexes — and the soul ages — quite spicy.

YET MORE SPICE

Another factor making life ever more interesting between the sexes is the fact that many people now are in the body they enjoy less, choose less often, and thus have less experience with. In your early lifetimes, you tend to take on more lifetimes in the body which feels more comfortable to you. By the time mature soul lifetimes come around, your essence begins to exert a mild pressure to get experience balanced. Old souls are under stronger essence pressure to balance out their male and female experiences, essentially because it becomes now or never. As the world begins to have large numbers of mature and old souls, it is more common to find people who have enjoyed the independence, strength and power of male bodies experimenting with women's bodies and, of course, paying back the karmas instigated in male lifetimes. Essences who have enjoyed the connectedness, creativity and procreativity of female lifetimes will now be balancing themselves by taking on more gutsy male experience and karmas.

It makes an interesting soup: women who are more used to being men and men who are more experienced as women. You can see the results of this everywhere in North America and Europe. This recipe for confusion has already loosened the confined ways female and male were previously expected to act. Madonna and Michael Jackson are strong, even blatant examples of what we are speaking of here. While they are each experiencing and learning from bodies somewhat foreign to them, they have become role models, perhaps we should say model breakers, for many young people. Most of the girls who idolized Madonna don't have her talent or acute instincts, but her outrageous strength is impressed on their psyches forever. She is nervy and masterful (with nary a martyred bone), unlikely to trip herself up as she takes on patriarchy. Michael Jackson, a gentler, more receding individual than Madonna, is not someone boys are likely to directly emulate, but he is out there living a soft, poetic, rather magical existence.

Typically, but by no means universally, it is the feeling, sensitive male who has had more experience with female lifetimes and the tougher, more determined female who has taken on more male lifetimes. As all this continues to be mixed on a greater-than-ever scale, evolution towards a socially more equal, more blended male and female quickens. In the meantime, it can be highly disorienting for all participants, for there are no clear guideposts and little steady ground; every time you think you have your bearings, the needle on your compass shifts again.

In the West, the most tumultuous part of this process is already complete. The warrior women have done their job; Western society has let go of a goodly amount of its sexist shoulds and musts, and no longer clings tenaciously to what is left. The tone is set for the rest of the world, when it decides to follow along.

HORMONAL WASHES

On planet Earth, the innate singularity of each sex is stronger than on ninety-five percent of all other planets where sentient life exists. Earth is an experimental planet: one of the biggest experiments for humans is in having many of the most powerful and interesting karmas take place between the sexes. Because of life experience, it is difficult for humans to understand how unusually wide the differences are between men and women. These differences make for disparate approaches to life, easy misunderstandings, and those intense and powerful karmas. Cetaceans, the other sentient, self-reflective species on Earth, exemplify the more universal androgynous, undifferentiated appearance between male and female. As mammals they have role demarcations, but cetaceans do not have the concentration of strong male/female emotional karmas which so color human life.[4]

Even though the demarcations between what women and men can *do* are getting erased, female and male body energies are always going to be quite distinct from each other. The hormones which infiltrate the two bodies are pervasive and highly influential, creating markedly different fields in which behavior takes place.

The unique hormonal wash each body gets lasts for about forty years each lifetime. Until hormones begin to swarm at approximately age twelve, children are in what we call an innocent phase; after age fifty-two or so hormones calm down, thereby enabling each sex to enter what we call the wisdom phase, a centered, reflective period of life no longer unsettled by hormones pushing the body and emotions this way and that.

FEMALE BODIES

For obvious reasons, women's hormonal cycles are easier to identify than those of men. A typical female body has a twenty-eight day cycle, divided into two parts of fourteen days each. The first portion of the cycle occurs in the week on either side of ovulation. (Birth control pills lengthen this part of the cycle and compress the next.) A woman will tend to feel inspired here. She will grasp the big picture, see the importance of love, of

---

[4] Their karmas are centered around compelling desires to innovatively and beautifully express themselves, and their understanding of life. See *The Michael Game* for more.

family, of peace. She will sense the purpose of life and almost automatically nurture human connections and communications. This inspirational segment is an easy, generally enjoyable, upbeat portion of the female cycle.

The second half of a woman's cycle is emotional and expressive. It encompasses the week before and the week of menstruation. Here, instead of the big picture, a woman sees details, especially any that have been politely or conveniently swept beneath the carpet. She feels more introverted and can get picky and moody, irritating everybody including herself. This part of the cycle helps to keep a woman conscious of what is really going on in her life. If she has been untrue to herself about anything, it will come bounding up now.

Civilized society encourages a woman to squelch this side of herself. But when she does bury this emotionally expressive, sometimes stormy part of her cycle — and nature — she loses. As she drifts further from her true feelings and true self, she becomes parched, a rainless woman. She may also end up with a menstrual cycle which calls increasing attention to itself through physical or emotional discomfort.

The ideal way to treat the expressive half of the cycle is to respect the emotions which arise and let them have a voice, even while realizing they may be overblown in the moment. Later, examine what came up to ferret out the underlying message. The more out of touch a person is with this lively, juicy aspect of herself, the scarier it is to let it out. Eventually life gets dry without it. While this part of a woman's cycle can be discomforting — nobody loves having to look at buried issues — it can tell her the truth about her life and keep her on course.

MALE BODIES

Men have similar problems with valuing the tricky-to-handle portions of their natural cycles. They pass through three discrete, approximately eighteen day, segments in their overall fifty-four day cycle. The in-charge hormone here is not estrogen, but testosterone, which creates more physicality and aggression, as well as a less emotional, more mental field for men. Because current western culture tends to value one, maybe two, parts of each man's normal cycle, individual men respond by consciously or unconsciously overriding those undesired parts of themselves. In addition to any social pressures on them, many men like to believe they are rational, considered beings not subject to cyclic mood changes — like women. These factors make recognizing and identifying male cyclical changes more difficult. But, just as with female repressing of emotionality, this male repression and denial creates dry, unbalanced men, men who are potentially dangerous. To be full, rich and whole, a man needs to experience each of the three major moods his cycles bring to him. Then, he's got rhythm!

The first phase of a man's cycle finds testosterone high. This is an action-oriented, extroverted, and sexy eighteen day period. We call it the aggressive part of the cycle. It is the easiest of the three segments to wake up to and identify. Women often notice that men smell particularly attractive during this period.[5] During this time men take on more projects and risks. They feel more romantic, protective, heroic even, sometimes becoming legends in their own eyes.

Knowing that aggression, like unrestrained sexuality, can often lead to trouble, modern western man may attempt to repress this part of his cycle and this part of himself. Men don't want to be unconsciously starting wars or having their other head lead them around for eighteen days when this period hits. But that is not much of a probability, especially for the man who is likely to clamp down on this expression in the first place. The point is to be able to use this energy positively. When a man cuts off this facet of himself, he is that much less vital, alive, or fun; furthermore, he is then prone to being sporadically and negatively controlled by this energetic, insistent aspect. The men's movement is rightfully attempting to redress denial of this side by

---

[5] When you sniff the back of his neck and it smells like ambrosia, you are here.

putting men back into positive enjoyment and harmony with the "hairy man" part of their natures.

Aggression in men is what the feminists of the 70s and 80s tried to tame or knock out with varying degrees of fervor and success. Few want to be with pushy, insensitive out-of-control guys, the John Bobbitts of the world; but the real point is for men to handle these energies positively. Many women who have been frustrated with their stale mates appreciate the new liveliness engendered by men's groups, even when the stability of status quo is threatened.

The second segment in a man's cycle is characterized by intellectual behaviors, by thinking. A man now becomes analytical about his life, his relationships, his actions, and times. He strives for understanding, making overviews as he goes. Suddenly he is communicating first, taking action later. Sex becomes more neutral here, not so important, but far from a dead issue.

This intellectual phase is the most acceptable part of the cycle to modern western men, who often try to stretch its cool focus over the other two segments of their cycles. The desire to remain lofty, intellectual, and in control at all times is understandable, but there are huge drawbacks to this one-sidedness. Many men pay for it with emotionally barren lives.

The final eighteen day period is an introverted, moody phase, an assimilative time. Turning inward, the man mulls over his life, his actions and times. What goes on here is a less conscious, more back-burner activity than the previous rational intellectual phase. A man may become melancholy and cranky; ideally, though, he is reflecting on his internal states. This is a catch-up time, and a time to rest in preparation for the activity of the upcoming aggressive period. The energy of assimilation feels like winter energy, and can be about as dynamic as hibernation. In fact, a man will probably be sleeping more here and be somewhat withdrawn sexually.

This assimilative phase in the cycle is the one men resist most. It is also as much in emotion's lap as their body cycles place them. Like gray weather, this can be a pleasurable time; but unfortunately men in western cultures are not conditioned to flow with it and brood. The training is to stay active and positive, quash those moods, get on top of them. Aside from Mr. Rogers, there are few cultural icons who help men understand the positive aspects of subjectivity, inertia, and stewing around. Men who re-think this one enrich their lives, but it takes courage, just as it does for a woman to let her emotions speak when she is not sure what will come out or how major the consequences.

Notice that men's and women's cycles will overlap every month at new junctures. Heterosexual couples cannot synchronize into predictable mood tangos. How male and female approach each other and how they are received will vary, sometimes from week to week. Perhaps the most hazardous phasing is when the male is moody and assimilative and the female brooding and emotional; then neither has much objectivity, nor ability to rise above arguments or issues. Homosexual couples (and often same-sex roommates) fairly quickly synchronize cycles. Communication is easier, but life may get more intense.

MATRIARCHY!

Because of bodily strength and embedded societal values, people long thought that women could never be men's equals. That view is now speedily changing, among women and men. The world is already rushing towards the sexual equality which will predominate on a generous portion of the globe during the twenty-first century. Pushing ahead even further in time, we see an upcoming matriarchal period, likely to last at least 1000 years, quite strongly in place by 2150. This is a period when those of you choosing women's bodies will have power and control over most social policies. Women will have the primary say in gov-ernment, politics, media and business, and over men.

How could life ever get from here to there? It is nearly im-possible for people raised in male-dominated countries and worlds even to imagine the physically weaker female gaining control over the stronger, more aggressive male, but consider a sequence of events similar to this: Men are progressively seen as responsible for the problems the world is facing, especially when their resistance to necessary clean-ups, changes in technology or behavior become painfully obvious. They will be held guilty for addictions to bigger and more deadly weapons, huge deficits and debts, leaking toxic waste, and the corruption of financial institutions and regulatory agencies. Women, untainted by these policies and scandals partially because they have had little power, will increasingly be the ones coming up with proposals for change. Many of the leaders who will initiate and build the human-sized institutions mature souls want will be women.

The elevation of women over the next century will happen in spurts and spikes. For example, the ways in which women commonly operate may "suddenly" seem to be more valuable to society than how men operate. You can see hints of this already. Part and parcel of the current consciousness change is a shift away from hierarchical organizations with their one-up and one-down power structures. Many companies are already searching for approaches that will make work situations meaningful, mutually satisfying experiences. Businesses are starting to design structures based on shared power, mutual aid and trust, because that now looks stronger and more competitive. Running an organization by rank, or a country by social violence, is less and less a viable option, for newer solutions are glowing too attractively. Neither mature soul societies nor workers are comfortable with iron rule from the top.

Consensus building, explored because of Japanese success with it, is something women tend towards naturally, yet was very recently seen as a spineless, indecisive way to manage a business. Sharing information, instead of withholding it, talking frankly with people, complimenting them, these too are typical female ways of being which are coming to have more coin in the management world. As values continue to change, women will more easily excel. In the new atmospheres, they will feel safer about expressing their opinions. And, feeling free to be themselves will make them more powerful. Instead of straining to stick to the language of men and business, a woman's natural way of communicating will suddenly have advantages.

People in women's bodies suffer less from the illusion of control. As baby-bearers, women quite intimately understand flowing with what life brings. They also tend to have more respect for life and fewer aggressive urges to dominate nature. As life-givers, women are more hesitant about war, even short, supposedly simple ones with few perceived downsides.[6] They keep communicating until they figure out other solutions to problems. For these reasons and more, the female sex is due to be viewed in a progressively favorable light.

Societies that increasingly value women, their ideas and input, will gradually and subtly cause men to feel less valuable. Lowered male self-esteem makes it easier to train them to stifle themselves, to be less active for their own good. In this way, men gradually lose power and become the second sex. If you make examples of those who don't fall into step by embarrassing and punishing them, fewer will risk those same behaviors in the future. Make men feel bad about themselves when they don't control their "primitive" aggressive impulses and they become self-monitoring, just like women before them who were long unable to grasp their own capabilities. Because this switch will be happening in a mature soul world, society will probably not experiment with the rougher, young soul control methods — like refusing them rights to property or inheritance or burning feisty men as evil troublemakers.

It is from this sequence of changes that power will gradually fall back into female hands. We are not suggesting that women are morally superior or that in the twenty-second century they are going to govern perfectly, peacefully, efficiently, and with good feelings all around, but the world will run differently, more hu-

---

6 Women are not immune to the politics and rationales of war. Margaret Thatcher, Indira Gandhi, and Golda Mier all led their countries into wars; they were all young souls.

manely, and with more respect for nature. It will be crazy in new ways. People in men's bodies will be struggling with their "innate" limitations. Given the mature soul climate, self-help books, groups, and therapists will still be flourishing as they attempt to assist men to process their feelings of shame and inadequacy.

In the West, you have twenty-five years of major flux behind you, and five years in front, where there still is chaos about how the sexes define themselves. In the quest for new balance, interesting karmas are created as women and men experiment with new ways of being with each other.[7] This is one more reason that being alive late century is as intense and exciting as it is. Your entire past history within common memory regarding men and women is being rewritten, with you the authors.

JAPAN: YOUNG WOMEN IN A MATURE WORLD

As mentioned previously, the current of consciousness is moving along at a faster clip than during prior soul age shifts. Music and other western media carry messages far, fast and wide. A world population in communication with all its parts speeds personal and cultural change. The Japanese are very aware of what is going on in the West and one result is that already some Japanese women find themselves unwilling to put up with traditional male dominance, especially in the form of traditional marriage.

Japan is an early young soul society. Women have until very recently been tightly under the male thumb, servants really, who dared not voice opinions or ideas of their own. They raised children, cleaned, managed money, and basically said yes to everybody, especially males, no matter how distant or demanding. Not a high self-esteem situation. The Japanese have long considered that a woman was ruined, as good as dead, if not married by age twenty-five. High tension still exists around this issue, but

---

7 Karma gets created when at least one participant feels intense about a certain situation, be it a quick robbery or 20 years of marriage. The real reason you "pay it back" is that each essence wants to feel and understand, completely, how that experience was for the other person by living it through in a body on the physical plane.

many women are doing the unheard of and choosing not to get married — this without the full array of career opportunities now available in the West. Yes, the men are in shock. They don't understand what has hit them. Reacting in true young soul fashion, they are ignoring emotions and focusing greater attention on work and company life.

These non-marrying women, numbering as high as twenty percent in major cities, would rather focus on their own lives than lead the restricted life of a wife. To hazard never having a husband in a traditional society famous for sexism and social censure takes courage of the first degree. To buck group-think, disobey your parents wishes, and risk being treated like a social leper is a big step even for an independent-minded young soul. It is an incredible change that women are making, especially given that Japanese society is still pulling away from its pervasive (baby soul) herd-mind era where willful individualism was unthinkable.

Do you see what else is happening here in this new global ambiance? The traditionally oppressed women of the most powerful young soul nation are suddenly able to angle for their own freedom and independent development. Japan, easily able to dominate world business, can no longer count on dominating its women. Nor, as it turns out, can it count on them to have enough babies to replace the current generation in the labor force. Interesting times.

The children Japan does produce are smothered with attention, clothes and toys. Children quickly given everything don't necessarily develop strong relational skills. Later, these youngsters are so pressured into performing at school that when their hormones start zooming they suppress normal adolescent craziness in order to pass tests. Adolescent emotional exploration is sacrificed on the altar of academic excellence. Remember, young souls like to excel, whatever the cost, so it is not just demanding parents causing this to happen. But by this repression, teenagers further arrest relational development and often end up emotionally abridged. Developmental arrest is one reason why phenomenal numbers of middle-aged businessmen read sado-masochistic comics on the train during the morning commute and why large numbers of women remain so childlike.

In Japan, you won't be seeing a maturation of the emotional bonding between the sexes as you will in North America, Europe, and other mature soul areas. The sexes will be getting more independent from each other, not closer. In a young soul country, relationships and family systems are bound to dwindle in importance. On the other hand, all that energy being directed into education and business gives an edge in the money world, which is "where it's at" for the young soul.

AROUND THE WORLD

We previously examined what happens to society when young soul men start getting born into heretofore baby and infant locales. Watch out status quo! It is a rare young soul who will stay on the bottom for long, no matter how the deck is stacked against him.

Quite similarly, status quo takes it on the chin when young soul women start being born into these same societies. They aren't willing to be slaves either. To work hard, gain little economic security, have no rights, and no hope of betterment becomes intolerable. No more resigned feelings about seven kids and a depressive husband who drinks or gambles the money away. Life starts reorganizing itself fast when young souls are around.

These women's inner lives give them little choice but to stand up for themselves; they will make men, laws and churches change. The lines will be drawn with feeling and a sense of urgency, "I am human and I am not putting up with this: Life must change." Men and society will try to slam doors on these women, but without much overall hope for success, particularly in Christian countries. In Islamic, Buddhist, and Hindu countries, life for women is not quite so ripe for transformation, nor are risk-taking young souls being born in such numbers.

Neither Latin America nor Africa will be particularly tumultuous because of the male/female restructuring that we expect. The underlying sense is that times have changed and people had better be moving along. Social programs, education, employers and husbands, fathers and boyfriends will all be shaping up as the newly uppity begin to change the climate for all women.

This reordering in the developing world will be provoked by small numbers of mostly lower-class women. Given the times and the substantial strength, stamina, and independent spirit of the young soul, the tide turns, not in a noisy revolutionary manner and not even with the amount of chaos the U.S. experienced around this issue. But the tide turns. Women gradually and irrevocably gain power, safety and say-so in their lives. These women are less likely to seek career empowerment than a personal sense of power, security for their children and families, and improved communities.

Most South American countries will continue to have baby soul majorities, but the atmosphere for women will shift. If the Catholic Church chooses not to support women in these changes, the church will lose adherents and power, home of Mary or not.

While the predominant soul ages in Africa are set to remain baby and infant, autonomous young soul women will be born there too. Traditionally, black African women have enjoyed greater independence than Asian or Latin women. Africa's influx of young soul women may want to forgo children, and instead create and manage businesses and make money. They won't be making huge changes in the way life looks for the average woman. Women's rights will be increasingly protected, though, and surgeries to excise the clitoris and labia will fall out of style. In the wake of the devastation of Africa's populations from famine and disease, women, conservative and responsible as they are, will come into more local control.

As India moves forward in the decade, some of its young soul women will courageously challenge rules, hoping to gain political footage and increased autonomy and safety. We do not see a quick or dramatic change here, more a slow struggle often pushed to the back burner. India's social institutions are so intricately multilayered and embedded that they are nearly impossible to (successfully) confront head on. Indian women have a fair chance of manifesting nearly equal rights and not-quite-equal opportunities by 2030. Male/female power issues take a long time to solve here, partially because the social training for women creates a great fear of independence, of even looking at life head-on.

The Indian women who intend to move the female sex forward will have to work hard and long, sifting through argument upon argument and the debris of lost battles. Most of the young soul women we see coming up are teenagers and younger now, but they are nearing twenty percent, sometimes twenty-five percent in the under-twenty population, again depending on locale. They will have the independence of thought, the drive and the nerve of typical young souls, but will know they must move carefully, with persistence, for the old ways won't disappear easily. This up-and-coming young soul country will stick with male rights and under-valuation of women for as long as it can. Right now, the push in India is towards creating a society where men can make it economically, and not towards a society that fully enfranchises women. India's citizens have had so little for so long that few can imagine a world with enough money, food, or opportunity for all.

Nevertheless, as women slowly gain more power in India, the unconscious way life now operates will change. Women will start looking at life with an eye towards rooting out the underlying causes of problems. Family size will be rethought, as well as the distribution of education, medical care, and wealth. And, women will be re-thinking the traditional marriage in which a potential husband is paid handsomely to take a girl off her father's hands. Not only do dowry systems humiliate and devalue women and leave them bought, vulnerable and exposed, at worst dowry systems place their lives in danger. Several thousand young Indian women are killed each year, usually in poorly investigated "kitchen fires." The woman is splashed with cooking fuel and ignited; the husband can thus marry again and collect another bride price. Usually he won't have any trouble finding another father willing to pay, even with the potential risks to his own daughter's life. The young soul crew would like to get this bit of tradition changed because it makes women's lives precarious.

In the Asian countries which will remain popular baby soul gathering spots, tradition will remain tradition, women unquestioning. But the position of women won't be rapidly changing even in those countries striding into materialistic young soul phases. Singapore, Taiwan, South Korea, Thailand, none of these will be adjusting themselves much on women's issues. Economies in these countries will continue to perk, money will be easier to make and there will be an abundance of material goods to buy. Women will be more frequently educated, hold jobs, and run businesses, but basically these countries will remain relatively tradition-bound in regard to how the sexes are viewed and treated. When either women or men manage to obtain any comfort financially, they will begin helping relatives to move up. Very few will be trying to fix society in order to provide the female sex with fairer breaks.

China, as usual, is running its own course. The government already insists that men and women are equal partners, with equal rights and responsibilities. While women do receive nearly equal educations and are forbidden from becoming baby machines, Chinese society is nevertheless pervasively sexist. And it is not a big issue. Life between the sexes has strayed far enough from traditional paths for now. The main movement we see in China is towards economic freedom, meaning relief from bureaucracy and police and more autonomy to do business and make money. Whatever elbow room women have gained over the last three decades appears to be enough to satisfy for the next decade or so. Much needs to be done in China for it to become the world power it desires, hence casting a critical eye on a still-patriarchal system doesn't carry much interest.

RUSSIA, ETC.

The former Soviet Union was another populous society where women supposedly had achieved equal status, rights and freedoms. Once again, actuality was different. Women ended up working their demanding jobs and doing their traditional tasks, performing twice the work of their men. They were factory workers or scientists too, and they were the people who stood in many long lines to purchase the day's supply of food, which they then cooked and served. They were the ones who most evenings washed out the day's laundry in the bathtub and cleaned the flat. To them, this extra burden was just one more requirement put on them by the monolithic system which ran everyone's life and was impossible to budge. These women are worn and beginning to feel their resentment.

The current political uneasiness and social chaos make for poor timing to address male/female issues. But, as life begins to find a new balance over the next decade, it will be seen that women have in fact gained more control over their lives and their men, without major confrontational squabbles. The main focus now is necessarily on political and economic issues, on how to co-operate and use freedom wisely. Sexism gets worked out peripherally.

EUROPE

Both Northern Europe and North America climbed out of rigid sexual stereotyping in the 70s and 80s. By the 70s, most European countries already had mature soul majorities making the process more gentle than in the U.S. Laws, customs and people changed, while the sexes continued to enjoy their polarities. Women allowed themselves their feminine allure and romanticism; many men retained their charm and gallantry. European men were not so beaten down, nor were the women so tough as in the U.S.

Southern Europe has yet to fix its traditional sexism, or to see much need. Greece and Italy, both with large mature soul populations, will continue to play with the divisions between the sexes, keeping the good girl/bad girl, virgin/whore dichotomy stirred up and their cat-calling, bottom-pinching males buoyant. The current pattern is still too full of excitement, intensity, and thwarted desires to release. For now, essences being born into those countries want the craziness of life as it is. Even the astral plane is voting for status quo.

Spain has quite a different scenario. It is pushing into its young soul era with thousands of its girl children being born as warriors, nearly forty percent. Mostly late teens and younger now, they will soon turn the men and the tight old Spanish system upside down, with little grace or tact.

With economies shaky in Eastern Europe, furthering equality between the sexes is understandably near the bottom of most people's agendas. However, these countries are now being heavily exposed to western media. which provokes changes in attitude and behavior between the sexes. In the meantime, as Eastern Europeans seek political and economic stability, increased rights for women will come along. Poland and Czechoslovakia particularly have many strong, grounded, practical women who are now unwilling to put up with recklessness from the male sex. For life to be good in these Eastern European countries, self-responsibility is crucial. Yugoslavia, engaged in warfare as it is, will, not surprisingly, hold women's rights in abeyance for a long time.

AUSTRALIA, ETC.

Australian women are definitely aiming for greater self-determination. While they may enjoy the macho of their men, they are after greater economic self-determination. The young soul woman here has swagger of her own. She wants to be able to put on her suit or overalls and prove she can run the bank or the ranch at least as well as the fellows. The hotter, more dramatic mature soul issues like rape, incest, and family and societal violence will receive publicity here, but the urge to dig in and fix these behaviors is small for the present. The young soul majority doesn't want to have its sense of freedom impinged upon by "excessive" rules.

New Zealand, stretched as it is between large numbers of baby and mature souls, is in a slightly different position. Mature souls have most of the power and run the show in a comfortable, laid back sort of way. The many baby souls add a stable, conservative element; nothing changes too fast. New Zealand is not an aggressive or competitive place, and few work too hard. Stable family situations are the norm and people feel secure, at home in their world. Women obtain enough respect and freedom already to make a restructuring of male/female behaviors unlikely. An essence now choosing New Zealand does so because a life in a comfortable, peaceful, non-hurried twentieth century place is what's desired.

VIOLENCE

Violence towards women and children comes under scrutiny with this consciousness shift because the mature soul wants life to be right for everyone and for justice to prevail. Abuse issues get talked about with an eye towards identifying and fixing the underlying social problems. Schoolchildren have begun to learn that it is not right for them to stay quiet if they are being hurt or sexually abused. It is only in the last fifteen years that a child anywhere would even have the vocabulary to make an accusation of sexual abuse.

Many people who were sexually maltreated as children are now being encouraged to let those memories surface so that they can be processed and healed. Therapists are digging in, exploring all aspects (except karmic) of abuse, and getting keener about spotting symptoms of early abuse in clients whose memories of it are buried.[8] Childhood abuse is primal, engendering lifelong pain and mistrust. Investigating all of this represents a huge shift in the power equations between men and women, between big

---

8 Even if your early childhood abuse had karmic elements to it, attempting to clear the sadness and rage out of your adult system is beneficial.

people and little people.

Violence in the form of physical, sexual, verbal violence is something fewer women are willing to blame themselves for. Women have been encouraging each other to pull out of destructive relationships, and not to assume their love for a man should (or ever could) heal him or cure a bad situation. Abused women are learning to put themselves first, to gather up bruised self-respect and get out. (The tricky part of this is that in the middle of a payback situation, you don't usually find yourself leaving until the karma is complete — even when you believe you should have left years earlier.) Women who have been pushed into sex are getting angry — instead of presuming somehow it was their own fault. College girls are sharing with each other, sometimes on bathroom wall lists, the names of fellows who get rough and won't pull back from unwanted advances. Men are being forced to become more conscious about sex, since if they don't back off when a woman says no, they can be shamed, censured and prosecuted. Society is less and less willing to provide cover for these behaviors towards women, another result of the consciousness shift in process on Earth.

If a situation exists in your family or neighborhood where violence may be occurring, you will be more inclined to overlook it, to put blinders on and not deal with it, if it's a karmic payback. Fresh new karma being formed right in front of your nose smells about a hundred times worse than karma which is wrapping itself up. People commonly feel much more passion about preventing new karma from being formed, and more wary about interfering with that which is being completed. Moral principles aside, your body and emotions will have you reacting to the differences very clearly.

Violence won't stop, but it will gradually recede. In fact, there may seem to be more violence short-term simply because it more frequently shows up for public discussion and condemnation. The day is not yet past when a woman reporting a rape may be poorly treated by police, doctors, and the courts, but as

UPCOMING CHANGES

women increasingly participate in those professions, shabby treatment will dwindle.

Violence in news reporting, novels, comic books, cartoons, television programming, and films entered increasingly into human circuitry throughout the 70s and 80s. Starting with the then-shocking brutality of *El Topo*, films of the last two decades became progressively more violent. Rambo and dozens of other macho heroes of wars, guts, guns, spears, and bombs created odes to the dark side of male strength and individualism. Similar to the way baby souls instinctively knew they had better jump up and fight abortion before time passed them by, young souls moved to get in their last licks before this testosterone-pumped gore fell from favor. Thus, the orgy of film, television, literary, and street violence arose out of the young soul's sixth sense that times were changing.

The 90s will at least see a turn from commonplace brutality and violent action in films and television. Once blockbuster action films no longer guarantee megabuck returns, Hollywood will find higher moral ground and put its money and its mouth into creative, positive visions of life. Already it has produced a surge of after-death and reincarnation stories and geared up for female "buddy" movies. Quite a change. As mature soul mentality takes charge, the consensus will be that it was a mistake to allow so much violence to be aimed at humans, and especially regrettable in the case of children. Healthful entertainments and ways to spend leisure time will be discovered. Hollywood will change its focus, make more money, and help the world realize a new future (at least while Southern California is functioning).

REGULATIONS FROM THE HEART
People will enjoy feeling more heart-centered and having their societies more heartfully support family life and community. To ensure that life falls into line with new ideals, mature souls often decide to steer and supervise even minute parts of life. In Germany, mercantile establishments aren't allowed to open

82

evenings, Saturday afternoons or Sundays so that store employees can be home with their families. This makes it challenging for singles, or couples who both work, to buy groceries or anything else. In Berkeley, neighborhood streets are barricaded to through traffic, creating a confusing, time-consuming pattern of block-ades, thus keeping neighborhoods basically traffic-free and more pleasant. Main traffic arteries are jammed most of the time. New Zealand voted itself a nuclear-free-zone, risking the wrath of the U.S. and loss of port profits, but found the stance to be worth it.

Mature soul societies will delicately and indelicately regu-late many heretofore "unconscious" behaviors. Already you have stronger laws against rape, sexual harassment, and domestic vio-lence, stronger protection for children and stronger anti-discrimi-nation laws in the workplace and in the banking system. The en-forcement of these laws is starting to encourage changes in think-ing and behavior.

Violence and pornography may be regulated out of films. Pornography has been under sharp scrutiny for years. Promises of self-regulation probably won't do. Overseeing ways of being and living will cut into the freedom of action many people now enjoy. The mature soul, while trying to work these matters through carefully, often feels that a small loss of freedom for the sake of society's greater good is worth the cost. Some policies and laws are bound to be picky, silly, and overblown, and will need continuing revision until people are generally satisfied.

WOMEN'S RIGHTS AND THE NEW WORLD

Laws that support women and aim to equalize rights will be promoted worldwide by Western countries because the political benefits start to be clear. When women get support and begin to feel confident, family size plummets. Poverty lessens, children are better fed. Support of women also cuts into machismo, which then cuts into power trips, dictatorships, and wars. National economies do better. When women start getting a fairer shake, their self-esteem grows, and they tend to influence their men towards higher degrees of cooperation in the world.

Environment & Population
Moral Problems / Political Issues

What have they done to the Earth?
What have they done to our fair sister:
Ravaged and plundered and ripped her and bit her,
Struck her with knives in the side of the dawn,
And tied her with fences and dragged her down.
—Jim Morrison

I had assumed that the Earth, the spirit of the Earth, noticed
exceptions — those who wantonly damage it and those who
do not. But the Earth is wise. It has given itself into the
keeping of all, and all are therefore responsible.
—Alice Walker

OMNIVOROUS BIPEDS

The intense, near-the-brink quality of the current ecological
situation has two major causative factors: long-time young soul
control of the world; and, skyrocketing human populations. With
an orientation towards the natural world which could by no
stretch be called respectful, young souls began "taking dominion"
over the Earth several thousand years ago. Their natural urge to

explore and dominate propelled them to take advantage of all they discovered in the world.

Five hundred years ago, Europe was in a state of ecological havoc, its environment battered. By the time Columbus left on his voyage, disease, plague, squalor, failing crops, malnourishment, and starvation were the miserable lot of the common man. In addition, a disabling and nasty sexism was heaped upon the ordinary woman. Animals were hunted to scarcity and even to extinction; nature was to be suppressed. Brutality from lords and landowners was commonplace, the Christian Inquisition in full swing. With this dismal downhill slide in process, only the exploitation of the New World's wealth kept Europe powerful and gave it the space, time, and resources to get its natural world in better order.

As the very systems that support all life are now dimming and threatening to crash worldwide, young soul consciousness — whether Rush Limbaugh[1] bragging that the sound of a chain saw is music to his ears, politicians unwilling to pursue needed policies, or corporate decision-makers with today's profit the only concern — strives to deny the facts that the Earth is daily presenting. The numerous recipes which appeared for spotted owl dishes and the many bounties offered for shot-dead spotted owls were, at best, semi-satirical attempts to put nature in its place. Subjugating nature was a perfect and understandable young soul quest. To subjugate it further now, begins to equate with a wish to self-destruct.

While it is normal for young souls to seek their own immediate advantage and yearn for more, they can be wrestled down at this historical hinge point and pointed towards more appropriate, planet-regarding ways of operating. Perhaps you are here now to hold a clear focus, press for appropriate action, and help heal the severe wounds the Earth has already sustained. If humanity chooses mass survival, young souls can't be given too many wiggle options here. (And old souls can't be too lazy!)

Humanity is being given a chance to gain the critical mass

---

[1] Many of the people who influence and appeal to baby souls are powerful young souls.

necessary to catch up with bad habits. When the evolving way of thinking gets a stronger grip and greater numbers of people clearly see that increased fulfillment comes from connections to people and community life, to nature and spirit, and not from more power or more stuff, there will be a different feel to making the same "hard" (i.e., ecologically sane) decisions. People will begin acting more collectively, uniting to help each other and the planet. Humans everywhere will band together to guide business and political interests to a more mature consciousness of stewardship. Adding to the excitement in the meantime is a large wave of virtually obsessed young souls aiming to stake their last claims, whatever the cost to nature, before time passes them by. Their natural reaction to go for broke makes the necessity of handling environmental issues quickly and with integrity the liveliest of challenges.

THOSE EXPLODING NUMBERS

Being inattentive or disrespectful of nature on a planet of finite resources is one side of planetary degradation; the other is burgeoning human numbers. If the population explosion isn't faced, other problems are guaranteed to explode. It's simple: The more people, the greater toll on the natural world. Industrialized countries have too many over-consuming people; developing countries too many under-fed people — and too little land to do anything about it. The environment copes with neither easily. Both groups are multiplying like lemmings before a suicide year.

As a result of climbing populations, developed areas suffer from disappearing forests and wild lands, farm land and soil. Plant species and animal species are lost every hour, every day. People are living with severe air pollution, mountains of garbage (plenty of it toxic), filthy water, vanishing fish, congested cities, and escalating crime. Because gridlock, crime, and pollution make large cities less efficient for business, young souls are experiencing concern and are more and more pliable about needed concessions.

The developing world, even without one car per person and lengthy commutes in from the suburbs, is so peopled that it has its own choking congestion. This gridlock comes from trucks, buses, cars, taxis, motorcycles, bicycles, donkeys, carts, and people, people, people. The surge in people has created squalor as well as a surge in the rats, insects, bacteria, and diseases that prey on humans. It has meant losing forests and rivers and soil, thereby creating miles upon miles of desert yearly; and it has meant air and water pollution more severe than in most industrialized countries.

Developed countries siphon off a huge percentage of third world resources, resources these countries can ill afford to lose. Even if coffee, tea, cocoa, sugar, tobacco and other drug crops were immediately uprooted, and the land given over to the production of real food for local consumption (and even if soils and climates weren't deteriorating rapidly), few of these poor nations would have sufficient arable land to feed their swollen human populations. Over ninety percent of future world population growth is charted to occur in these already over-stressed nations. The economic forward momentum of the 60s and 70s has been stopped and reversed in every area where human numbers continue to spiral upward.

Though Iowa and Bangladesh are equal in size, Bangladesh is considerably richer in natural resources. Imagine how poor and miserable Iowa would be if it had to cope with Bangladesh's population, which at 120 million is *forty* times greater than Iowa's. Any country can be rich if its population is small enough. Bangladesh, devastatingly overpopulated already, could double again in a short twenty-three years at current rates. But it isn't solely Bangladesh that gets poorer each year. Most every third world country does, because huge increases in people exert a downward force on living conditions, wages, and natural resources.

Downward pressure on living conditions is now occurring in

the U.S., the only industrialized country which has kept birthrates higher than replacement rates. California's phenomenal growth rate rivals many third world nations. If your age is over fifty, you have seen the U.S. population double; with continuing high immigration and high birthrates (primarily from first and second generation immigrants), numbers could easily triple in your lifetime. Central America, did not just double, or triple or quadruple in the space of fifty years, but rose by a factor of five. It was not alone.

From our perspective, it is clear that nearly six billion people greatly exceeds the carrying capacity of the Earth — if you want a healthy planet and humans with healthy futures. Even if the world were sensibly and fairly run, human populations in excess of four billion push the limits of Earth systems and resources. Not even at the height of Atlantean times was the planet's population so high, and never again is it likely to be.

On an essence level, you know that current population levels are unsustainable. The esoteric reason they are so inflated: Everybody wanted to be around, embodied, for this transition, to observe, participate, and perhaps even direct the way it will go. Yes, you are certainly right, sanitation and simple modern medicines greatly enhanced human ability to survive childhood diseases, and continent-to-continent food transfers have averted many famines. These factors all supported the ballooning of human numbers over the last four decades.

Yet, babies don't happen solely because of the joinings of sperm and egg (half of all conceptions are lost in the first few days), but because souls are pressing to become physical. Although you with the physical bodies are actually in charge and it is your place to say, "Yes, please!", "Not yet!", or "No way!", an essence wanting to become physical has the power to push people, and biology, around. (It won't surprise some of you parents to hear this!)[2] When millions of souls want bodies, there are more

2 Michael's viewpoint, as spoken by T.E. Lawrence: "Isn't it true that the fault of the birth rests somewhat on the child? I believe it's we who led our parents on to bear us and it's our own unborn children who make our flesh itch."

apt to be millions of new humans born.

Many of you catapulted yourselves into this dynamic era fully aware that the Earth would not continue to sustain five or six billion souls forever, and that you personally might not be lingering through to a ripe old age. What we are seeing is a probable twenty percent drop in population by the year 2000, provoked by a combination of earthquake and volcanic activity, poor crop years, challenged immune systems in plants and humans, severe problems with infections and diseases, and relatively localized nuclear contamination from several power plants.

Even a decline of one billion in worldwide population won't automatically "fix" the current environmental skid; but it will give the Earth a bit more breathing room, slow down the damage, and courteously give people a chance to rethink priorities and heal their natural world.

CRAZY STATISTICS

Shall we share with you some amazing feats of human multiplication and their noteworthy reverberations? In a long weekend, the world adds one million more hungry people (one million in excess of the death rate). In a decade, more than a billion (another China). India, despite years of half-hearted family planning, adds over 200,000 million a decade (almost another U.S.) to its crowded, malnourished space. It will top one billion by the year 2000, on its way to becoming more populous than China. Charmless new megacities, cities of over ten million and nearly unmanageable, are sprouting everywhere, especially in Asia.

Before the self-slaughter started, Rwanda had the highest birthrate in the world, with nothing positive being done to control its unsupportable, wild growth. In the Western Hemisphere, Haiti takes the high-birthrate cake. Tunisia, thanks to good leadership, has working population policies and peace. Next door, Algeria is growing like a weed at three percent a year, which could take its population from 15 to 32 million in a mere quarter century — and to 119 million in a century. Algeria is already tumultuous. Many Caribbean nations are so growthful that if the U.S. didn't absorb their excess numbers each year, they would explode, implode, starve — or bring their birthrates down fast. The U.S. with the fastest growing, least stable, population of any developed nation, chooses to spend more on defense each day than on family planning each year. The Vatican effectively promotes population growth on the continents which can least afford it, Latin America and Africa, blithely ignoring all its responsibility to future generations.

There are now 1.7 billion more working-age people in the least developed countries than in 1950. Many have never found regular work; one billion earn only malnourishment wages. On current trends, an additional two billion more working age humans are expected by 2025. Workers without work are pouring across borders, legally and illegally, everywhere, but especially into Europe, North America, Australia, and even into well-guarded Japan, this despite the fact that low-paying unskilled jobs are being shifted to the third world. The root problem is not lack of jobs or skills, but the number of people on a finite planet.

Extra fertilizer rarely produces extra food now. It's all been done. Pumping up yields isn't working, no matter what the new inputs. Twenty types of plants now provide ninety percent of the world's food, a shaky situation which could easily imperil the continuing existence of large portions of the food supply. In 1950, most countries more or less fed themselves most of the time. By 1990, one hundred countries regularly depended on the U.S. for grain.

Fisheries are depleted. Fish prices are soaring around the world; oceans are no longer a source of cheap protein. Per capita food and income levels are currently falling nearly every place in the third world — even though governments are a little less corrupt than a decade ago. Less food and less cash take a terrible toll on people — malnourishment, increasing sickness, and less education for children. Development has been overwhelmed by the population explosion. Countries find it an impossible task to keep up with, much less improve, important services such as sewers, water, electricity, roads, education, and healthcare.

ON THE EDGE

On an inner essence level, you are all aware that the 90s are a hinge period, an impactful exciting stretch of life on a very thin cutting edge. Which path will the Earth take? The fairly stable preceding four decades which supported this big-time population increase, are now jolting towards some kind of finale, maybe grand, maybe not.

From the astral plane, your essence plans many growthful, exciting lifetimes that alarm and shock your body and personality — once you catch on.[3] Personality must become attached to the body in order to play out the physical "game" (or most people would, on a bad day, have a lapse of attention and walk too close to an oncoming bear or truck, thus doing themselves in well before adolescence). Because the personality does get attached to physical life, it only reluctantly leaves a body. And twenty percent now have leaving on a nearby agenda.

Ecological systems are so quickly and dangerously weakening that without this rollback in human numbers and a concomitant shift towards responsible living, there is little chance for mass survival very far into the next century. With major consciousness and behavioral changes and declining numbers, the Earth will soon be the recipient of much needed help.

How exciting to taunt the natural world and peer into the abyss! "How close to the edge can we get? Can we still make it?" We hear this from you! Inspire and organize yourselves quickly or humanity will face an austere future (and austere future lives). Humans always create the future by design or by default. Playing too close to the edge is what we would call default, and can easily lead to destruction.

---

[3] The astral is the plane closest to the physical plane. When your body dies, more of "you" lights up on the astral plane, where you heal yourself from the pain of physical life, grow in emotional understanding, and plan future lifetimes with your family of friends.

BASE OF LIFE

Loss of soil is one of the problems we see as most threatening to sustained human life on Earth. The land itself is disappearing and not just from its burial beneath roads, parking lots or buildings. U.S. soils have been so poorly husbanded that something like five tons *per person* are lost *every year*, blown and washed away. Chancy levels of soil loss have, in fact, already occurred all over the world, chancy because topsoil doesn't come back. Good deep soils take thousands of years to build; loamy, dark and beautifully fertile, they maintain moisture between rains and nurture abundant, healthy crops.

Disconnection from the natural world is so common that city people (North Americans particularly), even just one generation away from the land, have difficulty grasping the importance of dirt. Good soils are the backbone of U.S. and Canadian affluence; they not only produce the steady supply of affordable food on your table, but also maintain health and strong bodies while freeing energy to create all you do with your lives. Like other resources, soils are being depleted at a much greater rate than renewal can occur. Oil and coal, also non-renewable and on their way out, will eventually be replaced by better, cleaner energy sources, but what do you replace dirt with? World-wide greenhouse hydroponics?

As chemically dependent agribusiness and short-term economics replaced the practical family farmers who did their best to nurture their land, problems multiplied exponentially, even while food supplies rose. U.S. soils have already lost nearly *half* their organic material and minerals and furthermore are full of the toxic residues of "modern" agriculture and the "green" revolution. A rather insane ten pounds of pesticides per person, children included, is still applied to soil in the U.S. every year, with residues which hurt all life, including the important microbial life in soils. Let this worsen further and you "create" sterile soil, soil which won't support life. With good stewardship the organic and mineral content can be slowly rebuilt, while cover crops, hedgerows, and trees can keep some of that five tons per person from being blown and washed away. However, topsoil that is already lost is gone forever. It can't be rebuilt and there is no place from which to truck it in. Neither fertilizers nor nice organic compost can pinch hit for missing topsoil.

Saline soil is showing up in all areas of the world which have been subject to chemicals and heavy irrigation. When irrigation water can no longer drain through the soil, salts build up there and in the ground water below. Most plants abhor salty soil. Their refusal to grow causes further desertification. The solution? Quit using chemicals; pesticides, herbicides, fungicides, and chemical fertilizers. Restore the health of those soils; add minerals, add organic material, grow cover crops, appeal to nature spirits and devas, and replant forests, for even those forests hundreds of miles away help create more rain and deeper, spongy drainage. What is being done? Nothing of the kind. Bizarre technological "fixes" are plotted; (young soul) mechanistic science aiming to trick nature into a few more years of productivity.

Soil erosion is equally a developing-world problem. Even tropical soils that start out good won't support the intense agriculture being asked of them now, so they too are degrading and disappearing. As human populations boomed, many wildlands were taken over by people attempting to feed themselves. Grasslands were burned and forests that helped to create regional rain were cut; less rain in these trickier climates can quickly equal drought, then famine. When thin soils are intensively farmed for even a few years, they quickly stop supporting life, and sometimes can't even create cover for their bareness against a blazing sun or rain and windstorms. When nothing can grow and water doesn't soak in, the dust storms grow fierce. Then it is said, with a helpless shrug, "The desert is encroaching; the climate has changed." The climate has changed, but it is human activity that causes deserts. (Though deserts, because they adversely affect rain patterns, do tend to self-perpetuate and expand.)

So far, problems with soil aren't even a glimmer on the map

of Western consciousness. But, as the climate becomes less benign, the marginalization of once good soils will play to a larger, more concerned audience. Poor soil quality will then be seen as tightly related to poor crop years and caloric shortages.

BREATH OF LIFE

Trees make the atmosphere breathable and help create rain and manage water. They soften the weather and provide food and shelter for a myriad of creatures. Beautiful, dignified, and admirable, trees are absolutely vital to the continuation of life on Earth. Trees are disappearing too, and not only from excess logging and development; they are dying everywhere, on their own, through climate change and disease, weakened by the modern world. Germany's Black Forest is no longer abundant enough to support a devic fairy tale.

The deck is stacked against trees; many species are so sensitive to polluted air that they weaken and die. Acid rain is hard on the finish of your car, but it kills trees. They can often survive some climate change, a summer's extra heat or lack of precipitation, but they are weakened for years afterward and have a more difficult time fending off insects or an aggressive new fungus. Humans cut trees because they are valuable for paper, fuel, and building projects. When they cover land that developers, road builders, or farmers want, they are considered expendable. With their ecosystems dismantled in newly denuded areas, trees struggle to regrow.

Forests around the world are under stress, their life force dimming. This situation is critical. Humans are not sufficiently technological to be able to live without them. Keep your options open: Plant trees, nurture trees, protect their habitats.

BEVERAGE OF LIFE

Water loss is another looming issue on the planet of six billion. Aquifers, the huge underground chambers that have gathered water into them over millions of years, once seemed inexhaustible. Worldwide, people are pumping this ice age water at much greater rates than it is replaced. In the U.S., three billion gallons of water are removed every day, not to be replaced. In Arizona, it is often illegal to dig a well because the water table has sunk too drastically to allow unmetered use. Half the wells in Beijing are dry, with the water table dropping six or seven feet a year. Mexico City, still growing by a million people a year, is losing eleven feet annually from its aquifer. In India, old, always-productive wells must now be dug deeper or the village loses its water; many can no longer be dug deep enough to find year-round flows. People are making extraordinary demands on thinning water resources.

Because of deforestation, each year less and less water soaks into the ground to be tapped for use. Fewer trees also mean less water evaporating into local clouds and less local rain. What rainfall there is more easily floods as it quickly runs off towards streams and oceans (taking plenty of topsoil with it) instead of soaking in and enhancing groundwater supplies. Water is simply not as available as it was five years ago, much less twenty or one hundred years ago. This resource is literally being drained away.

Humans and their lawns, landscaping, agricultural, washing, and sewage needs have simply outstripped the amount of water available. Fossil water is near exhaustion and the skies don't rain as predictably. What do you do for encores? Young souls say desalinate ocean water, dam everything, and colonize Mars if necessary. Mars isn't even in the equation. The world, though, is learning that there are limits to rerouting and damming rivers if you don't wish to put ecological systems in havoc. Desalinization on a large scale costs a fortune — ask the Saudis why locally grown strawberries cost twenty dollars a pound. It is also beginning to make Arabian seas too salty for fish.

Severe water shortages will continue to be problematic, making life less lush in all parts of the globe. Shortfalls of water can mean shortfalls of food — not just quick, every-other-day low-flow showers. Water is important enough that wars will start over it. Many countries now share water more or less peacefully, but what happens when water is less abundant? What happens to Israel, for example, which now takes nearly half its water from an aquifer under the West Bank, when it succumbs to pressure and gives back the West Bank? What happens anyhow when that aquifer is drained? Fiery flare-ups provoked by water issues are highly likely during the 90s in the Middle East.

Water is also increasingly polluted — bad for people, worse for children, hell for fish, and more often than you might imagine, so foul even industry cannot use it. Pollution of fresh water is an elementary problem compared to lack of water. Stop putting garbage, sewage and chemicals in it and, after awhile, the water is better; the river or stream or lake begins to heal (unless it is being made acid by airborne forms of pollution). Sane, ecological solutions appear to cost businesses and cities a great deal of money, so they come slowly, amid heavy foot-dragging. In reality, these changes cost nothing compared to the cost of procrastination at this moment in time. The more conscious humans are, the easier the changes will be — and the greater the future.

GREEN THINKING

The problems caused by the Earth's changing blend of atmospheric gases are alarming and have rightfully received much attention. People are alert and interested as they notice unprecedented droughts, heat waves, fires, snowfalls, floods, and storms stacking up. Greenhouse effects and ozone depletion could overshadow all other ecological problems by creating sudden and dramatic jumps in the magnitude of storms, temperature extremes and, in the case of ozone depletion, a vast general breakdown in biological immunity — meaning your immune system isn't so competent; neither is the tree frog's nor the tree's.

Because of people, industry, cattle, and new chemical compounds, the atmosphere's composition has changed, and continues to change. In turn, the Earth is changing because its heat can't so easily escape. The young soul mentality waits for all those greenhouse predictions to prove irrevocably problematic before making consequential change in the business-as-usual machine, just as George Bush waited for an ozone hole to form over the Northern Hemisphere, his hemisphere, before mandating substantive U.S. action.

Europe, Canada, and even the occasional Latin country are doing better, making commitments and taking action with the intention of creating solutions. Here, the U.S. and Japan have been the fiddlers, making do with whitewashes, greenwashes, more studies and obfuscation. Struggles between those working to protect personal and environmental health and those seeking to protect business and jobs whatever the cost will be tense until near the end of the decade, when the obvious dependence of humans on a healthy biosphere makes it too scary to muck around any further.

When the world's heat gets trapped by these greenhouse gases, what happens? Weird weather. Exciting weather. Difficult weather. The first half of the 90s had some of the most violent weather on record. The pattern of change, as you know from your personal lives, is rarely smooth and uniform. Given the continued high releases of greenhouse gases, these are the weather patterns and events we see closing in: fiercer summers and winters with more erratic springs and autumns; rain in deluges, or dearth, with widely varying annual amounts; stronger, more damaging storm cells with increased lightning, more forest and grassland fires; warmer tropical oceans and monstrous water-borne hurricanes, typhoons, and cyclones. Increased difficulty in growing crops is obviously going to be one direct result of changing weather cycles.[4] Increased volcanic activity will counter the greenhouse warmth with temporary cooling effects. But volcanic debris is not a perfect balancing act for greenhouse gasses; rather it is just another factor pushing weird, undependable weather patterns.

When society finally becomes serious about fixing the environment, the will and the way will be found to take the profit away from practices that pollute the world or deplete finite re-

---

[4] Crop failures were prevalent world-wide in 1994. Only the U.S. produced surpluses.

sources. The cost of environmental damage will start being fully factored into public decision making. The cost of lost resources and pollution will be factored into the prices of goods. This is called green thinking and green taxation and makes elegant good sense. Those who are profit-motivated regardless of downline costs (whether Mom & Pop at their corner grocery or the most multifarious multinational) will balk at making change despite myriad warnings. Environmental protection does often impose some short-term costs, often surprisingly minimal, but long-lasting benefits to life and finances can be great. Sometimes nature's blessed lulls in the action are too optimistically taken. It is not that suddenly there is no provable problem or that the need for global maintenance has receded: It is that you have been given a couple minutes more to get moving. Your choice is to promote sane attitudes and ecologically based action or to bask, unconsciously, in the fading sunshine of a passing era.

STRATOSPHERIC GASES

High up and very thin, the stratosphere has had a fairly constant amount of ozone layered in it. Life formed on Earth while this stratum conveniently protected plants and creatures from what would have been harmful amounts of the sun's ultraviolet rays. Now the composition of the stratosphere is changing; human activity has chlorinated it, thereby destroying ozone and creating ever widening gaps in this protective layer. Chlorofluorocarbons or CFCs, the chemicals at fault, are on their way out thanks to worldwide legislation, though still broadly used in aerosol cans, refrigerators, air conditioners, plastic foams, and in the cleaning of microchips.

Major volcanic outbursts also reach up to the stratosphere and literally blow holes through the protective ozone layer; these holes traditionally last for a couple of years before knitting back together. All that extra CFC chlorine up there changes the picture considerably. When this chlorine mixes with volcanic sulfuric acid, the combination more potently destroys ozone, creating bigger, more dangerous permanent holes. The sharp rise we expect in volcanic activity over the next four to six years is horrific news for the ozone layer and the protection it gives most life.

The problems connected with ozone destruction are sobering, skin cancer being probably the least perilous of the bunch. Phytoplankton instinctively retreat from extra ultraviolet by going deeper into the ocean; there they get less light, but then can fix less carbon — so the atmosphere gets more greenhouse gases and potential heat. And you get less oxygen. As one-celled plants, plankton will be able to adapt to some degree, but because they are at the heart of the oceanic food chain, the entire ecosystem will further deteriorate as they weaken. Plants, trees, and most food crops are also hurt by ultraviolet radiation, this unfortunately meaning less green life overall, more greenhouse heat and diminishing food supplies. People, animals, and plants will find their immune systems weakened by this extra ultraviolet radiation. Immune system degradation causes increased susceptibility to bacterial and viral diseases and will be a major contributing factor to worldwide declines in population.

Ultraviolet radiation eventually clouds the crystalline lens of the eye, the lens through which you focus on this page. Australians already are being strongly warned to protect their eyes from this hazard, although when humans get cataracts it is a simple enough procedure to replace the clouded lens with a decent artificial substitute. Not many animals will be the recipients of lens replacements. Animals and insects, unless they are nocturnal, have all-day, everyday exposures without the protection of sunhats, sunglasses, or sunscreens. Farm animals in Australia and New Zealand are already developing lens problems. Large-scale blindness would wreak havoc on the entire animal kingdom and the ecological balance of the natural world.

It has been fifteen years since the warning sounded. Because damage by these CFC chemicals is so straightforward and nightmarish, it should have been possible to get rid of them fast. It is much simpler, after all, to root one chemical out of industry than to retool the internal combustion machine or to leave forests intact. Many countries, usually the mature soul ones, saw the danger from these chemicals as so extreme that they unilaterally began phasing them out (when they could not get the support of the U.S., the major user). It seemed the moral and prudent thing to do. This is the kind of courage necessary for a save here. Waiting for everyone to climb on board is not possible, even when it is crystal clear that a global undertaking is inescapably necessary. Future security depends on commitment now. Sometimes you must act first and alone.

POLITE CONVERSATION NO MORE

The sun, which goes through its own cycles, looks as if it will be getting stronger and hotter over the next fifteen to twenty years. With a brightening sun, the greenhouse blanket already in place, and the many (unfavorable) feedback loops which tend to keep the fires stoked, the world is due for more violent and extreme weather. As normal weather patterns fall apart, the meteorological schizophrenia of El Niño years begins to seem normal. Beyond weather being increasingly unpredictable and hard on humans (and animals, insects, and plants), it is oddly difficult to predict whether the next ten years will actually heat up. The planet is in a unique, complicated, grab bag situation. Greenhouse gases could provoke cooling, if newly warm oceans and air create more high cloud cover. Add to cloud cover by a mere ten percent and you have started an ice age. Flip a coin: Fry or freeze?

If the weather in the late 90s manages to heat up despite atmospheric volcanic debris, we do not see much of an upwards bump in temperature nor a significant rise in the seas from melting glaciers or ice shelf collapse. If ecological sanity is not found and carbon dioxide, methane, CFCs, and nitrous oxides continue to be released, then the early 2000s will be rougher and tougher weather-wise than the current decade.

MORALITY AND RESPONSIBILITY

The U.S. has yet to see the wisdom of becoming energy efficient. After Ronald Reagan weakened mileage standards for new cars, with nary a squawk from the public, he then dismantled alternative energy research (and Jimmy Carter's solar panels on the White House roof). As an oilman, George Bush was more thrilled about drilling the fragile Arctic than about changing the type of light bulb used in government offices, which would have saved an equal amount of energy. Business interests in the U.S. are lobbying hard against any energy efficiency measures Al Gore and Bill Clinton advocate, managing to scare the public with fears about cost and lifestyle changes. These lobbyists do their best to equate ecological thinking with anti-business, anti-job, eco-mystic nonsense.

Though most Western European nations, and also Singapore and Japan, are far ahead of the U.S. in energy efficiency, delinquent U.S. technologies have received scant attention from the media. Many poor decisions in America are driven by the false view that being kind to nature is unnecessary because of America's huge resource base. The corollary and favorite mantra of lobbyists, that ecological practices will cost jobs and competitiveness, is equally wrong-headed. These false notions have already cost the U.S., and the world, dearly.

When citizens become either sufficiently frightened or inspired to deal with these issues, fuzzy thinking about energy use will sharpen right up. Energy efficiency is an area ripe for quick, positive results, green gold for the companies and countries which invent, produce, and sell the technologies. The U.S., if it falls further behind, risks becoming a big, broke old dinosaur.

The farther along the evolutionary path a nation is, the more likely it will concern itself over the whole. On energy use, the U.S., for example, has not taken the high moral ground, having been more inclined to stall meaningful change than to create it. With a sluggish economy, Reagan, Bush and other business-first proponents found it simpler to ease up on environmental regulations. Unless people are naturally thoughtful or educated by good leaders, they will be more fearful about job security than world ecological security. Although the Clinton administration has done its homework, combating the fears provoked by corporations and popular loudmouths has not been a top priority, so pro-nature legislation has been slow to appear. Europeans, in contrast, pushed their governments down the path of integrity and action years ago. Germany, with over twice the people and productivity of California, uses an equal amount of daily energy. The very traditional Japanese are energy efficient (and rich) thanks to their planning, which looks further downstream than today's quick profits. Singapore is proud of how energy efficient it is, and poised to reap many benefits in Asia on that note alone.

For an example of what people-power can accomplish, look at what happened with the nuclear dilemma. In the 70s and 80s, the probability of nuclear annihilation was palpably higher than it is currently. What happened? A few focused souls, primarily (mature soul) women, started moving with commitment and power to goad citizens into awareness, change the scenario, and release the planet from the grasp of (young soul) male fantasies which could have easily pushed the button on global thermonuclear war. As more and more people joined in, future world scenarios began to shift. This was no small thing. Making it through the late young soul period without a fatal, self-inflicted wound is predictably tricky on a planet as aggressive as Earth.

When enough of the general populace finds the same intent to fix the environment, an immense amount of attention will be focused on straightening out laws, taxes, lifestyles, birthrates, and technology. Politicians and industry will have no choice but to get real and get moving. Unfortunately, the environment is perhaps a thousand times more complicated and difficult to repair than nuclear annihilation was to avert or inefficient energy technologies are to upgrade.

UPCOMING CHANGES

HUNGER, DISEASE, SQUALOR, RESOURCES

There are many, many places in the developing world where malnourished populations barely sustain themselves. One way people survive on a short-term basis is essentially by committing national suicide with whatever natural resources exist. You can watch this happening in many ways, on many levels. Population pressures push people everywhere into encroaching on traditionally wild areas. When the forest is used up for fuel or cash, or the last bird or bear or monkey killed, or fish poisoned from mining run-off, the noose around everybody's neck tightens, with local populations always feeling it first and hardest. Usually these men and women are not exploiting their country's resources to bank a dollar profit from teak office furniture, ivory bracelets, or cheap rainforest hamburgers, but simply for their own basic survival needs. Unfortunately, with human numbers being what they are, wild resources don't have a chance to renew themselves. What was sustainable is long gone, and one-time resources like wood and land and water and biodiversity are being spent, gambled away. Suddenly, fewer people can be supported each year. Ask Haitians what happened to their once fertile country after turning the last tree into for-sale charcoal lumps.

Occasionally, there exist simple, ingenious solutions which can help shift these seemingly impossible situations so that nature can be saved while people find new, sustainable ways to provide for themselves. Birth control is a necessary part of any solution. As the decade moves on and the World Bank and third world governments are increasingly held accountable for their actions, we expect more success on local levels and more innovative green-science, grassroots, Peace Corps type activity to support positive solutions. The ideas and money to nurture green changes must usually come from outside, from people or groups dedicated to finding remedies for apparently hopeless, painted-into-the-corner situations. The poor don't usually have the overviews or knowledge to be able to jump outside their survival frame of reference and dream up solutions; the rich, educated third world elite, who enjoy the fruits of the present system, rarely pitch in money or good ideas, especially if the poor could in any way become empowered.[5]

While Oregon loggers worry over the survival of their way of life, they are not facing malnutrition, disease, or death, which is what the third world person may face if she can't get at that forest. The onus of responsibility is greater on the first world where there are many more alternatives, more freedom of choice, more education, and often more consciousness. Displaced loggers have options if they are willing to be flexible.

Multinational corporations have their hooks into the resources of undeveloped countries, often with more loss than gain for the locals. This multi-national activity, akin to the deals which send old-growth Oregon forests to Japan to be processed into woodchips, is often about convenience and short-term profit.

COLONIZING MARS??

Earth will, with high certainty, remain the place humans call home. No new planets are in sight. The human race will stick with Earth, bearing the many debts of mismanagement now and in future lives. Dolphins and whales, though, are gradually being "seeded" onto another planet because, through no fault of their own, the oceanic environment, their environment, is no longer healthy enough to live in. The aim of their suicide beachings is to demonstrate how intolerable the oceans have become; they are emotional pleas for humans to expand their consciousness and change their polluting ways. From the standpoint of the whole universe, the two most uncivilized behaviors possible for a sentient species are: one, blowing up or poisoning your planet past the point of habitation; two, harming any other sentient species on your planet, whether mindlessly or purposefully. Humans are guilty on both counts, and the Earth is consequently viewed as an

---

[5] A marvelous exception: The 93 year old Princess Mother of Thailand who in 1988, frustrated over opium growth and addiction in the hill tribes, started a project to substitute coffee crops, macadamias, and flowers, and then got Buddhist monks involved in detoxification programs for the tribal addicts.

uncivilized cowboy-like planet that is best to be wary of, a wild experiment at a far edge of the galaxy.

What is not yet clear is how much more austere and empty of life the Earth will become, or how much less diverse it can possibly become and still support even a couple billion humans. Currently, nearly six billion human mouths are killing off 150 other living species everyday. Variety is the staff of life, not simply the spice, and humans have been spending their biodiversity as rapidly as other nonrenewable resources.

New consciousness is growing, but it is not yet dynamic enough to achieve the most favorable possible outcomes. A tilt towards slowing down and cleaning up exists, but human will is not yet sufficiently focused to plow deeply into the adjustments necessary for ecological systems to regain health. Put worsening population pressures into the equation and you have pushed yourselves right to the brink. Is the planet going to find new balance or push onward into a disastrous, dangerous loss of diversity? Humans have abundant free will to work with on that one, but it would help to be fast.

Even though you are witnessing the passing of the exploitive young soul phase and are clear that the currently embedded materialistic way of life is dysfunctional, changing your lifestyle for a dream, an ideal, or a question mark is a maverick idea, never popular mass activity. People do not like giving up anything they have gotten comfortable with, whether it's Roundup on the front lawn, slaves, fossil fuels, cows, antibiotics in chicken feed, or blowing all manner of smoke into the communal air. Few choose to live more simply or more ecologically because they have been rationally or morally swayed to do so. Usually a shock must act as a catalyst to make change unavoidable, creating behind it a broad-based desire and mandate to get moving. Politicians soon act or get pushed out.

Bundled right up in this ruinous crescendo of environmental disasters is a noticeably more humble way of life. The financial system is already unstable and will grow worse. Spurred by events, many of you will see the future and choose simpler lifestyles and be happy about elementary things like not putting your car's weight of carbon dioxide into the atmosphere each year. Others (of you?) will be kicking and moaning, regretting the loss of material distractions to changed circumstances and policies. Bright sides to reorganizing your world will be apparent, but feeling forced to surrender, forced to make change never feels great — even when convinced there must be a silver lining in there, somewhere. While life may seem harder with fewer gadgets, luxuries, imports, meat meals or whatever, the sense is that Earth has at least received some time to heal and push the detritus of the twentieth century out of its body. Respect for the fragile threads of life, for the beauty of the planet and its creatures with their myriad interconnections becomes an awesome experience for many. New ways of thinking, feeling and being emerge. People learn that cooperation, not competition, sustains all life. This is a gigantic step away from young soul consciousness. The everyday world begins to feel more sacred. Freshly in tune with nature and grateful for the good that they do receive, many people will come into a deep, profoundly sensed connection with the Earth.

IF YOU'VE SEEN ONE REDWOOD TREE...

One occurrence that regularly shows up at the end of a young soul era is environmental degradation. Earth is right on schedule! Any sentient species will be most abusive of the planet which supports it during the young soul era. If dolphins and whales had available a clean, life-supporting environment, they could also have had overpopulation problems and other self-caused problems with their natural world (though never the technology based problems now confronting human tool-users). Once mature souls start gaining control, the issue is focused: Will the natural world continue to be degraded without a second thought? Or, does the alarm sound loudly enough to reverse the situation?

The swing to mature consciousness means increased environmental awareness, but the eventual outcome depends on how quickly problems and habit patterns are tackled after the young souls lose clout and prestige. Do the sentient beings sit on their collective hands or tails and keep easy, old habits, or do they initiate quick policy changes?

"If you've seen one redwood tree, you've seen them all." Not many Californians have forgotten their then-Governor's remark to conservationists wanting to preserve a few of the remaining original stands of the planet's most immense trees. When mature souls of Ronald Reagan's timbre are in charge, or in the majority, the loss of biodiversity will be swift and stunning. At Earth's current juncture, if each aspect of life isn't guarded and treasured, if the means to protect what exists aren't created, losses will pile up at a vastly accelerated pace.

Do you keep your wetlands or allow more to be drained? Do you keep your ducks and other insect eating, seed-dropping birds? How many wild areas do you accept being clearcut, dammed, or transformed into mini-mall, golf course subdivisions? Is it acceptable for a paper company to pollute a river valley because then more people have jobs? Risks and benefits must be weighed, but decisions made now have critical impact. Neanderthal ecology won't take humanity much further into the future. The time to protect biological diversity is now! Either you forge ahead, letting go of "entitlements" to nature, and do the right thing because you know it's right, or you continue to make compromises and paint yourself into corners where there are no tomorrows.

Diversity brings beauty to a planet, pleasure and excitement to its inhabitants — and security. Diversity is a safety net for all inhabitants, a guard against extinction. Sometimes those in charge will allow a planet to skid towards austerity, losing up to ninety percent of its original life forms. Even fifty percent of biodiversity going down the drain would keep humanity extremely limited. A species which allows such a loss to occur and manages to survive carries forever after a great emptiness. Life is never again as rich and they know it. No planet can continue to support life in the customary way after such losses; only highly technological societies survive such destruction of their natural world. Humans are not currently that technologically advanced.

NO MORE INFANTS, FEWER DEVAS

At some point during the mature soul period, nearly all planets with sentient life stop admitting new souls. Nearly simultaneously, new infant souls stop desiring to come because an already-mature world, like Earth, looks a bit worn and frayed. The wild devic settings for early lifetimes have almost vanished. Why choose a depleted Earth to begin a cycle of lifetimes? Also, playing catch-up to a majority three or four levels ahead is, at best, an uncomfortable strain. With so many advanced souls, infant souls get pulled and stretched to grow faster each lifetime and can't easily choose their own pace. Potential new souls also consider what scope they would have during their young soul period a thousand years hence. Would their creativity have much range or impact? Already, the game is more refined and confined, with fewer conquests, dictators or even dictator's statues left.

While this closure to new souls moves planetary consciousness along more rapidly, nature has a difficult time because there are fewer devas and nature spirits. Souls considering a cycle of lifetimes on any planet always first blend with the planet energetically as nature spirits to determine their affinity for it. The investigatory process tends to be lengthy before any commitment is made to a whole cycle of lifetimes. In the old days, when Earth was loaded with nature spirits, people noticed them more easily and gave them names like sprites, fairies, and elves. They were rightfully seen to be protective energies or spirits.

When in devic form, one has consciousness, intelligence, a total oneness with both nature and the Tao, but no physical body.[6]

---

6 Michael uses the term Tao, which means God, Goddess, All-That-Is, undifferentiated oneness, to avoid confusion with the image of a bearded Father-god in the sky.

To explore and know a planet, devic forms of life bind with different aspects of nature; these bonds help keep nature whole, strong and happy. When there are no longer large numbers of souls investigating a planet, nature is not as protected and consequently biological diversity is lost. Some helpful devic activity will always remain, regardless, but never at earlier levels. When devas thin out or abandon an area, nature looks flat, tarnished, as if its magic, vigor, and vitality had drained away. The deva deficit is always a part of the mature soul problem. How do you keep nature together without abundant devic help? (On the other hand, just because devas aren't dancing around every tree, doesn't mean you can't ask for their help with your garden, trees, and part of nature — and get it.)

On Earth, just as on any planet at this critical juncture, there is diminishing help from the unseen world at the very time all the bills from the young soul era come due. The preservation and nurturance of life is now up to the sentient species inhabiting the planet. Global maintenance is a major responsibility, and can be a major fork in the road. If those in charge don't intuitively sense the need to protect the biological bank account, much diversity is inevitably lost. With "alarmist" types (like Al Gore) at the helm and backed by consensus, a greater variety of life is saved for future generations.

While the planet has many people rooting for sensible energy alternatives, like solar and wind, and others putting time, creativity, and money into new, clean technologies, and yet others committing to saving forests, threatened species, native seed stocks and so on, current trends do not yet favor nature. But, you do have a saving factor coming up, a shoe thrown in the works, some sabotage against man's "progress" by Mother Nature. "Sabotage" is not a precisely correct term, of course, but these natural events will help clean house and buy time.

ARISING VISIONS

When the world can't do business or sustain life in the same old way, something new must be born. One advantage arising out of the trauma of the late 90s will be the inability of nations and people to continue in their current ecologically blind, self-destructive ways. Humans are being challenged to find a way of life which does not relentlessly take from the planet or steal from the children of the future. A sustainable economy, which neither poisons nor depletes resources, must be created. Politicians (Ronald Reagan, George Bush, and Newt Gingrich among others) will no longer be able to appeal successfully to the lowest common denominator by arguing, for example, that cheap fossil fuels are a rightful part of your standard of living or that environmental and labor safety regulations must be relaxed because the economy is stalled. It will soon be obvious to most people that economic and ecological health are inextricably linked.

Adverse environmental changes, ongoing weather catastrophes, and waves of illness will gradually push people into developing new ideas about how the world must look. We believe that by the end of 1996, a pervasive and powerful vision will be forming, with large numbers of people sensing what must be done. This vision is, of course, an ecological one. The critical mass necessary to make healthy choices in the U.S. will have finally collected itself. Western Europe comes to this point sooner; Australia, Asia, Africa, and Latin America make the leap a little later.

No longer turning their back on the Earth, humans begin to change their actions and ways of living. A beautiful sense of connection with the Earth takes root. Gratitude starts coming up when things go right — when crops grow well, when the rains seem "normal", and your community remains healthy. Most now take these gifts from nature unconsciously, not acknowledging the source of their abundance. A more reverent, appreciative, tuned-in state of mind is on its way.

With people no longer seeking highly materialistic goals, a

111

pensive, even depressed interval will necessarily occur, followed by a determinedly inspirational re-visioning stage. Many will feel compelled to examine and modify their ideas about life and to find new meaning. No one wants their reality to collapse into being solely a scramble for survival. As part of reinvesting in life and making existence seem worthwhile again, new concepts, ideas and images start arising and being discussed quite avidly, in day-to-day life and in the media.

A major worldwide reassessment will necessarily occur regarding the environment. How do jobs, industry, chemicals, technology, biotechnology, land use, agriculture, human and non-human life-forms — and cars — relate to the health of the natural world and to the health of humans? This new vision necessarily involves respect for life's network of interconnections, and includes the understanding that whether you are pulling apart the fabric of life in a rainforest or in your own backyard, you are pulling apart needed human support systems. Very soon it is only too obvious that the ecological fabric must not be further picked apart. Many of you will be involved in carefully weaving it back together.

ENVIRONMENT VS. MONEY

Silent Spring, Rachel Carson's seminal book, first stirred environmental consciousness in the early 60s. For three decades the spirit of materialism clearly beat out any spirit of deep change. The 90s will bring profound changes in point of view. Even highly educated, pridefully-rational Westerners are bound to become more mindful of their spiritual linkage to natural systems. Many will feel a need to take the wonder of nature into their hearts by gardening, hiking, watching sunrises, sunsets, full and new moons. As odd as this may now sound, many people will be searching for a way to express their appreciation for and unity with forests, wild areas and wild creatures. This will be done with ritual — and, increasingly, with political action aimed at protecting and healing nature.

E N V I R O N M E N T & P O P U L A T I O N

Those who live on the land, whether in Bali, Kansas, or rocky Afghanistan, have tended to be more mindful of their connections to natural systems than those who have lived in their heads. Now, more and more humans will begin to see that saving wildlands, waterways and species will help save humans — another threatened species, endangered, ironically, by sheer numbers.

What we see here is not so much a redirecting of society from above by the ecologically-minded, but a grassroots movement, filled to the brim with young people, which shakes off the shackles of status quo, and will no longer tolerate politicians or business leaders who lack the courage and common sense to make needed corrections. This movement may not spout words like sustainable or regenerative, but revitalizing nature and creating a world with a better future will be the essence of what is naturally sought. As people become aware of the value of replanting forests and letting certain areas revert to wilderness, governmental dollars are likely to be channeled into these projects. The crucial importance of funding programs to heal the natural world finally becomes plain.

BIOREGIONALISM

While national support systems shift and flux, people will come to identify more strongly with their local areas. The Republican intention to decentralize and reduce the size and role of the federal government will put power and money back in state hands and will encourage and accelerate bioregionalism. Buying regional products will receive heightened emphasis simply because it works well on so many levels and helps the environment quite a bit. As an area starts to consciously depend more on local food production, regional diversity is supported because fewer monocrops are grown for export to other areas; from pesticides to trucking, the load on the environment lessens dramatically.

Thinking local roots you in your area and makes you more committed to its health. The movement towards

113

bioregionalism, like the talk of California dividing into three states, will grow louder. Mature souls enjoy having both strong community identification and strong global consciousness; when the two intertwine comfortably it feels like perfection. Urban or rural, you are happiest when you feel connected to your place, your land, your own region of the world and when you appreciate the local people and culture, the woods, hills, streams, lakes, animals, even your area's unique blend of weeds and insects. Tuned in like this, you know what needs protecting and fixing, and are more likely to be willing to fix it or fight for it. Politicians like to complain that no one wants anything (usually meaning something potentially odious like an incinerator, dump, or halfway house) in their own backyard, but even convinced that it's all one backyard, the only place that most people feel absolutely compelled to protect is usually close to home.

Living in cities where water, food, and raw materials are in short supply and disease easily spreads is not an ideal situation at this time. Some entire nations, like Japan and Holland, survive solely by virtue of imports. While both create much of value for the rest of the world, neither could exist at anywhere near current levels of abundance if developing nations feed themselves first. (Similarly, if rural areas in developing lands were allowed to feed themselves first, most third world cities would quickly collapse.) In North America, as in Europe, the food situation is not currently critical, but it could be as food production falls with climatic strain and blight. Even though rural locales will generally be more comfortable during these changes than cities, no place is totally immune, remote, or risk-free. This is a worldwide event; all humans and habitats are involved.

FOOD FOR THOUGHT

As we see it, if food could be distributed equitably there would be minimally enough for everyone only if Westerners would drop their daily caloric intake to below 1500 vegetarian calories. With current habits and systems, that is most unlikely.

In any case, with world population increasing a billion a decade, feeding everybody at these minimums could last only a few more years, and does not take into account unpredictable climates or ecological problems, both of which will make food production progressively more difficult. That aside, within a few years of sharing those daily calories equitably among all people, challenges would be greater than ever. Relentless agriculture would worsen the weather, soil, water, and forests and the planet would be reeling from the still bigger crowd of human mouths.[7]

The bloat and heart attacks of Europe and North America are caused by food choices, but are also related to malnutrition elsewhere. Expect much debate, worldwide, as to whether poor countries should continue to export food (cash crops) or whether they should feed their own populations first. The mature soul will be very concerned about moral correctness here.

If these countries can't feed themselves, does it make sense to take their bananas? Or for prime agricultural land to be used for export sugar or cocoa instead of down-home beans? Or to continue to collect interest payments from a country teetering on disaster, magnanimously giving back a small percentage of that money as aid?

Europeans will be at the forefront, ending the practices they see as injurious. They may do so with boycotts or by placing high tariffs on tropical food imports to discourage use. Wealthy third-worlders will struggle to hold their cash-crop system together for as long as possible, simply because it keeps them rich. The multinational corporations controlling this trade will continue to exert strong behind-the-scenes pressure to maintain trade as is. But the pragmatic and moral issues won't disappear. Rather they will be hotly discussed and impossible to hide.

In the developed world, the sentiment will grow for third world countries to be given a fairer chance to feed themselves.

---

7 Growing food on the hoof generally means there will be less food and water for humans to share. That, and the problem of methane gasses released by cattle adding very significantly to greenhouse problems, will make meat less appealing over time.

Seeming to contradict those intentions will be strong feelings in first world, food-producing countries to keep grain "at home" to ensure supplies in chaotic times — even if that means people going without food elsewhere. Soothing consciences by sending shiploads of food will no longer be considered an option; public debate over what to do and what is fair will pick up considerably. The English may wonder about giving up their tea, but if the tea bush monopolizes land valuable for food growing, it will seem the correct thing to do. The same with Americans and their coffee. At the very least, foods imported from countries not able to feed themselves will seem more a luxury. Purchasing them may feel as shameful as buying fur may already.

Concern and guilt over famine in the third world will enliven the search for answers. Attention will go into analyzing systems and rooting out unjust practices. For example, the world will severely censure any government which is buying weapons and raising armies before attempting to feed itself. Population policies, conscious or unconscious, will come under intense scrutiny because they must be part of any solution to decrease hunger.

The emergence of mature soul consciousness will make the excesses of the West embarrassing and hard to stomach, especially as conditions in the third world become more pitiable. Western lifestyles will be seen as subsidized by the resources of poor nations. Again, the older the soul, the greater responsibility felt for correct action — and the greater sensitivity to the blind spots of one's homeland. Thus, mature and old souls will be those most conscience stricken about the increasingly awful state of poorer countries. Moral action will seem imperative.

The realization hits that U.S. deficit spending is part of the problem, and must be curbed; that third world debts need to be traded-off or forgiven to protect everyone's future; that the practices of banks and multinationals need scrutiny and immediate modification; and that third world leaders must be held accountable for what happens under their watch. This is not a short-term project, but it begins because the world is ripe for change.

Messages from the heart can no longer be easily neglected.

POPULATION

Because the first world has both the favorable land and fewer to feed, famine and pestilence will create more havoc in undeveloped, less powerful countries. The third world, especially, will see significant increases in malaria, leprosy, tuberculosis, cholera, diphtheria, dysentery, AIDS, and other infections and plagues. (If the weather warms significantly early in the next century, diseases from the tropics will migrate north with Europe particularly vulnerable.) With the burden on health from increased ultraviolet radiation, uneven food supplies, increasingly problematic parasites, worsening sanitation, crowding, fear and stress, even once simple flus can and will take deadly turns.

As ultraviolet radiation gnaws away at immune system strength and integrity, diseases will more commonly jump species barriers, before now an unusual event. AIDS has already transferred from monkeys to humans. In another very unusual event, Soft Brain Disease, an occasional problem in sheep, became Mad Cow Disease in Britain as the remains of infected sheep were used to feed cattle. Cats then developed their own brain softening disease, thanks to the infected beef in their pet food cans. The British Isles now have, understandably, many more vegetarians than previously.

Farm factories, which raise animals with cost as the only bottomline, engender problems that will become more obvious as human health deteriorates. When animals don't get sunlight, movement, or healthy food, their bodies don't exactly become healthy food for people to consume. Quality of life issues for the animals on these factory farms won't be ignored in a mature soul world, though when people are malnourished or starving, this issue drops lower on most agendas.

What with food and disease problems, along with natural and ecological disasters, populations in Australia, Europe and North America will likely decrease by fifteen to twenty percent before the end of the decade. In Africa we expect at least a twenty-five percent decrease in population, with potentially up to forty percent possible; Asia and Latin America will likely decrease by twenty to thirty percent.

Does the reduction of worldwide population by twenty percent overall reduce malnourishment? Sure, in some places, but for food to grow the weather must help, and even with bumper crops, politics must change or many people still won't have food. Asia and Africa already don't have enough food to go around. All possible tracts of land are being cultivated; Green Revolution or not, there is still not enough food.[8] If the number of mouths to feed is decreased and the weather doesn't deteriorate, more food becomes available per person if, and this is a big if, it is fairly distributed and not hoarded by the few or exported to richer places.

Latin America (excluding the Caribbean nations and Central America) has enough land to feed itself even at current population levels, but a good percentage of that land is tied up by landowners who won't allow it to go into food production. Rather, it lies continually fallow or is kept as expensive rangeland, a hard-edged, young soul tactic ensuring high crop prices and a desperately needy labor force. When crop yields sag because of worsened growing conditions, fewer people will not mean more food per person, unless more agricultural land is put into production.

POPULATION 2000
What with Nature weeding her garden, Earth has an opportunity for some quiet healing. Souls on the astral plane will not be pressing so strongly to return. There will be no groups of newly arriving infant souls, and humans will be more conscious of their breeding habits. Though populations plummet initially because of disaster and disease, most nations realize the thing to do is to

---

[8] The poorly-named Green Revolution of the 70s aimed to feed the world through scientific agriculture, but created myriad problems because of its heavy chemical emphasis and its discouragement of diversity.

keep their numbers down and avoid the usual, unconscious after-the-disaster scenario of breeding like crazy in order to affirm life. Some religious leaders are bound to start crusading for the small family, pointing out how low birthrates help squelch human misery.

Social awareness of population-provoked disasters will create pressure to keep numbers down. Freedom is never unlimited; human welfare is more gravely undermined by cancerous growth than by limitations on family size. Population control becomes more talked about, more participatory and more creative in the new century, not more draconian. Social pressure and government promotion of the two child family tends to work quite nicely, especially when the economic incentives and disincentives (i.e., no tax breaks with three kids) are there. Birth control continues to improve and becomes increasingly easy to obtain and use.

Abortion, also, will be more easily available. The emotional issues surrounding abortion will be carefully examined. Abortions always contain an element of sorrow because the soul trying to come in is usually an old friend, but it is not being allowed into (your) life, at least at that point in time. Calling abortion murder is not actually accurate because the soul is certainly not killed.[9] It is not yet embedded in physical life. (It may even come right back to you in another pregnancy or as that little niece or god-child you so adore.) The soul of the child-to-be hovers around the pregnant mother, but does not enter its body until birth, and even then it is only lightly attached for the first year or two, having some chance to opt out if life looks too difficult for it to manage. By early in the new century, abortion will be freed from its shrill fundamentalist context and instead seen as an option, one that is nobody's first choice.

Most mature souls realize that unwanted pregnancies can lead directly to too rapid population growth, poverty, child ne-

---

[9] Murdering a person doesn't kill the soul either, of course, but it is a highly karmic situation because a soul becomes attached to a body through living in it. Also karmic is the fact that other people have become attached to that person being in his body and are shocked and pained when he suddenly and violently is no longer.

glect, child abuse, and a dozen other unacceptable social problems, and that women who don't want to continue with a pregnancy ought not to be forced. The ability to be responsible, feed, and pay for children will loom larger as communities seek to protect themselves from socially irresponsible behavior by discouraging it. Self-responsibility may be encouraged by wiping out public monetary support for teenage pregnancy. Self-responsibility of citizens is an important element in any successful society and one that mature souls, in their rush to protect everyone, sometimes leave behind. Social pressure and welfare reform will soon remove teenage pregnancy from an American girl's list of interesting options. Worldwide laws preventing early marriage and promoting women's literacy and education would tend to delay the age of first pregnancy, thereby decreasing the number of children. Strong laws against child labor would prevent couples from bearing numerous offspring to reap economic benefit.

The methods by which population can be kept "low" are myriad, but one big element is always self-esteem, how women feel about themselves. As the female sex's sense of power in the world rises, the need or desire for numerous children drops drastically.

Both governmental programs and social pressure will combine to keep head counts down. The content of public programs will stir debate in the coming decades. It is already felt that taking destitute people and enticing them into sterilization is just one more demeaning action that takes power away from the poor. How then do you get women to have one or two children, and not their culture's typical five or seven, when children (sons especially) are viewed as old age security? Already in Brazil, specially plotted, long-running soap opera dramas are educating viewers about the value of small families, all within the context of an enjoyable storyline. Birthrates are falling dramatically as people see clearly, in characters they love and hate, the positive side of having fewer children. Simple advantages like less yelling, less exhaustion, more food, and more time for love are pointed out and start to impact female and male viewers on feeling levels, causing them to rethink the traditional more-is-better scenario. Male ego fulfillment through unlimited pregnancies and childbirths can be easily disassembled with these soap operas too. The media has the message. Given a little encouragement and another vision, both sexes are usually delighted to side-step the seven children option.

Getting to the root of the problem means giving poor women some sense of control over their lives. Enticement to sterilization will certainly still happen, but offering something more in return than a transistor radio or a half-month's wages to a person on the edge of starvation will seem vital. Rural water systems, sewers, schools, and clinics — these are the services that help make lives better and support couples to choose fewer offspring.

In fact, offering clean water, agricultural help, schools, road repair, etc., to local communities as a reward for low fertility rates will be seen to be more conscious and workable than the forced child quotas and sterilization being used in China. Local people immediately realize how their lives would be enhanced and enriched by these services. Let them figure out systems to cut birthrates — condoms or sterilization, rewards or penalties, education or shame — and then give the promised help as birthrates actually fall. The community has then tripled its security: It has a more supportable growth rate, the successful experience of pulling together to solve problems, and more security about sanitation, health, and the future. Coupled with the memory of what it was like when the world was so crowded, these tactics can continue to hold down human numbers.

FIXES ON CONSUMPTION

Consumerism becomes possible for those who have economic and political clout, but it is a young soul reward which puts tremendous pressures on world resources. People begin to realize this, but doing the right thing gets trickier when lifestyle, job, or savings may be threatened. Many people are so overwhelmed by the problems presented by conservation, including threatened price increases and unemployment, that they fail to see the benefits accrued by backing away from polluting technologies and relentless consumption. One sunny morning before long, politicians will discover that it doesn't take turning Texas on its ear to support solar research — or even to make a partial switch-over to solar.

Young souls go for expansion; mature, baby and old souls can appreciate the value of conservation, of taking care of what exists. Conservation is not glamorous and is usually pushed aside by politicians because even though you keep the world, it takes effort, money, and commitment — and someone's always yowling. The good news is communal will to adjust lifestyles and technologies to save the planetary home will soon arrive. Then, unless politicians are clearly on the side of conservation of resources and non-polluting technologies, they won't be electable. Not that there won't be frantic fear-based arguments against the supposed costs, but taking care of the environment becomes one more bottomline from which most refuse to budge.

Freedom clearly is not about the ability of an unregulated business class to destroy the interests of everyone else. Corporate leaders often fight conservation measures, complaining that regulations mean unwarranted government interference — meaning interference with their assumed freedom to exploit resources. Business will rarely do the ecologically correct thing until it either gives a competitive edge or everybody is forced into it. When world environmental situations drastically change, newly insightful politicians will find the necessary courage and stamina to tackle business interests and lead forward on environmental issues.

So how is it that environmental degradation can get turned around? Suffering. People get less resistant to changing status quo when life doesn't seem to be holding together anyhow. Suffering takes people to deeper, more thoughtful layers of themselves. The prior opulence of Western lifestyles starts to seem more distant and less appealing or ethical. Conservation starts to feel correct, not so bad. After all, you have already cut back! Sufficiently worried by crop failures, pestilence, plant and human diseases, consumers grow willing to take the cure, bite the bullet, and do whatever is necessary to regain planetary health.

Despite all that is missing emotionally in America, nearly everyone in the world wants its consumer lifestyle because it looks so powerful and glamorous.[10] Modern educational systems promote consumerist values and cleverness without wisdom. Children are taught to look down on self-reliance and on self-reliant indigenous cultures. But before long, social pressure against non-essential consumption will be strong and there will be less advertising to swell and exaggerate everyone's desires. Beginning in 96 or 97, blatant propaganda to encourage ecological thinking and sustainable living will be evident. People will be sobered by interesting facts now pitched at them, such as, "Tiny Switzerland puts twice the burden on planetary resources as bulging-at-the-seams India."

The puzzle of how to manage the planet so that it can regain health and stability will grab many people's interest. How do you support life now and insure that your great-grandchildren can be supported too? Just as the baby boomers somewhat successfully attacked racism, sexism, and war, the major task of this teen to mid-thirty generation, whose voices are beginning to be heard, is to tackle governmental reform and environmental issues. This will be the work of the next several decades.

THE NEW RELIGION

As the 90s move along, large segments of the general population will acquire a certain reverence for nature. Tribal people are usually conscious of the web of life, the sacred connections between all aspects of life. Peasants and farmers generally feel har-

---

10 The U.S., because of its size and consumption habits, is, ecologically speaking, the most destabilizing entity on the Earth.

mony with the natural world. However, once urbanized and mentally sophisticated, connection with the environment tends to slip away. By the late 90s, it starts to mend.

Humanity, long disrespectful of its human stage setting, now senses that something is very wrong, so wrong that the chance of a big save by science is mighty slim. Ill health and nature's ferocity make people fearful, but more willing to swallow the antidote. The survival of the physical world becomes such a looming issue that, along with acting more ecologically, men and women start doing more beseeching, whether it is through prayer, rain dances, earthworks, medicine wheels, communing with nature spirits or asking for help from the Goddess. This surge of feeling for the Earth has strong mystical and spiritual overtones. Individually and collectively, a connection with nature suddenly seems a vital anchor. This new animism will help balance the weather over time; it will also help bridge the gaps between science and religion. The Rush Limbaugh types who might prefer to kick creation in the pants to show who is boss will pillory this budding movement (as will some unconverted religious organizations), but sincerity will win the day.

When Truth is in the air, as it noticeably and increasingly is between 93 and 97, the need to examine beliefs and assumptions of society grows urgent.[11] Thrilling, but hard work. It will seem a comfort to connect with nature, move back to basics, back to the Earth. There is a new willingness to throw off stagnation and corruption and go through whatever clarification or detoxification process is required. To connect with nature is to unite with a whole that is quite complex and sacred. This tuned-into-nature focus will be a theme picked up by many religions over the next thirty years, a major turn away from the Biblical directive to take dominion over nature because God put it there for man to

---

11 From 95 on, the focus shifts from inward truth to outward. Republicans are suddenly chipping away at what looks out of integrity to them — welfare, teen pregnancy, school lunches, the Departments of Energy and Education, "frivolous" lawsuits against corporations and a thick environmental bureaucracy. Environmental and business reform is not their forte, but those reforms will come too.

use. Manifest destiny, conquest of nature, resource depletion — all that goes; these failed concepts fall right out of politics, religion, and the way most people think.

Greener churches will form to reflect changing consciousness. Religions will soon arouse and excite people's respect for the natural world, or they will lose appeal. Catholicism may do itself in on this, and on population issues. After all, fewer and fewer people will be needing yesterday's rigid sets of rules about life. Mature souls, especially, are seeking emotional unification through love and communion with one another, higher forces, and the whole wide world. They want ways of tuning into the living breathing Earth; they want to be part of its healing. Earth-centered activity and love help create a healthier, more harmonious Earth.

An unprecedented *group* of infinite souls, Buddha and Jesus-level beings with immense, infectious spiritual force fields, will become noticeable on the planet around the turn of the century. Their luminous and powerful message: All life is one. Honor it all — plants, humans, cetaceans, animals, streams, mountains, and galaxy. These messiahs and avatars with their varying sexes and races will help all people unite more deeply with each other and with nature. They will be challenging the holiest of vested interests, outdated beliefs and rigid ideas still buried in society and religion, just as Buddha and Jesus did in their times. Their impactful collective influence accelerates mature soul consciousness.

ENVIRONMENT 2000
Right now the planet is burdened; strained, pressured, chemically afflicted, uneasily reeling from distress. And soon to reel more. By creating a ruckus, though, the Earth begins a cleanse. Ridding herself of a portion of out-of-control bipeds will decrease all manner of polluted inputs. Hard as this shake-up is for all living things on the planet, it will buy some relief. We believe that the natural world will start perking up near the turn of the century. Though ecological systems are still precarious, the

Earth starts to feel more comfortable, stable. She's on the mend, but there are still big questions. Will life support systems be able to detoxify and come into new balance? Will water and soil and air ever be able to sustain life as before? Will the lessons of the 90s be absorbed? Will humans become ecologically respectful (and vigilant) or go unconscious and take whatever else they can? All possibilities are available. Because thinking and feeling are evolving, action is likely to become more attentive and intentional.

By 1998, agriculture should be more sane, meaning practiced with fewer chemicals and more respect for the health of the soil, people and planet. Poisonous herbicides and pesticides will be falling out of use because public outcry against them is so severe; they are seen as heavy-handed, not nearly clever enough. Clean food and vital soil are in. Safe, clever, biological controls against pests and weeds will be sought after. Scientists putting attention on food production will be approaching it from a more healthful, less arrogantly manipulative chemical standpoint than previously.

After devastating blights and annihilated crops, people will come to instinctually realize that supporting healthy life all over the planet means less trouble with the weather, pests, plant and tree diseases — as well as less human disease. Even a clever, nontoxic fix for corn blight or Dutch elm disease is different than actually creating healthy environments for plants to grow in. The morality and safety of genetic manipulation will continue to be debated, with the ethics and potential problems of these projects being carefully scrutinized. Temptation to try one more technological fix (Gorilla genes to keep the wheat stalks strong against fiercer storms?) is countered by increasing wariness and caution.

CFCs will be banned in the mid-90s. Fossil-fuel use will be heavily taxed and will decrease. Safe, alternative energy sources will start receiving adequate development money. Around 1997, frightened by blights, epidemics and other breakdowns, in hopes of turning adverse situations around, people are finally willing to do whatever is necessary to detoxify the planet. Clearly, this means getting chemicals out of the Earth's veins, getting rid of polluting practices, and living in a tuned-in fashion with new values to modify and replace current materialistic ones. Humans will be discovering what non-material fulfillment means, looking to intimacy for it and to playful camaraderie, spirituality, creativity, adventure, and especially to community involvement and service. By 96 or 97, the majority is quite aware that the planetary crisis won't be solved by one more chemical or technological miracle, and that the only way out is through hard questions, good answers, some grace, and working creatively with decent politicians to get things done.

When confronted by nature gone awry, the mature soul world will clearly see that humanity is part of nature, that nature is necessary to survival, and that they had collectively better get a move on. Spirited local groups start to successfully counteract vested interests on local, as well as on national and international levels. Citizens will be concerned enough about their communities to fight misguided business practices, politicians and policies which do not conserve, make healthy or restore. The not-in-my-backyard syndrome, in which people gather together to fight degradation of their local area, is fierce by the year 2000, and is an important component in halting the skid into worse problems.

GAIA

The living, breathing planet does have consciousness of itself and its parts, as well as ability to adjust and regulate itself. This consciousness is now popularly referred to as Gaia, Goddess of the Earth. The Gaia energy is far more personal than the neutral all-inclusiveness of the Tao. We see it as a large coalition of devic beings, a collection of souls who eons ago chose not to be physical at all, but to be the keepers of nature and protectors of the Earth. This coalition of energies acts essentially as an overseer for the planet and is, in a manner of speaking, its heart and soul. It appears to us as a million points of light that hover close, all around the planet on a mesh-like triangular grid, and also as the light radiating from the core of the planet to each of those points of light. The living grid has give and flux, even as it helps keep the Earth stable. At this moment, however, the grid is losing cohesiveness; it is shabby, not in great shape. It has lost ability to sustain and protect. Patches of it have come loose, like shingles on the top of a house.

This human experiment could simply be allowed to go where it goes, even if it shoved the Earth towards the freezing, arid conditions of Mars or the cloudy, boiling conditions of Venus, either of which are possibilities. The Earth could easily become too poisoned and toxic for life, like any number of previously pleasant planets. But those scenarios do not seem to be what is preferred, or likely. The Gaian urge, as we sense it, is to keep the planet relatively stable by keeping temperatures consistent, water flowing, air fresh, gases mixed normally, and photosynthesis hopping so that most aspects of life may continue to thrive.

On one hand, the Gaia energy is like the Mother Nature you imagine, nurturing, giving, caring, non-judgmental, easily accepting whatever all the kidlets are doing. It has provided teeming abundance, beauty and grace for all to enjoy. Earth is a planet glowing with life. However, within the heart of the planet there is growing frustration over the inability to maintain life systems in a balanced, smoothly functioning manner; too many humans and too many polluting practices continually intensify the strain. With holes in every ecosystem, and much of life going awry, it is not surprising to find uneasiness and agitation within the planet itself, within Gaia.

The core of the planet is no longer stable and in balance. We find stress, aggravation, restless, thrashing energy pushing to let go, but also restraining energy struggling to maintain some balance. Molten magma is newly pressured and stressed, searching for suitable release. This will provoke the great quakes of 96 through 98 and the awesome volcanic eruptions. It has already weakened the magnetics on the planet, making fields less cohesive, more scattered, and more vulnerable to polar shifts. (When the planet's field isn't strong, a nearby comet or asteroid can more easily be the cause of a flip.) The magnetic poles are already on a fast track, so much so that aviation maps must now be adjusted every few years, not every ten or twenty.

Letting the planet's more primal energy loose with earthquakes, volcanic action, and storms is essentially a reassertion of Gaian power. It is the power of the planet unleashed to effect its own healing. Through this organic, chaotic process, a smoother functioning whole will be created, in time.

Like a tossed pebble rippling the water around it, what one person does makes a difference. As the planet seems more arbitrary and haphazard, each person who can remain stable and centered makes a difference in the way life feels for all. If you find yourself longing inconsolably for the past, have a good cry, and then a good laugh. At yourself. Your attachment to what was won't bring it back. Restore your own spirits by honoring the sacredness of the process, of all life. As you ground and heal yourself and shed personal chaos and sorrow, your new level of wellbeing, and your example, helps others heal and grow. You may now find yourself a person with something important to say and to offer — a leader.

Two Consciousness Exercises

EXERCISE #1
Ponder what you want in life. Discover how much money can't buy.
In interchanges with others, point out what money can't buy.
Educate yourself and others by inserting the phrase, "You sure can't buy that with money," as often as possible into your conversations.
Have fun with this and your life will become more abundant.

EXERCISE #2
The following is a simple, profound consciousness exercise designed to plunge you into deep layers of yourself. Pair up with a friend to do it. Sit across from each other and look into each other's eyes. Maintain a gentle eye contact throughout.
The younger person will ask the older a question, then quietly listen as the person responds. Time this for five minutes. The questioner is to give no feedback at all, simply be present and still. If the respondent stops talking, gently repeat the question.
When five minutes are up, quietly switch roles, with the older person asking the younger the same question. As before, the questioner stays quiet, receptive, aware, and non-responsive. When that is complete, do another round with the same question. This may seem ridiculous and impossible, but do it to get the experience.
If you are feeling adventuresome, you may wish to do yet another round with the same question, or a round using one of the alternate questions.
(Any of these questions are excellent to bring into meditation. Though the process isn't as pushy, insight and wisdom are still available.)

THE QUESTIONS
Where do you find happiness?
What is contentment?
What is Earth?
What is Gaia?
Where in your life are you wasting energy?

S I X

Political Change/Earth Change
The World Report

Men and nations behave wisely once they have
exhausted all the other alternatives.
—Abba Eban

We must dare to think "unthinkable" thoughts.
—James William Fulbright

SOUL AGE PROGNOSIS

Adding soul age information to the given social and political conditions in a particular area can lead to clearer perceptions of how a people and their society or nation might adjust to increasing economic stress and to the onslaught of ideas now coming into focus. In any country it makes a huge difference not only what the largest soul-age group is, but also what group is second largest. For instance, Haiti contains primarily baby souls but has nearly as many infant souls, making it little able to take developmental leaps forward. India and China, also primarily baby but with their next strongest input coming from surging young soul populations, are firmly planted on the developmental road.

Checking to see what's in the wind, we'll scan the world, first taking a look at infant soul areas, then at the whole globe, continent by continent, specifically examining many individual countries. Special attention will be focused on the up-and-coming batch of young soul countries, which are usually interesting and always potentially troublesome.

INFANT SOUL AREAS

Countries with large infant soul populations are quite naturally undeveloped, affording those souls who are beginning their human experience the slower, simpler lifetimes they desire. Nevertheless, infant souls often find themselves in skirmishes with wildlife, climate, marginal food situations, marauding neighbors, and with young souls who want their resources, labor, or ancestral lands. Enduring these types of hardships are part and parcel of learning about survival on earth.

To economically develop a nation composed primarily of infant souls is hugely challenging. The population simply doesn't have the backlog of experience or skills on which to build. This inexperience can make a big difference in even such modest arenas as producing crafts for possible sale to the many tourists now exploring these (See it before it's gone!) primitive areas. Even if a culture is an art-and-craft producing group, infant souls have rarely developed the craftsmanship or discipline to make the objects that sell. Neither do they have the business pizzazz to take advantage of this source of customers and potential influx of cash.

When an infant soul area is comfortable and doing well — as the Amazon Basin has for thousands of years — early lifetimes can have an exploratory, magical one-with-nature feel. All over the globe, tribal areas are now shrinking, encroached upon by the modern world. Many indigenous Amazonian tribes are losing their traditional lands. As their land shrinks, so do their buffer zones of protection from the outside world — as well as from each other. Losing territory also means a diminishing food supply. Amazonian tribes will continue to lose ground throughout the 90s, though at declining rates because the area has found many, many protectors in the form of ecologists, journalists, rock stars, and even the occasional politician. Tribal peoples, currently about forty percent infant and thirty-five percent baby, are seeing increasing numbers of young, mature, and old souls born among them, people who desired front row seats — or starring parts — in the fight to save these cultures, their knowledge, and the rainforest itself.

Tribal lives in Borneo, New Guinea, Irian Jaya, and Australia will remain fairly static throughout the 90s, neither horribly plagued by development nor batted about by climatic changes. In the fifty years it took Central America to quintuple its population, its infant soul tribal peoples were progressively squeezed into smaller, more marginal areas. In fact, tribal populations were decimated as everyone else multiplied. The Sudan, Ethiopia, and Somalia contain many infant souls, and are in dire shape with little chance for improvement over the next twenty years due to internal warfare and chronic food shortages. This area of Africa is so severely overpopulated as to be ecologically devastated. Climates are already drastically altered. Sri Lanka also descended into warring with itself, with its population changing from the baby/young ferment of twenty years ago to the baby/infant combination of today. Being unwilling or unable to pull itself out of the fighting pushes this country, or any country, more deeply into impoverishment on nearly every level. Sri Lanka could be an island of delight — but so could any place.

Infant souls understandably don't have the confidence or knack for changing much about their world, especially when it is going awry. Nor do they have the power to stand up to young souls, the landlords, warlords, shopkeepers, or government officials most likely to be making their lives more wrenchingly difficult. Infant souls have little interest in or comprehension for politics, but it is politics which nevertheless often makes their lives insecure and wretched.

Ambitious young souls doing their thing in equatorial areas are the folks most likely to be bumping up against the infant soul and causing pain and anguish. Young souls are pushing into the

Amazon to farm, ranch, and mine; they are sparring for power in Central America; vying for control of more land and resources in Peru and Columbia; and playing politics with food in Ethiopia, Somalia, The Sudan, Zaire, Nigeria, Liberia, and much of Latin America. Remember, though, everybody who is now mature or old has had lifetimes of terrorizing peasants, serfs, peons, natives, slaves, factory workers — and women. Karmic behavior, you bet, but part of young soul turf.

Latin America

We have to expect a day when the balance
of nature will be lost.
—Quetzalcoatl

Music has been my playmate, my lover,
and my crying towel.
—Buffy Sainte-Marie

South America, Central America, and the twenty-two
Caribbean Island nations are predominantly poor baby soul
countries run by the usual gang of rich young souls, clever and
intent on maintaining the social policies which have kept the
money in their family pockets for generations. Status quo is
usually easy to maintain with baby soul masses who tend to prefer
the comfort of tradition over change. Change seems risky, like
dangerously tipping the boat when you are not completely sure of
your ability to swim.

Typically, baby souls will think exactly along the lines they've
been taught and do what leaders say to do, because what they are
working on internally is learning to obey a given society's unique
set of rules. Old rules which carry the weight of custom feel better
than any newfangled ways of looking at life. If the religion says do
this, and has been saying that same thing for millennia, then it
must be right. This soul age can get anxious just listening to

someone railing against a landlord, much less someone proposing political change, because that might mean recasting the traditional order.

Because baby souls are the largest group in Latin America, politicians, the clergy, businessmen, and landowners have had a relatively easy time taking profit from their complacent, low-paid labor pool, giving little back in the way of salaries or services. Though their churches may be ornate, the underclasses don't ordinarily get paved roads, sewers, electricity, healthcare, educations, or even enough regular work to purchase steady, adequate supplies of food. Nevertheless, baby souls are likely to remain loyal to their leaders and often view them as superior people or strong fathers who had best be obeyed.

Igniting a revolution with this kind of majority is like using damp kindling to start a fire. In baby soul countries, established leaders tend to be admired wholeheartedly (unless poverty and corruption glaringly increase or, on the other side, a leader attempts to fast-forward the masses and push modernization too rapidly).

These soul age patterns in Latin America have been fairly stable since colonial times. What is currently happening in about half these countries is a shock to tradition; an increasing number of young souls are being born into underclass families that have been poverty-stricken for generations. Many, now in their teens and twenties, can neither imitate nor abide the stoicism of their parents. Young souls tend to be all here-and-now; praying for a better afterlife does not make sense to them. Many have experienced heartless landowners, seen siblings and cousins die from lack of medicine, or parents sick and weak from grueling work. The group knows what it is to have too little food and fuel. Their gangbuster young soul energy is pushing them to get out there and make something happen. But, what's to do? How can they possibly shape life to their liking?

Finding few decent work opportunities in rural areas and no place for their individualism or ambition to go, these impoverished young souls are migrating in hordes to large cities. Few jobs await them. Even an informal street business, like selling fruit, juice, or handicrafts, requires some capital, savings they don't have. Banks aren't famous for lending to the illiterate poor. Soon these migrants to the city discover that the police often bleed street businesses nearly dry anyhow. The cards are stacked against the underclasses in the cities, just as they were in the countryside. These desperados don't even dream of job training or other educational opportunities, but when they discover no jobs and dismal business prospects, the only door open may be petty crime.

Up-and-coming young souls are hard to control. If continually frustrated, they can get mean. Increasingly, they are making life miserable for the rich all over Latin America, most particularly in Brazil, but also in Argentina, Peru, and in an organized-crime fashion, in Columbia. Chile and Costa Rica, to their credit, have taken the opposite route and are educating and opening work and business opportunities to the poor.

While Chile and Costa Rica move forward, life in many Latin cities is not only hard on the poor, but becoming an increasing headache for anyone with money. In Rio, one dares not wear jewelry or carry a bag or package. Nothing is safe, anywhere, not even your person. It used to be that tall stone walls with glass shards atop them would keep the poor out, but now around-the-clock guards at your walls may not be enough. Everything gets stolen. Car alarms protected cars until thieves figured how to get around their noise, in seconds. So the rich bought systems which closed down gas lines within a few miles should their vehicle be hot-wired. Subsequently, more cars were stolen with their owners in them, at knife or gunpoint, some crooks taking delight in leaving car owners naked on isolated roads — not prudish baby soul behavior!

So many fractious characters being born into lower classes means times have changed; the masses can't be so easily controlled. The police in Brazil have killed many street kids as one way of holding down crime. Now, these children of the streets are protesting, marching by the thousands, grabbing headlines. It is a revolution starting to happen, a punch from below which will force rich Latin families to create openings and opportunities for at least some of the poor. If these wretched masses don't find new healthy ways to participate in society, the crime wave will turn uglier yet.

The ruling families are nervous, but not changing their ways — except for taking more pains with security. In an attempt to protect themselves in case everything blows, many transfer money outside their country and continent instead of investing at home. This drains cash from local economies, tending to make everybody poorer and the situation more tense. Argentina, Brazil, Columbia, Peru, Venezuela, Mexico, and most Central American countries greatly need to make sweeping social, political, land, educational, and economic adjustments in order to avoid descent into internal chaos.

Transformation is going on already in Latin America. Military dictatorships are falling away, one by one. Two countries, Brazil and Chile, have popularly elected presidents for the first time in twenty years and it looks as if democracy is holding, inside and out. The fellows with uniforms and guns are minding their manners and the U.S. and its CIA are also minding their manners, not interfering as they did twenty years ago when both Brazil and Chile's democratically elected leaders were murdered. With the U.S. and the Soviets no longer fighting wars of influence in Latin America, Latin politics are being left alone to a much greater extent, which allows for more freedom, more creativity, and better self-regulation.

The birth control question in Catholic Latin America is still too mined to tackle effectively, but because cities are at such bursting points it is finally clear that doing whatever it takes to support rural people to remain in rural areas is a good deal for everyone. People need life support services in the countryside. These services always go to cities, capitals first, to keep city dwellers placated and away from presidential palaces. But to be viable, rural areas need support in the form of schools and electricity, sewers, health services, and so on. Latin governments won't find the money to make extensive improvements overnight, but many are finally seeing rural services as useful and important. Times have changed.

The U.S. has pressed hard at Columbia, Peru, Bolivia and Ecuador to destroy drug-producing crops and laboratories. With a peasantry barely able to eke out a living when cultivating easy-to-grow, high-payoff illegal crops, how possible is it to switch crops? How could government authorities bomb the countryside with herbicides and defoliants if people's ability to eat is then destroyed? To effectively lower drug production, alternative crops that people will be able to extract a living from must be found. These four countries are now more interested in rural reform than they are in responding to heavy-handed requests from the U.S. to spray the land with poisons and put the peasant growers out of commission. Evolutionary change is in the making.

Most Colombians, including many politicians, now wish to get rid of the dark shadow cast by drugs, drug deals, and drug money. Columbia is sophisticated and rich enough to transform itself from a drug money capital into something more diversified and positive. To pull this off, both determination and vision are needed. Columbia has enough solid young souls, creative mature souls, infrastructure, and new-found vision that it is likely to be able to do this and avoid the descent into chaos.

Only a few years ago Peru was on the brink of chaos. Years of weak leadership, corruption in the government, police, judiciary, and upper classes, plus high debt and the destructive efforts of Shining Path guerrillas looked like they would pull the country apart. But, look what happened! Alberto Fujimori, a brilliant mature soul planner willing to take a lot of heat, got himself elected president, against all odds, and then re-elected. He canceled the legislature for a year or so (too-bought off to approve needed reforms), took on near-dictatorial powers, gave the International Monetary Fund a fit, and tackled corruption and all who stood against reforms. The legislature is now back, re-formed, the Shining Path guerrillas imprisoned, and the country beginning to flourish. One determined person with vision, energy, and great courage gave fresh life to an entire nation.

Venezuela is a much richer country than Peru. It has a large (nearly twenty-five percent), stabilizing group of young souls determined to hold onto their money and country. They intend to manage the poor and the military in whatever way necessary to insure their future. However, with nearly half of Venezuelan citizens so poor they can only afford one meal a day, economic reforms are clearly required to avoid uprisings. Venezuela will keep itself stable, either by making sufficient reforms or by becoming increasingly authoritarian and brutal.

Latin countries which are not already being pushed politically and socially by segments of their poor are likely to remain fairly stable during the coming economic crunch. Most of the stable nations have large proportions of baby and infant souls, who tend to remain quiet and conservative, even when burdened by increasingly extreme poverty. The potential that these countries could be inflamed by some brand of political righteousness is there, but unlikely. Baby souls have a desire to fit in and live closely within the confines dictated by their society. They need to feel right about what they are doing — in Latin America and Africa this usually keeps them quiet. (In Arab countries it is getting them noisy.)

In most Latin countries, mature souls account for at least twenty percent of the population. Mexico is unique in that it has had a stronger mature soul influence spread throughout most areas and strata of society. Over the last two hundred years it has had essentially equal numbers of mature and baby souls. This influence gave Mexico vibrant music, arts, crafts, and it's warmth of family and community. While mature souls are usually able to boost a country's economy, in Mexico they were not able to because of the low priority this non-intellectual society puts on education.

POLITICAL CHANGE / EARTH CHANGE

Under the recent presidency of Carlos Salinas, Mexico did move forward on material and educational levels, and many more people were able to fund small businesses and prosper. Salinas was brilliant with economics but played corrupt old power games. He manipulated people, facts, and hid inconvenient figures from his party, Mexican citizens, and the World Bank. As the old order breaks down, all levels of truth are coming out. Disgrace caught up with Salinas soon after he left office. New consciousness is breaking open cover-ups and Mexico is suddenly investigating fraud and corruption in the government, the ruling party, and in the upper classes. Aiming for truth and honor in the way a government does its business will become a familiar cause in the late 90s as mature souls wrest power from embedded systems.

The border between the U.S. and Mexico is the only first world/third world land border on the globe. That it has been peaceful is partially because it leaks so well and partially because of traditional Mexican docility. When times get rougher and drought and severe food shortages arise in both countries, the border will become a sore spot as the U.S willfully attempts to close it in order to feed and care for its own population first.

AN ASIDE
Now, while it is true that the fifteen percent who are wealthy in Latin America (or anywhere) have tended to be young souls grabbing easy birthrights on their way to experiences of power and wealth, there are always exceptions. Any soul age can take a silver-spoon birth, but because money and power are a quintessential young soul experience, these wealthy families tend to be more wearing on the other soul ages. Hard to believe? Imagine yourself the daughter of Donald Trump, or a Latin son expected to continue the family business, where high profit is based fairly directly on the misery of many workers. Being born into situations like these is a piece of cake for the young soul, but compromises both the morality and freedom the later soul ages

141

hold dear, and often forces a difficult rebellion.[1]

Young souls, of course, choose to be born poor also — sometimes just to get going with a body, there being too few rich parents to go around. But also they do it in order to challenge themselves and gain strength by willfully rising above miserable circumstances. This is similar to a baby soul's choosing to test her mettle by incarnating into a rich, competitive family in order to be pushed toward greater responsibility.[2] People always experiment to gain experience; some individuals even specialize in doing the unusual.

Old souls tend to choose their birth locations carefully so as to have some degree of comfort and freedom. Nevertheless, old souls will assume care-taking positions in primitive populations, becoming teachers, shamans, storytellers, herbalists, midwives, and healers for their communities. Sometimes old souls also choose powerful, wealthy parents in order to put themselves in a good position to get things done in the world. The danger lies in becoming too content, lazy, or compromised to challenge the family conscience, come fully into essence, and get that life task completed.

Mature souls exist in every culture, too, at about five percent minimum. They incarnate wherever they can learn, express, and create with emotion, which is basically worldwide. Some mature soul gathering spots, like Hollywood, Rio, Amsterdam, or Rome are much more pleasant than others, say Prague or Rangoon, but growth through emotional intensity is universally available, so mature souls aren't usually as picky about their birth locales as the old soul becomes. Of course, what has tired the old soul and made her prudent and selective is the intensity of experience in her recent mature soul lifetimes.

---

[1] John Robbins, author of *Diet for a New America,* is a good example of this, plunging forward to improve the diet of America as he rejected the "karma" of the Baskin-Robbins ice cream fortune.

[2] Queen Elizabeth epitomizes this.

Africa

It takes a whole village to raise one child.
—African Proverb

We are not to expect to be transported from despotism
to liberty in a featherbed.
—Thomas Jefferson

SUB-SAHARAN AFRICA

From most every angle, sub-Saharan Africa looks to be a sad, increasingly difficult place to live. Africa will continue to experience adverse climatic changes, worsening drought, pestilence, famine, rampant AIDS, and the usual tyrannies inflicted by leaders interested primarily in their own personal aggrandizement. The first world (with its hands still in Africa's pockets) will increasingly turn its back on Africa, with the "Operation Restore Hope" intervention in Somalia being an obvious turning point. Over the next two decades, Africa will find few success stories, rebirth, or renewal.[3]

It is for several reasons that the world will increasingly let this continent falter and drift. First, the developed world is having a difficult time itself and is thus pulling attention homeward. Second, it is increasingly possible to ignore Africa because wars

---

[3] North Africa is covered later in the chapter under, "The Muslim world."

143

between the Soviets and the West are no longer being waged there. Without foreign military help and money, no sub-Saharan African country is big or sophisticated enough to be a major threat on the world scene. Third, Africa appears depressing to the Western eye. AIDS has spread like wildfire. Corruption abounds. Nothing seems to work or improve easily. Africa appears to be a sinkhole to Western governments which are increasingly dubious about throwing money into it, despite mammoth suffering. Development money and business loans are heading toward Eastern Europe, which needs to be brought forward by only twenty years, not twenty decades. Africa has been set adrift, left to its own internal wrangling, chaos, and pain. The unspoken first world feeling is: Let it sink; perhaps it will cleanse itself in the process.

In general, it is fair to say that Africa's leaders have not been stewards who helped their countries along. (The few who did were undermined by the West, which was fearful of strong leaders with social and political change in mind.) Rather, they have tended to be a corrupt, fanatical, and unusually maladroit bunch. At best, they have tended to skim off personal fortunes from government monies, institute a few grandiose building projects, while ignoring the basic healthcare, education and infrastructure needs of their citizens. (Still, their money-grabbing looks puny compared to the ways Western policies have squeezed the continent.) But despite bad leaders and poor treatment from the rest of the world, Africa's most horrendous problems are now coming from a disastrously worsening climate and booming populations which have come close to exhausting the land.

Some places, like Mozambique, had excellent leaders and could have developed beautifully but for the policies of the West (and South Africa), bent on keeping any potentially strong socialized (or black) country down. Mozambique received incredible pain and injury in the "destabilization" process, but might still recover as South Africa's disruptive policies are halted and the West pitches in with aid money. This country, which recently hired the Transcendental Meditation organization to help it stabilize and move forward, is obviously looking for creative and positive options. Mozambique must fix its broken infrastructure, mend war wounds, and, like the rest of Africa, find a way to staunch intertribal warfare and heal deep ethnic disharmony.

South Africa, very wealthy and very long controlled by legions of thick and stubborn white baby souls, is finally beginning to create breathing room for all races. Will it manage? Many here are doing their honorable and willful best to insure that their world does not descend into gross chaos. The reins of leadership have been turned over to blacks. Nevertheless, fear, anger, and stinky, corrupt politics abound, among both whites and blacks. The country has the wealth, the resources, and much of the determination it needs to move carefully forward and avoid the all-too-easy slip into total, bloody mayhem.

Over half the country's remaining whites are relieved about the downfall of apartheid and convinced that their world must be carefully opened to blacks. It is a scary process requiring courage and a great deal of moral strength. Among whites there is a reactionary, almost totally baby soul contingent of nearly fifteen percent who would rather see the country in war and ruin than co-ruled by blacks. They exude a frightened, stubborn vigilante mentality, angry in that inimical baby soul way over the traditional order shifting so radically beneath their feet. Other whites can't decide which is worse, a possible bloodbath or opening up their world to blacks. They waver back and forth, tortured inside, but are basically flowing along with the new changes. Happily for everyone, the mature soul leadership of Nelson Mandela is proving balanced and positive.

South African blacks have been so suppressed, repressed, and shoved into corners that many who are politically active tend to be angry. Blacks, like the Zulus, who believe they have been pushed from mainstream black politics are extremely angry and volatile. To take advantage of the new openness, blacks now need to avoid getting mired in righteous anger, resentment, or impatience.

UPCOMING CHANGES

Many individuals have consciously let go of anger and bitterness towards whites and the old system because they know instinctively it is the best way to move forward now. Many others could use support with anger, with self-esteem issues, and in getting creative with the new possibilities starting to appear. The black townships could greatly benefit from traveling consciousness teachers, whether Werner Erhard's workshops and teachings or Maharishi's Transcendental Meditation, or any other motivational teachings which preach self-responsibility, forgiveness, and moving forward with vision. Because so many South African blacks are mature souls, they can be reached relatively easily with this type of support. They are living historical, transitional lifetimes as the world opens up in this way; it would help them to have a sense of themselves in history and to gain perspective and understanding about how transitions are normally two steps forward and one back. They need overviews and they need the understanding that their self-esteem will gradually heal itself. With realism and psycho-spiritual support, and some focus on black ethnic issues, this community will well prepared to move forward as opportunities open. Potentially, South Africa could be very glorious.

After dry conditions in the early 90s, the weather in South Africa remains fairly benign. The country will be shaken by several earthquakes with a Richter force of 7.0 or higher during the decade, and will need to cope with problems caused by the lack of ozone protection. It may also need to cope with famine-starved masses pushing in from the north looking for food.

Though still an extremely difficult situation, at least South Africa's white leaders were called on their tyranny and forced by world opinion and economic sanctions to relinquish power and join the late twentieth century. Africa's black leaders, many of whom are even more tyrannous toward their own race, have not yet been pushed to their knees by world pressure, the governments of Kenya and Zaire are beginning to experience the discomfort of the world spotlight. Both the West and Saudi Arabia have a strong commitment to keep Kenya stable. It is being spurred to become responsive to all classes and tribes of people — democratic, in other words. Though Kenya has primarily baby souls (thirty-five percent), its nearly equal proportions of ambitious and competent young souls (thirty percent) gives Kenya the ability to forge ahead of many other African countries.

The whole inner core of Africa is most affected by AIDS, which will continue spreading and decimating populations. Too little food and protein combined with high rates of venereal diseases bode poorly for immune-system strength, making the march of AIDS and related problems easy and swift. The pain in these central areas is already intense and is due to worsen considerably.

West Africa has several countries which are heading towards young soul expressions: Ghana, The Ivory Coast, and Liberia. When young soul majorities hit, there are always choices to be made. The usual ones: whether to get expansionistic and make war or to get educated, industrialized and make businesses. Choosing the latter route, The Ivory Coast and Ghana will be trying to knock down the one-sided trade policies which have drained resources and raw materials from them and given little back in the way of money or jobs. These West African nations might start fighting back, for instance, by sitting on their raw materials and produce (and debt payments if they dare) until Western trade policies are changed. Liberia, however, is tending to busy itself with bloody ethnic disputes over power and with war, making attempts to gobble up neighboring territory. West Africa looks fortunate in that it is likely to retain a climate that supports steady food production.

Nigeria, also heading towards young, will likely become increasingly militaristic, authoritarian, and difficult for its neighbors. Cameroon looks as if it will be ripped apart by its own military forces.

Asia

Better to abolish serfdom from above than to wait till it
begins to abolish itself from below.
—Alexander II

I was raised the Chinese way: I was taught to desire nothing,
to swallow other people's misery, to eat my own bitterness.
—Amy Tan

INDIA, CHINA, ET CETERA: MOVING TOWARDS YOUNG

Many Asian nations, including two countries, the Goliaths of
world population, are negotiating the boundary waters between
passing baby and upcoming young soul phases. India and China
are ready and aching to become gloriously materialistic; India,
especially, would enjoy military glory also. Each has had a top-
down, traditional baby soul society in place for several centuries,
with the majority of citizens simply doing what parents, elders,
ancestors, peers, political leaders, and religion called for. Neither
has yet exhibited much technical innovation or put business needs
over baby soul, kinship-oriented bureaucracies, but they will.
Despite China's vaunted left-turn from warlords and corrupt rule
by a few rich families, it still has capricious top-down rule and its
ruling families remain rich, powerful, and insulated. And China
still has a near-impossible, multi-layered (use those back-door

connections if you want to get anything done) style of bureaucracy. India's justly famous layers of official red tape finds bureaucrats stalling on everything, rarely a cause for criticism, instead of taking on the responsibility of making even simple decisions. Corruption on all levels is accepted as a fact of life in both countries, as in most of Asia.

As China is making its shift into young, capitalist elements in the economy are growing and the socialist elements shrinking. State factories have become a drag on China's economy, not the engine they were supposed to be, pushing development and prosperity. Intellectuals and workers alike are longing for democracy and personal freedom. They see democracy as the freedom the West has to make money and be individualistic; the freedom to say what you want and have it count. Worldwide (excepting the Middle East), people are tending to view Western democracy as an appealing, materially successful model on which to base new societies.

The energetic, enterprising Chinese are itching to be productive, make millions of products, billions of dollars, and enjoy the prizes. Primarily because China has so many young souls, socialism did not stunt commercial instincts as it did for so many in Russia. When given a chance, they will be superb at nurturing their businesses. The desire to do business, to create comfortable lifestyles, is much stronger in China than any pull towards militaristic adventurism. They had enough adventure with Mao! People are biding their time and strength until key members of the old guard pass away, making way for moderates to take over from hardliners. Few Chinese were pleased with their government's actions in Tianamen Square, but without uselessly sacrificing more people, there is nothing to do but wait. The time for major reforms has not yet arrived. If people feel they are making economic gains and moving in good directions, they understandably don't have a keen desire to turn life on its ear. Linear forward movement looks more appealing than another righteous revolution.

UPCOMING CHANGES

In the meantime, new opportunities to make money are continually opening up. Economic freedom is coming at a faster pace than political freedom, interestingly just the opposite of what occurred — and caused chaos — in the Soviet Union under Gorbachev. There is now a high degree of probability that Hong Kong will retain most of its economic freedom, and a good deal of its political freedom, when it merges with The People's Republic in 1997.

Though many of China's frail, octogenarian leaders will be gone soon, significant social and political change in China will not happen rapidly. Governmental structures will remain very authoritarian. The difficult economic times of the mid to late 90s will tend to favor strong governmental structures (and give one more reason to keep the Hong Kong economic powerhouse on full power). While people have had it with authoritarian excesses, these coming years are, by necessity, so survival-oriented that agitation for change will likely be mild.

Some major problems will have to do with, what else, ethnic minorities. Minority areas in the North and West will begin to stir, and over the course of the next decade will be restive and difficult for the central Chinese government to handle. Tibetans will, of course, continue to wrangle to get their country and autonomy back — with the world behind them in spirit, though not with sanctions or guns. The Chinese are too emotionally attached to dominating and taking the wind out of Tibet's aerial sails to let it go easily. Controlling this remote, lofty Himalayan kingdom is always a tremendous ego boost for them.

Trouble will be brewing between the poorer, less-developed ethnic areas in the West and the richer, more young soul areas along the Eastern seaboard and in the South. There are several possible courses of action China may take here, even including dropping bombs to subdue its Western provinces, but eventually, certainly within the next twenty years, we see this part of the country being split off, separated politically from China proper. This region will have much internal warfare, and at this split off

150

point, looks as ragged as Afghanistan did in 91 when the Russians pulled out. Given the temper of the times, China may decide not to spend the military money needed to enforce her present whole and simply let those conflicted western areas go, choosing instead to invest in its own productive capacities.

Food in China will definitely be problematic; it nearly always is. Many food shortages will be localized, based on regional climatic doings, but two years of severe widespread drought with occasional quick damaging rainfalls will bring on widespread famine. Peasants in food growing areas will not be so likely to let themselves starve first (as they were forced to do under Mao in order to feed the towns), and there may be an unusual amount of agitation in the countryside. Already peasant riots have erupted over industries that are so horrifically polluting that whole villages fall ill. China in its rush towards industrial development is blindly poisoning its air and water, sometimes to levels not even seen in Eastern Europe under the communist system. Although most agricultural land is well cared for, a blind eye is turned towards the toxins of manufacture which increasingly foul the air and water and menace the health of human populations.

Some high magnitude quakes (near 8.0 on the Richter scale) are likely in the North in 96. These are huge quakes, but because the area is neither heavily populated nor economically crucial, it will not greatly affect productivity or economics. The rice belt in the South comes under stress because of dry weather and looks severely blighted during several mid-decade years.

High population, less than ideal weather, and famine have been concerns in China for many centuries. Unlike India, China has a strong inclination towards rational development policies. With very little arable land compared to population, it works hard to be self-sufficient in food production. A strong population policy was seen as the only way to possibly maintain the ability to feed itself. In its attempt to do that, China now uses more fertilizer on its soil per acre than any other country in the world. It has a traditional respect for land, regarding it as a resource to be sustained, not plundered or abused. China's leaders make sure rural populations are continually taught new, improved agricultural techniques, but production still ultimately depends on luck with the weather.

Planners in China have also shown greater respect for their population's health and education than the rulers of India, a democracy. But of course, in a democracy you can get swept out of office for unpopular policies — as Indira Gandhi found when she suggested that all government workers with three children be sterilized. Two decades ago, the Chinese woke up to the fact that their population was unwieldy.[4] Plus, they saw an unbelievable explosion in numbers still coming at them if nothing was done. That's when the two-child policy was instituted. When years of that proved not enough to stop the onslaught of new mouths, the even less popular one-child laws came into effect. These family-planning moves were not presented to the populace with much discussion or civility but, nevertheless, there are now "only" about fifteen million new people to feed each year.

Fixing population in India is trickier because, as mentioned, it is a democracy. The poor, who hope their children can support them in later life, do not like to give up what they often see as their only hold on security. Eventually though, as ambitious individualistic young souls continue to be born, India's birth rates will start to head down simply because young souls are risk-takers who tend to see security in their own ingenuity, not in children. But even if India could hold its galloping birthrate to its current rate of increase (which would be difficult given the huge proportion of people under twenty-five), it would still surpass China's population soon — on even less arable land. As you could predict, this would be a major disaster, though it is not the likely scenario. Systems and situations won't be pushed quite that far.

Like most developing nations, neither has much of a track record in keeping pollution down, though both are seeing plenty of public health reasons to begin. The well-fed, healthy person is

---

[4] Twenty percent of the world's people on seven percent of the arable land is tricky, especially for a country not rich enough to import food.

capable of producing far more than the small cost of keeping her nourished and fit. Ignorance, malnutrition, and toxic overloads create a weaker, less productive work force, while access to clean water, doctors, and education do just the opposite. Most countries heading towards young are ready to discover and apply that truth. China supports the health of each individual with widespread public health measures. India's attitude is less careful and less conscious. Feeling helpless about having too many people on too little land has numbed India to the pains of extreme impoverishment. "Natural" corrections, like high death rates from early childhood diseases, famines, epidemics, and unprepared-for but predictable natural disasters, are common and tolerated.

It is a very different human experience to be among milling throngs competing for every tiny resource, including sidewalk sleeping places and garbage, than to have too few people to "subdue" the land, as was occurring just two centuries ago in North America. Humans like variety in big packages; however, this Indian bundle of experience has now pushed Mother Nature to the edge.

China and its freshly young soul neighbors — Singapore, South Korea, Taiwan, and Hong Kong — have accomplished the unusual over the last decade by managing to close some of the gaps between the privileged and the poor. As populations have risen over the last thirty years in typical undeveloped countries, the poor have received less and less a share of the national wealth. India follows that pattern; China does not. With poverty in India measurably worsening year by year, and disparities continuing to widen between top and bottom, the poor are forced to scramble more frantically each year simply to stay alive.

China and India, rich culturally, but painfully poor and populous, are heading into their young soul phases very differently, and will create different effects in the world. Despite pervasive,. long-term human rights offenses, China is in more integrity with its people as it heads towards a technologically inventive, materialistic phase. India, with its exuberant, lavish art and music scene, could become fantastically creative, artistic, inventive, and make itself rich. It already makes more movies each year than Hollywood. However, because of lack of planning and an exceedingly top-heavy distribution of wealth, India is heading for trouble. Ethnic and caste rivalry, longterm bitterness over religion, governmental favoritism, the tension created by bounding populations and shrinking resources will continue to take a huge toll in this country.

India's internal chaos will no doubt cause a bit of external chaos with its neighbors, and quite possibly with the world at large. With newly bulging armies, India has become progressively more militaristic and inclined to push around the smaller countries which border it — Nepal, Pakistan, and Sri Lanka have all felt that muscle recently. India is having expansionistic dreams, and could well use an incursion into another country to take attention from internal problems. Like the people of Iran and Iraq, India's educationally and nutritionally handicapped masses could, for a period of time, enjoy the adventurism of their leaders. Anything which would make them feel powerful as a people could have attraction, even if it means a war in which they and their brothers may die.

Pakistan is also moving into its young soul expression, with its own set of angry feelings and expansionistic dreams. Under severe land pressure because of fast population growth and severe drought, it is likely to try some encroachment of its own. At the very least, Pakistan would like to have more of Kashmir, a rich, primarily Muslim area now mostly within India's northern boundaries.

While expanding proportions of the very poor and exacerbating their misery, India has also been adding to its middle class. City people are managing to get jobs or create businesses that pay well enough to buy consumer goods of every stripe. For the first time ever, consumer credit has been made available and large numbers of people are using it, abandoning the traditional modest savings programs most families previously maintained.

POLITICAL CHANGE / EARTH CHANGE

Generally, of course, it is the young souls who are pushing themselves up the monetary scales — whether on credit or not. Typically, the newly rich view the poor with little compassion, often as cheap labor or a backward embarrassment to their country.

India's ravaged environment is on a fast downward spiral. All the fresh young souls who want a chance to get at the country's resources are not likely to allow any law protecting the environment to come into serious enforcement. Poisons abound on land, in water and air. Agricultural soil is in terrible shape, much of it becoming desertified. Deforestation is not likely to stop despite a growing peasant-based tree-hugging movement; erosion and flooding will worsen. Water is severely short; ground water is not replenishing itself. Both mismanagement and lack of management shrink positive possibilities for the future.

In India we see extreme weather as the major coming assault. Hotter and dryer weather for most of the country, and then flooding as precipitation gets compressed into shorter wet seasons. Harsh, late monsoons will cut into growing seasons and cause crop losses. Severe food shortages are likely here for many years, with little hope of sufficient imports to save the day. Generations of pervasive calorie and protein shortages, unclean drinking water, and parasites have not created terribly strong constitutions. Increased food shortages mean a further weakening of the human body, more disease and a severe reduction in the average person's productivity. Food riots based on frustration and anger at unfair distribution practices will occur in many cities. The poorest classes (castes) will experience increased intolerance and prejudice towards them and have even more difficulty surviving as they become the scapegoat targets for the frustrations of the luckier castes above them.

155

UPCOMING CHANGES

SOUTHEAST ASIA[5]

Vietnam now has an equal number of young and baby souls and is heading, with great energy, towards economic development. It wants to be back on the world map as a thriving place. Burma, with its equal numbers of infant, baby, and mature souls is still lolling around in the 1950's with a military dictatorship disinclined to open the country to the world, but people are strongly desiring more personal freedom. Laos and Cambodia are predominantly baby and infant. Before its holocaust, Cambodia had many young souls, but killing everybody with glasses, money, or an education basically wiped this group out. Cambodia easily beats out Afghanistan as the most booby-trapped place in the world — mines and the exploded and unexploded poisonous debris of war are everywhere. It will be an extreme challenge to grow food and build healthy people or a strong nation on this toxic waste.

Thanks to the consciousness of the Thai people, who absolutely did not want fighting on their territory, and plain good luck, Thailand avoided becoming embroiled in the recent wars in Vietnam, Cambodia, and Laos. Like many nations, Thailand tends to concentrate its baby soul populations in the country, while its cities magnetize young and mature souls. Thai city-dwellers, particularly, have an entrepreneurial spirit and a strong taste for business and money. They will continue to agitate periodically for increased political and economic freedoms. The worst problems we see here are health issues created by massive population increases, pollution, shrinking food supplies, high levels of HIV and AIDS, and intensifying problems with tropical diseases, especially incurable malarias and leprosy.

Earthquakes will bring problems for all countries in this area. Weather looks as if it will be a bit hotter and harsher in Southeast Asia, but the rice crops usually come in.

---

[5] Indonesia and Malaysia are covered later in this chapter under, "The Muslim World."

POLITICAL CHANGE / EARTH CHANGE

SOUTH KOREA AND TAIWAN

South Korea is one overt example of the pressure young soul masses in Asia are exerting on their ruling elites. Koreans insisted that their government allow more personal and economic freedom, and willingly fought riot police whenever they had to in order to underline their demands. They wanted the possibilities to be open for their hard work to translate into personal monetary success. These young souls fought relentlessly to win ground, foot by foot. Since young souls will not quietly stomach one more life as a peon, these situations can get explosive if rulers do not make way for their enterprise.

Taiwan, another economic success story, is getting richer, feistier, and more nervous about China's making a grab for it. Who would protect it? Taiwan practices careful diplomacy and more than a little magic to keep itself free and independent. A Chinese military incursion here is unlikely in good times, but gains probability in hard times.

JAPAN: YOUNG AND ON TOP

Japan is definitely enjoying its still-new young soul status and success. People are having a wonderful time spending their money, doing it with increasing elegance and style. Even though their lives were changing rapidly, the Japanese were able to take comfort in their culture's rock solid baby soul roots. However, as time passes and people risk more individuality, that safe baby soul solidity is beginning to slip away. Lifetime employment is no longer guaranteed. Politicians are being regularly rocked by scandals. Some teenagers are loudly rebellious. Local, home-brewed forms of corruption are showing up more often in government, finances, business practices, and in organized crime. Handgun use is increasing, so are grisly murders. The fascist far right is noisier and richer than ever. And then there is cult leader Shoko Asahara's madness, and his 17,000 Japanese followers. Squeaky clean is soiled, frightened, and humbled.

Japan will also be experiencing problems with the

environment and food supplies. It has poisoned itself with modern technologies and its (young soul) disregard for the environment. Like the U.S., it searches for technological ways to get around necessary cleanups. One interesting example: Ocean waters have become so polluted that not enough sunlight can get through to produce the seaweeds of which the Japanese are so fond. They are experimenting with masses of nighttime grow-lights focused on the seaweed banks, hoping this extra light will make up for the reduced penetration of sunlight. Of course, it can't make up for polluted seaweed, but that is not the issue, yet. While traditional Japanese food choices (fish, rice, vegetables, tea) tend to support the health of this population, their food and environment are being increasingly chemicalized with little regard for the health problems bound to be created. These are typical young soul goings-on.

The gravest problem with Japan, however, is great geological stress. It will be the recipient of many high magnitude earthquakes in the 90s. It has already had very dangerous 8 point quakes in the North. As these strong quakes move south, industry and even rice growing will become disrupted. Tokyo looks as if it will sustain a devastating mid-8 point earthquake, most likely in 97. This and other great quakes will put the most industrialized country out of business for awhile. Investments around the world that can be sold quickly will be, for the Japanese will need to get their money home to rebuild. But, as they do this, it will cause chaos on international stock and real estate markets. Tokyo's demise is going to be crushingly hard on the rest of the world, one more reason that these mid-decade years will be so difficult.

RUSSIA AND ITS FORMER REPUBLICS

Mikhail Gorbachev released people from the stranglehold of political repression, intending then to slowly instigate economic reforms. The energy got away from him, though, and life started surging forward without a plan. The breakup in the U.S.S.R. was so sudden that much chaos resulted. While the young souls are rushing about making money and crime, most people are unused to the new energy and freedom and unsure about how to handle it or where to take it. Life in Russia, as in most of the former republics, is full of confusion and uncertainty, with pain and worry everywhere. Yet, underneath, relief exists and excitement for the future too. The strong mature and old soul influence makes these areas react uniquely to the new set of problems. As political, military, economic, and legal structures fall apart, many new experiences will come to life, and many new social experiments be ushered in — some more consciously designed than others.

Russia itself, and the Baltics, Mensk, Ukraine, Georgia and Armenia are full of mature and old souls, now often emotionally drained and full of complaints and fear. People feel overwhelmed with the number of changes that need to be made, but there exists a powerful backbone feeling which insists: we are strong enough to handle this and to create more interesting, fulfilling ways to live. The problem is that no one really knows, for sure, that they can actually accomplish anything of the sort. People are hardly daring to give voice to their hopes and longings. In the meantime, the economy is a disaster and preventable and deadly communicable diseases are running rampant.

In contrast to the mature/old predominance of Russia, the newly unleashed Eastern Europe countries are full of young souls in a hurry to make money out of change and chaos. In China, too, the many young souls are enjoying new economic freedom and entrepreneurial experiments. Russia has too few ambitious young souls to energetically push the nation into action. Instead of losing themselves in mercantile activities, many Russians have become depressed (mature) or thoughtful and inward (old). Once they have felt their way through the current situation and have a course more fully in mind, these populations will feel more empowered and secure. The area is bound to see a spiritual renaissance, one so powerful that it will strongly effect the rest of the world.

However, the darkness of young-soul organized crime is penetrating Russian society, government, and business so deeply as to bring much negativity into play. This then attracts negative astral influences which can cause situations to worsen instead of brightening. While we see it unlikely that this area will fall dangerously into negativity or evil, it could use support and help. Economic aid of course, but emotional and spiritual support particularly. You can make a greater difference than you might imagine by holding Russia in your mind and seeing universal light, love, and white-gold clarifying energy gently raining down and soaking into people, buildings, institutions, and the land. With your feeling nature encourage the people and the land to soak in this beautiful energy. See people enjoying this light and beginning to shift to more positive, more buoyant ways of being.

Moving away from the dark yoke of 2000 years of oppression takes processing and time. Your love and effort can definitely aid the process and help support the most positive of outcomes, a lovely and powerful spiritual resurgence. (Also of help is the nourishing presence of an infinite soul, now a young teenage boy in eastern Siberia.)

The Baltic states will remain fairly stable, as will most of the former European republics. Food growing conditions in this area will actually improve. The Ukraine and Georgia, already fertile grain growing areas, appear to remain in good shape weather-wise, with politics being, unfortunately, a trickier matter.

Russia's eastern seaboard, north of Japan and across from Alaska, will be prone to numerous high magnitude earthquakes, tidal and volcanic activity. The republics adjoining Turkey and Iran — Georgia, Armenia, and Azerbaijan — will continue to experience many problems. These areas are very vulnerable to strong earthquake activity, which would temporarily quiet their internal wranglings. Turkmenistan, which borders Afghanistan and Iran, and Tajikistan, which shares the Farsi language with Iran, are both likely to be wooed by Iran and either seduced or overpowered. These countries, too, are in a hot earthquake zone.

POLITICAL CHANGE / EARTH CHANGE

Many of the former Central Asian republics are on a slow slide towards social chaos, fighting, and authoritarian regimes. These areas are primarily Islamic and are bound to be attracted, pushed, and pulled by the fundamentalist tenets and drama of the Middle East. Rich in resources and baby souls, but not in education, technology, or development, we see the probability of strife in these areas as strong. People here are less decided on which way to go and what to do than in Russia itself, where at least there is a n unspoken, but clear, determination to build a secure and unique society out of the ashes of the communist experiment.

China may try moving into the three republics which neighbor it, but would have trouble holding on as local sentiment is too strong against it; ultimately, China is likely to be giving up territory on its west, not expanding it.

Australia, New Zealand, Antarctica

Truth is the only safe ground to stand upon.
—Elizabeth Cady Stanton

It must be so pretty with all the dear little
kangaroos flying about.
—Oscar Wilde

AUSTRALIA & NEW ZEALAND

Australia and New Zealand will be among the easiest places to ride out world changes. It helps that neither nation is profoundly overpopulated. Barring increased ice breakage in Antarctica, weather changes won't be as severe in the Southern Hemisphere and food shortages and disease won't be as problematic as in Latin America. Nevertheless, both Australia and New Zealand are on the planet and will be subject to some extreme weather and unusual geophysical events. Australia is already experiencing severe punishing droughts and increased desertification. Harsher ocean-borne storms are another new reality. Australia will also be subject to some unusual earthquakes, primarily in the North, but Sydney will be rocked also.

Both nations will remain solid, socially and politically, however rough times get. Australia, because it has large numbers of strong-spirited, practical young souls, will manage well and keep business together much longer than one might expect in such a world-dependent economy. However, stress from drought, heat, and a pushed-out-of-line ecosystem allows room for plagues of grasshoppers, mice, and widespread grain disease. Food shortages are likely mid-decade, leading to increasing health problems and ultimately, more death. Psychologically, Australians revert easily to a hardy-pioneer mind-set, which makes hardships seem less onerous because they are tackled with high spirit as interesting challenges.

New Zealand remains something of a safe haven, an oasis from the world's storms. New Zealanders are primarily mature, with nearly as many baby souls, both full of old-fashioned friendliness and community orientation. They will watch out for each other emotionally and physically, in all the ways that they can. Crops and weather look as if they will do amazingly well here, helping keep community spirit high. Lack of protection from the ozone layer is a big issue this far south, and excess ultraviolet radiation will create health alarms for humans as well as problems with the numerous sheep and other grazing animals being raised here. Crops don't do quite as well with extra ultraviolet either, but agriculture looks manageable.

ANTARCTICA

The volcanoes under this continent are now active, though showing no obvious signs like steam or lava because they are deeply buried under mile-thick ice. Antarctic vulcanism is but another symptom of the worldwide increase in geological activity. Much of Antarctica's ice, while hinged to the continent itself, lies as a thick sheet hanging over the ocean, displacing no water. If volcanic activity melts or violently disrupts a good portion of the ice sheet's hold on the continent, watch out, because sea levels will rise to Noah significance as the ice shelf falls into the water. Global warming could, of course, cause the same splash.

We see the likelihood of a major portions of the ice shelf breaking away in the next two decades at a little less than twenty percent probability.[6] But, this ice shelf is so immense that the one part which is in most danger of becoming unhinged, a mere ten percent of the continent's ice, would raise ocean levels twenty feet. This would be absolutely devastating for all islands and low-lying coastal areas — the very areas which shelter the majority of the world's people. Every coastline would be radically changed by such an increase.[7] The world's rich delta areas, such as most of Bangladesh, Egypt's fertile and populated Nile region, and the Mississippi delta region and Louisiana, would be swamped.

If all Antarctica's ice were to melt, say from global warming, the rise would be nearly 200 feet, making an intensely oceanic world. This extra water weight would press the ocean floors deeper and create, in reaction, an even higher level of geological activity. Equators bulging with water would make the Earth's axis of rotation unstable. World climates would be in mass confusion and, Southern Hemisphere winters longer and fiercer as the ice drifted northward.

Again, at present, we see these Antarctic occurrences at a relatively low probability. This would be such a momentous event that living on the coasts wouldn't be much more disastrous than living anyplace else. This scenario would certainly be one loud way for Gaia to insist, "Let's reinvent everything."

---

[6] A Rhode Island size piece broke away early in 1995, a pea-sized chunk compared to the whole shelf. Months later, a forty mile crack on the same peninsula of sheet ice turned a huge monolith of sheet ice instantaneously into ice cubes.

[7] It is generally figured that each one foot rise in sea level translates into the loss of 100 to 1000 feet of coastline, depending on the fierceness of the sea and tides and the incline of the coast.

Canada and the U.S.

Those hills hold nothing now. .Lawns instead.
Deeply disgusted by lawns.
Stupid flat green crew cuts.
Nothing for anybody to eat.
—Chrystos

If Rosa Parks had taken a poll before she sat down
in the bus in Montgomery, she'd still be standing
—Mary Frances Berry

SIMILAR BUT DIFFERENT
The U.S. and Canada, both strong (young soul) countries, are
now in the process of creating new (mature soul) expressions in
the world. Canada has traditionally been more compassionate and
supportive of her citizens through social programs, community
services, childhood and old age safety-nets, while the U.S. has been
the mightier, jazzier, more competitive place to live. It is easy to
see that Canada's transition into this new consciousness era is likely to be smoother sailing than that of the U.S. Though both have
spent themselves into holes, the U.S. will be more keenly regretting
its decline as an economic powerhouse. For Americans and their
leaders, this change will take time to assimilate.

MINORITY LIFE

Both Canada and the U.S. have large ethnic groups which are currently calling attention to themselves, wanting bigger slices of the pie, more protections, more consideration. In Quebec, the French are increasingly vocal. They want autonomy and respect from the sea of English speakers surrounding them — or they want a totally separate state; no longer will they put up with what they see as second class citizenship. In the U.S., African-Americans are too widely scattered about the country to be calling for a separate state, or surely they would. Blacks have been set aside to stew in their own juices for a long time and are genuinely angry and increasingly volatile. America seems a racist world that allows them little room for success. The U.S. certainly does have a strong element of racism and has, especially in the past, purposefully gone out of its way to undermine thriving black communities. Current high immigration levels eat away at the job base of poor blacks, an unnoticed but important factor in rising African-American poverty and desperation. Affirmative action programs were originally instigated to help open doors and compensate blacks for damage done over centuries. Giving other minorities equal eligibility undermines the original intention and has further undermined blacks — as will abandonment of the programs entirely.

In North America, the people who have become most successful — meaning rich and respected — typically have been intellectually-centered individuals, focused on professional goals and willing to persevere against great odds. The "winners" have come from all soul age groups, but most often have been young souls or their offspring, imprinted with go-get-'em values. They have come from all races and nationalities, but particularly from Northern Europe and, more recently, from Asia.

Blacks in the U.S. most typically are baby or mature souls and lack the focused drive of the young soul. In addition, African family systems traditionally put emphasis on the organic collective whole, and little emphasis on education or individualistic striving for success. Blacks, consequently, have not been as well supported to go grab success by their own cultural traditions as either Asians or Europeans. Moreover, most North American blacks have chosen to be moving-centered (helped with athletics and dance) or emotionally-centered (which helped gain success in music and acting). But, these favored centering choices do not help them swim with mainstream, in-your-head America.

Each lifetime before reincarnating a decision is made to be intellectual, emotional, or moving-centered. (A secondary center is also chosen, with the remaining center then becoming difficult to access.) Worldwide, people divide themselves equally between these three choices. North American populations, however, have consistently been fifty percent intellectual, forty percent emotional, and a mere ten percent moving. Half of all African-Americans are lively moving-centered individuals who express themselves through the body in a way that feels foreign, if not threatening, to a staid, sedentary, intellectually-centered white. Being moving-centered makes sitting still in school a challenge. The body wants to move and the mind isn't entranced with what is being presented.

Now, seeing that you choose your lifetimes, why would anyone choose a black skin in a white world, an emotional or moving-center in an intellectual world, and a locale where your soul age was not the main player? Challenge and growth, of course; to incubate qualities like humility and compassion, perhaps. But, spending a lifetime marked by your skin color and hounded by messages of social inferiority are nobody's prescription for a good time. In fact, one reason for the attraction of drugs in black culture is that the experience of life is often much harsher and intense than expected. Ambitious astral plans for growth through cruel trials can feel overwhelming once the body manifests on the planet. Drugs numb pain; unfortunately, they basically block growth and evolution.

Minority life has a way of being intense and difficult in most areas of the world. Humans truly push this method of growth to interesting, unusual extremes. Being outside the mainstream throws you squarely on your own resources; for one, you must either accept what the dominant culture says about you and suffer self-loathing, or go against the predominant mind-set, think for yourself, and figure alternative explanations for your predicaments. That process is strengthening; you are personally enhanced because you have explored yourself and contemplated the ordering of the universe. Because it induces the doubts which fuel emotional growth, plugging into a minority community experience is a recurring mature soul scenario. In North America, as elsewhere, the experience likely to remain potent and wrenchingly difficult.

We are not implying that because people "choose" a certain life experience, whether being a Kurd in Iraq, a Jew in Moscow, or an African-American in Detroit, that they will feel invigorated by their adventure or delighted and enlightened by the growth required of them. Nor are we implying that the social structures which make those experiences so formidably uphill should remain unchanged.

It is the essence that chooses a difficult lifetime, not the earthly personality which, in most lifetimes, would select not only the same color skin and religion as the in-charge majority, but also a kindly father who owns a candy store and bestows a sleek red car and trust fund at age seventeen. Sometimes it is hard to figure what in the world essence had in mind for you. When something difficult happens, the personality often gripes, "Why me?" But even the essence is occasionally upset about the mess it finds itself in. Children under two sometimes "opt out" with a sudden, inexplicable death because their essence sees the task ahead as too overwhelming.

Hamburger jobs are about as dead end as drug jobs and teen parenthood. Pain and poverty have made too many in America's underclass give up on life and settle into bleak despair. Blacks are currently being pressed by Republican forces to become more responsible, to move away from dead-end behaviors. This will become another insertion point for discussion of rights versus responsibilities. Social disapproval and the taking away of monetary incentives from behavior that does not pay off is a start towards weighting the responsibility side of the equation.

However, the existing playing board for blacks should be set more level. As mentioned, it would be helpful for immigration levels to be adjusted downwards. Debates and discussions in schools over values would be useful. Are responsibility, perseverance, truthfulness, or showing respect for others useful qualities to cultivate? What happens without them? Personal growth workshops emphasizing taking responsibility for your self and world, widely popular among whites in the 70s and 80s, but expensive, would be a huge help, perhaps in modified form, for high school students, welfare moms, or anyone who has lost hope, vision, and self-discipline. This may sound visionary but visionary is exactly what is required to help these communities bail themselves out. Black culture has a tremendous opportunity coming up to heal, re-energize, and begin creating new, interesting options. Assistance and structural support to nurture this process is important, as is the encouragement of new ideas and new black leaders as they emerge.

Given that moving-centeredness tends to impart lots of energy, providing blacks with the mentoring support to launch and nurture small business ventures and other money making projects would bring on many wins. Entrepreneurial skills ought to be taught in schools, along with basic business and investment know-how. Perhaps it should be possible to begin a small street enterprise or, at least, be faced with less red tape and permit expense in opening a storefront. The availability of small loans, seed money, and business support groups is very important.

All societies incubate prejudices against minorities, but now these judgments will be more frequently exposed to the light, which will help ease minority life. Most often, it is mature souls who put energy and emotion into rooting out social evils in order to make life more equitable for everybody — including themselves, in future lifetimes.

MONEY AND THE AMERICAN CLASS SYSTEM

Getting the U.S. more equitable in regard to taxes is going to be a very interesting process. The 80s witnessed the dying grasp of young soul mentality with both the Reagan and Bush administrations creating widening schisms between rich and poor, and serving business interests, the military, and the ultra-rich to the detriment of the middle and lower classes. Laws relaxing banking regulations, for example, opened the gates for outright thefts by executives at savings and loans, with the total amount so grandiose that it will drain fifty to sixty dollars every month from each American household for the next twenty years. Failing banks, stock trading companies, corporations, and insurance companies are certain to add more to that bill. The ultra-rich have considerably more wealth than they did ten years ago; almost everybody else has less — less income to spend, less social support, less education. The numbers on paychecks may have risen, but spending power and support services for the average citizen have been diminishing since the mid-70s.

Theoretically, the Reagan windfall tax-cuts for the rich were to trickle down into research, development, more factories, more jobs. They did not. Instead, tax-cut monies vanished into junk bonds, real estate speculation, leveraged buy-outs, art auctions, yachts, and luxury automobiles — the magic stuff of the materialistic 80s. The country is less competitive than ever before, and under Reagan's leadership the U.S. became a debtor nation for the first time, and by the end of his watch, the largest debtor nation in the entire world.

Most Americans, except the already demoralized poor, don't like to admit that they are increasingly threadbare, and thus tend not to bring the issue into focus. In fact, some prop themselves up by identifying the poor class below them as the culprits who have taken their money. The public in the U.S. so strongly identifies with material success (or potential success) that, even when unable to buy what was affordable last year or finance a child's education, people are loathe to admit their status has changed. And if they can't afford to travel to Europe or Japan, they don't get the first-hand shock of what it feels like being the poor cousin. The well-off American of recent memory, flashing greenbacks, happy on top of his world, still exists but only for the richest Americans, those few who control about seventy percent of U.S. wealth.

Americans also don't like to believe they have a class system. The myth is that everybody could be rich if they were ambitious, smart, and persevering (though often now all hopes are pinned on the lottery). This skewed version of reality is one reason Americans rarely consider acting in a bad-mannered way towards the rich. Hardly anybody points vigorously to the corruption of banks, savings and loans, insurance companies, or stock trading companies, companies which have bilked the public of untold walloping sums. Very few realize what proportion of money the rich control, or the extent of their and social and political advantages and tax-rule favoritism. (In Mexico, the top ten percent also control seventy percent of the wealth, but the average worker is aware that income disparities are supported by high levels of corruption. No one claims a classless society in Mexico, nor believes that everyone can get rich.)

Though people grumble about taxes and politicians, they haven't been willing to actually tackle the tax structure — or the political system beneath it. It is easier to let the welfare mother remain the scapegoat, or for liberals, the Pentagon. Thinking in terms of economics seems so complicated.

Canada has been taxing itself for social programs and easing into a mature expression, while the U.S. has been tearing off in the opposite direction, making middle class life progressively more difficult to attain and maintain. The set-up in the U.S. is exquisite, at least in its ability to create upsets, drama, and social divisions in need of mending. Little urgency has been felt within government to do anything about worsening poverty or the increasing collection of wealth by a few. There has been no leadership on either side of the issue, just band-aid patchwork schemes which quiet voters and allow politicians to retain privileged lifestyles.

While bureaucrats and bureaucratic regulations are not as corrupt or labyrinthine as in India or Egypt, the U.S. does need a thorough housecleaning to restore vitality. The Newt Gingrich led Congress is going for it in unprecedented fashion, and has been dauntless in its willingness to tear into many social and economic structures, most of which needed a good shaking up. It takes fortitude, clarity and lots of communication to successfully tackle systems that were structured into place over many decades. Tackling programs which aid and abet the already wealthy is challenging because lobbies for the rich are more numerous and more powerful than those few that lobby for the poor. In addition, politicians are not happy about voiding their own good deals or hurting the interests of their richest contributors. Clinton and Gore and Gingrich and Phil Gramm and Bob Dole all know that gasoline deserves a European-sized tax, one which will support conservation, public transport, and leave room for the development of clean technologies, but so far all lack the political courage to make it happen. No one is planning for the inevitable transition away from oil, harmful and as close to running out as it is! Crisis management has become the usual form of governance. Longterm planning is a challenge for anyone, public or private, but is especially difficult for elected officials with short terms in office.

Even with the general public beginning to sense that environmental security may be more important than military "security", politicians are not yet willing to get too radical, especially if it means closing bases or losing jobs in their home states. However, as money gets tighter in the mid-90s, people will start to zealously guard how it is spent. Unless the U.S. chooses to go bottoms-up economically, as the U.S.S.R. did to keep its huge military in place, military spending will be cut, chopped, and shredded despite worries and Pentagon threats of pending disaster. Supporting a gargantuan military and weapons research program is not a major thrill for mature souls who know intuitively that there's got to be a better way. How public monies are spent will be analyzed endlessly; suddenly, economic restructuring is no longer "too complicated" for the average citizen, but a subject of great interest.

REDESIGNING HEALTH SERVICES

The mid to late 90s will see a truly radical economic overhaul, an overhaul provoked by debt, deficits and downturns, and fueled by the clear need to get life systems on a better track. When money looks as if it is being misused, people will yelp, loudly and to good effect. Along with subsidies to any group (including farmers, foreign countries and the military), the U.S. will be reevaluating its technology-heavy healthcare system, which costs an inconceivable amount for delivering so meagerly. Hard moral and practical decisions will finally get made to ration healthcare dollars in a fair and sensible way. Organ transplants may start looking too expensive, and most heart bypass surgery like a hi-tech rescue for those who haven't bothered to care for their bodies. Keeping a million Americans alive, year after year, in vegetative comas from which they have no chance of recovery won't be seen as a needed service, but extremely wasteful. The same for throwing $200,000 worth of aggressive treatment at a near-terminal cancer patient to extend life by a few uncomfortable months. Bailing out premature crack babies with meager lifelong prospects from their multiple crisis situations to the tune of $50,000 to $150,000 each won't be seen as a useful way to spend public monies.

Once these issues get into national debate, the pro-life crowd is certain to have an interesting time. Broad, general right-to-die laws are bound to be passed amid much discussion of how a person's last years and weeks should look — and whether thirty percent of the healthcare budget should be spent on the last few months of life.

While mature souls like to make sure everybody is cared for, they aren't so phobic about death as the young soul, who will often hold on to life at all costs, convinced that this one body is the only chance there is. The mature soul gets the idea that there may be more to life than the physical body and begins to view the death process as a part of life, sometimes better greeted than put off. Six years of operations, interventions, drugs, and decay, or staring at the ceiling of a nursing home sounds horrifying to anyone; the young soul, though, may do it all, clinging tenaciously to life in the body. The Danish, looking death squarely in the eye, no longer fund major medical procedures for those over 70; the American medical/legal system insists on saving people, sometimes again and again.

The mature soul may find letting go more courageous and appealing. After all, death is an interesting, mysterious passage into another adventure. Without denial or fright (or a foggy, drugged mind), you have some degree of control over how and when you exit; buying a lot of treatment, however, often forecloses on your ability to make death a beautiful and magical experience.

Self-responsibility for health is a concept which will come on stronger and stronger, particularly in the already puritanical U.S. Certainly, the average guy will be feeling more concerned and responsible for his own health when hi-tech fix-it money starts drying up. Television will have blatant propaganda promoting "eating right," exercising, and quitting bad habits. The U.S. will likely follow California's lead and tax tobacco heavily enough to pay for hard-punching anti-smoking campaigns on television and radio. Canada already places sufficiently high taxes on tobacco products to discourage use (and encourage smuggling). It could be that soft drinks and sugar will also receive punitive taxes to discourage their use. Healthy people will be seen as an important asset, part of any country's bankable wealth.

Expensive options will surely be rationed so that more money can find its way into the areas that have high payoffs, like prenatal and preventive care and health-promoting strategies. Many Europeans enjoy easy and insured access to homeopaths and herbalists because these non-toxic modalities work, stave off more serious problems and, being low-tech, cost very little. Because they make sense monetarily, the U.S. may bring these health strategies into mainstream despite the predictable catcalls of quackery from the American Medical Association, fighting to retain a monopolistic hold on health dollars.

CARING FOR EACH OTHER

The number of impoverished youngsters, impoverished by lack of money, nutrition, and aspiration is huge. As money gets tighter, social and educational systems will increasingly falter, until redesigned to include more community input and participation. Early childhood education is especially likely to shatter in many pieces as a voucher system opens the way for primary school experimentation. Education will become a hot issue. How can you best train and educate children and evolve them into thriving, productive adults? Can education dare neglect children's emotional, religious, or spiritual lives, their self-esteem issues, and the different ways they learn? How do you inculcate kids with positive attitudes and values — and stop crime and self-destructive behavior before they start? Americans are clear that drilling children as stressfully as the Japanese do will never work; so, what is the best way to help young people be whole and vital, and to find zest for what they do and keep the U.S. afloat? These are some of the sizable questions a concerned citizenry will be raising in just a few years.

A perspective coming in strong by 96 is that people, both individually and collectively, need to act to encourage responsibility and to care for each other. From the lofty heights of religion all the way down to the correctional system, all aspects of life will be examined freshly. This is a quest for the truth at all costs, even when the holiest of assumptions go up in smoke. Politicians who dance, shuffle, or throw money band-aids at problems won't last. By this point, the public will go for bottomline truths knowing that foundations need rebuilding.

Times remain difficult. The world keeps throwing boomerangs; bad luck unfortunately starts to feel normal. But this new urge to reinvent social and political life keeps these years from feeling dismal, like the years of the Great Depression. People sense that out of hardship a better, more workable society is being built. The outer world gives few choices; life can't go on in the same old ways. Clearly, though, many positive changes are being forced by harsh circumstance.

THE CLINTON ADMINISTRATION

The Democratic Party has been in a long crisis with little excitement going on or truth coming out since the Kennedy era. The great social programs of Lyndon Johnson were found unwieldy, too expensive, and perhaps stultifying. Jimmy Carter was seen as a kind man but an anemic leader. Little attractive, fresh, or practical emerged until Bill Clinton and Al Gore, elected for their ability to clarify certain ideas for the nation and to help move it forward to a better future. Clinton's people-skills and consciousness perspectives would allow him to lead well, but his difficulty in grounding and centering himself causes serious leadership problems.

Clinton was elected as the mature soul focal point for needed structural and attitudinal changes. As such, he also became the focal point for all who resist change and growth. Unfortunately for the President, he governs at a time of enormous backlash and fright at the momentum of change. Moving from young soul willful individualism to interacting in your community with an open heart necessitates a big, difficult leap in consciousness. Furthermore, baby souls particularly, but young souls too, relish having enemies. With the downfall of "evil communist states," they've targeted Clinton and big government as the new twin evils.

However, Clinton was given the opportunity to do some useful and radical things. To succeed, he had to rally the public, to get it to care about an energy tax, re-investing in America, reducing violence in the culture, healthcare reform, or creating a healthier environment. Sadly, he chose the insiders route, making deals for small incremental changes, trying not to upset too many applecarts when what was needed was fresh air and big movement. Though he did initiate some useful scaled-down programs and steered the country well in many respects, most of his major tasks were pushed aside for the sake of day-to-day political expediency. Clinton's choice to not go the public route and not capitalize on his good heart and considerable communication skills to educate the public and help move policies forward, turned out miserably for him. "Stay safe and make your party proud," has meant accommodation and abdication of responsibility. Clinton's economic reform plan did not even attempt to balance the budget. He gave up on grazing fees, and on mining fees. He lost the energy tax, and waffled on his promise to gays.

It takes great courage to risk upsetting advisors and voters, to follow your inner truth and not the shifting winds of opinion polls. No president will be able to change anything without fighting for it by educating and wooing voters. Consensus building does not mean caving in to special interests or the lowest common denominator. It means firing people up with a sense of the future they can flow with. By backing away from leadership, Clinton handed the mantle of power to Newt Gingrich. Gingrich does not have the mature soul heart, but does have the courage, organizational abilities, and drive to threaten sacred assumptions and tackle structural change.

NOVEMBER 1996

If Clinton should get himself responsibly grounded and work from his core with integrity, the election will be his. Obviously, there are a few ifs and buts to that becoming a reality. An additional challenge he may face in 96 would be the need to decisively use power to keep some areas in the West stable. At issue may be how harshly to respond to militias or gangs or even armed cattle owners. Exercising top-down authority is not easy for Clinton. The country will need a strong hand, someone willing to take a lot of heat for stepping on individual freedoms in an attempt to keep the whole together.

The 96 U.S. election is bound to be interesting, as the Chinese would say. By November 96, the emotional and financial drain of natural disasters is just beginning to be felt. The economy is worsened, the dollar weak, (losing thirty to forty percent of its 1994 value), and people nervous. Earthquake and volcanic activity is kicking into gear and weather is peculiar. Californians are pouring out of the state to the increasing distress of those in nearby states, particularly Colorado. Some Western states may be rumbling about secession. People rightfully worry that 97 will mean a quantum leap in problems. Life is faltering already. No one wants chaos or anarchy, yet trust for the federal government is low. With conflict and contentiousness and increasing polarization, it feels like the country is pulling apart at the seams.

The 96 election is likely to further crack the two party system. Disputes break out, people are hot-headed on all sides of issues. Clashes arise everywhere. Candidates will be running no-holds-barred races with widely differing agendas. All claim to be knocking away dross to maintain a semblance of smooth functioning. At issue is, what exactly needs to go.

The fight that shapes up between new consciousness and old will be a thriller. How can everyone agree to work together with these changes versus withdrawal, gangs, booby traps, refusal to give an inch, and police state tactics in reaction. The majority, contrary to how it may seem, actually wants a pragmatic policy that can help pull life together. Few will be interested in hearing from the ACLU about individual freedoms being infringed upon. The community now has prime importance. What heals the country is cooperation, flexibility, and an intention to find positive solutions.

EARTH AND WEATHER CHANGES

California, unfortunately for the entire U.S., is at the top of the list for trouble. Already it has been suffering extraordinarily; first it was years of drought and major economic downturns, then came fires, and then months of rains so torrential that huge portions of the state were ruinously flooded. And always small and medium earthquakes, and the threat of the Big One. Nature in California used to be extremely lively and devic, but no more.

Earth-level misery is high.

The level of warning given to Californians, both via events and inner sensing mechanisms has been quite high: This is no longer a safe, stable, beneficent area. Migrations out of that state have already filled up Oregon and Washington (to the point that locals are hostile to new arrivals), and are in the process of filling Colorado, Nevada, Arizona, Utah, Wyoming, and Idaho. Nevada, much of it fairly harsh desert, has the virtue of being close-by and empty; it is now the fastest growing state in the U.S.

Whatever their reasons, those leaving are heeding their intuitions. It is important to take action on your insights, particularly in times of instability when life can change with lightening speed. Furthermore, acting on your insights and intuitions keeps them coming smoothly to you; ignoring them stalls the process of communication from your soul.

It has been said that those remaining in California are doing so because their life force isn't strong, that they don't want to live, or that they have death-wishes. Perhaps all true. But also it is going to be an exciting ride — thrilling and survivable for many; for others, it will be a fascinating way to go. Life and death intensity, panic and survival — people are utterly curious what this will all be. Will it invoke heroism or cowardice? Certainly the eyes of the world will be on these California events; great attention is already focused on California because it is the harbinger of so much. There will be glory in being there, surviving, and in having the stories to tell.

Yet, we foresee problems with refugees getting settled in other areas. People will have lost physical possessions, equity, jobs, loved ones, and equanimity. It does not look that they will be welcomed en masse into nearby states where citizens are nervous about crime, space, economics, and further fraying the social fabric.

Beginning as early as August or September 95, intensifying movement in the ground is likely in two target areas: the greater San Francisco Bay area and a large portion of Southern California.

The Southern California area we see as problematic runs from Oxnard and Ventura inland to San Bernardino and to the desert communities Joshua Tree and Yucca Valley, to Riverside, Fullerton, and towards Newport Beach. We are seeing a sequence of fairly strong quakes here that will lead to inundation of one-third of this total area as early as 97. Southern California volcanic activity, probably near Mammoth, will act as something of a precursor to this devastating quake. The earthquakes leading up to this will be large, in the 7 and 8 range of the Richter scale, none of them safe or pleasant. Riverside, Long Beach, and Bakersfield all look hard hit before 97.

The quake which allows such inundation seems to be predicated not on tidal waves per se, but on a breach in the land which allows slippage or a tilt, and then ocean water to surge in. This slippage is not isolated from the continent or from other plates and will trigger many more quakes, in parts of the country that normally don't have them. This event has nearly a ninety percent probability now, and this close in on time, the energy tends to get locked in place.

The nuclear power plant in San Clemente will cause problems here, but out of this disaster (or one in Cuba) comes a powerful worldwide grassroots movement to close these plants down. Scientists will be reassuring people that the damage was contained very nicely considering the size of the quake and that a quake that large is an isolated event, a very rare occurrence. Similarly to how people know the weather is weird by 95, they know this earthquake was not an isolated event. The Earth is in an internal uproar, hard not to notice. A huge push to get nukes shut down around the world occurs. Despite oil supply problems and worsening economic situations, people are willing to decommission these plants.

The San Francisco Bay area is due for fairly strong earthquakes in 95, 96, and 97. Eureka, San Jose, Hayward, and Visalia will all be strongly rattled, but without overwhelming damage. Santa Rosa and St. Helena are likely to have a powerful quake, probably in 96. This one is very destructive. We are also seeing what appears to be a large scale industrial accident out of the Richmond, Antioch, Pittsburg area that allows poisonous gas to drift over the Bay Area. This kills people and adversely affects the health of many for a long while. The accident flattens nature, people's spirits, and the economy.

Oregon is not immune from West Coast problems, but it is not a hot spot center of activity. Washington, however, will be full of excitement. There will be quakes in Eastern Washington and around Mt. Baker and Mt. Ranier. These latter quakes will lead up to an awesome eruption of Mt. Ranier, most likely in 96. Mt. Ranier is a massive, magnificent and dangerous grandfather volcano. The explosion will be breathtaking. Because of helter-skelter winds created by this firestorm, heavy ash is likely in both Tacoma and Seattle. Ash, devastating to mechanical objects, will sour the economy and make it hard to boost back up. This eruption will effect Northern Hemisphere weather and sunsets for years to come.

The next dozen years will see a startling amount of volcanic activity, particularly in the Northern Hemisphere. In North America, this will be occurring up and down the West Coast from Central America to Alaska.

Victoria and nearby coastal areas in British Columbia are in danger in the coming years. Vancouver will have difficulties and many people will leave, but it is not destroyed. The inland valleys of British Columbia look basically safe, even though shaken by earthquakes. Many people will choose to move further east into Alberta.

In general, it is the coastal areas of the U.S. and Canada that are subject to the most hardship. The West Coast and Gulf of Mexico coastlines are particularly vulnerable. The lower third of Florida and a portion of Louisiana and Texas coastline appear to be under water by late in the decade. The Boston/New York area is the critical Atlantic Coast area because of building geophysical stresses. The area is likely to experience damaging earthquakes as early as 96, though probably a year or two later. One New York quake will be strong and immensely destructive, causing great pain and economic damage. Coastal areas are usually highly populated simply because they are active, alive, attractive places to live. That they are more dangerous does not mean every piece of coastline will be quaked, flooded, or nearly blown away.

In the early 1800s, the New Madrid fault, which runs along the Mississippi Valley, spawned the mightiest set of earthquakes (8.6 Richter) ever in the U.S. The fault is stressed again, and active. While it is too unsettled to forecast clearly what will happen, this fault has some possibility of achieving a release as early as the summer of 95 or the 95/96 winter. The following two years also have some peaks of possibilities. The event we are seeing here, a mid-6 or low-7 Richter scale event, is strong enough to cause damage in adjoining cities, cities which are totally unprepared for tremblers.

New Madrid is a dangerous fault not only because of its recent history but because of the thousands of square miles one quake can adversely affect (from Louisiana to Illinois and over to Pennsylvania). Midwestern towns have few protective measures against earthquake damage written into their building codes or consciousness. Memphis and Saint Louis are the most endangered cities, but towns much further away can be damaged. Even a Richter mid-6 quake here would sap economic strength from the center of the country.

VOID THOSE PROPHECIES?

Many who are familiar with catastrophic prophecies for the 90s, are quite confident chaos and cataclysm have been averted. The thinking is that because people have changed, grown and become immersed in new consciousness, pure love, light, and heart, life on the physical plane need not get rough. True, many, many people have shifted and do help lessen aggression everywhere and hold the planet peaceful. But what new consciousness has not yet done in numbers is nip consumerist habits, vote, make plans to replace fossil fuels, get violence out of entertainment, or get to work on population policies. Inner peace, love, bliss, and a willingness to cooperate and creatively search for new ways of being are of primary importance. But people need to move their feet too, act on their love, intuitions, and insights, and work from their beautiful cores to heal the world. Indifference to the planet is a curable habit, and while being loving and visualizing world peace and stable ground certainly help peace and stability, on the physical plane it is only half the equation. Many who have developed this peaceful inner light are laying back, as if waiting for the world to collapse so that they will have something inspirational to do.

Europe

We have just enough religion to make us hate,
and not enough to make us love one another.
—Jonathan Swift

Sharing is sometimes more demanding than giving.
—Mary Catherine Bateson

WESTERN EUROPE

Western Europe, with the largest enclaves of mature and old souls now on the planet, naturally tends to be at the forefront of social change. In many ways, this area will be more comfortable simply because it has already successfully put much of the new social agenda into action.   France, Germany, Italy, England, Denmark, Finland, Sweden and Norway have high proportions of mature souls in their populations, high taxes and kindly governmental policies, as does Holland with its high proportions of old souls. Greece has matching numbers of mature and baby souls but is so poor that social policies have not caught up with consciousness. Switzerland used to be old, but is fast becoming more young-influenced, serious about business and banking. Belgium and Austria are gradually winding down their young soul phases. Spain is freshly, proudly young and Portugal, still stalwartly baby.

Mature souls usually feel it is important to support each other and help the underdog, so that guaranteed health and welfare services, decent educations and trade schools are generally available. Europeans also support mental and creative health by making four to six weeks paid time off customary for all workers, including even nannies and maids brand new to their jobs. Europeans have a hard time understanding how anyone can keep family or soul together on one or two weeks of annual vacation, a quandary with which old souls can surely identify.

Europeans also ponder why the U.S. allows so much social violence. They refer both to the obvious extravaganzas with guns as well as to more subtle forms of social violence. Allowing so many homeless people to exist, much less starve or freeze seems inexplicable. Hearing about U.S. families being bankrupted by medical expenses sounds like a medieval horror story to them. Europeans are convinced that communal action to provide social safety nets for each citizen seems the only right, morally responsible, self-respecting way to proceed. Of course, until quite recently, most countries in Europe had fairly easy homogeneous populations who shared the same values.

Some European nations have a gentle, grandmotherly feel to them which sets an example for the rest of the world about how life can work. With experience, these countries have become more sophisticated (and realistic) in their handling of healthcare, social programs, immigration, and educational systems. When economies slump (as they inevitably will), there will be agonizing as consumer lifestyles disappear, but Europeans will rapidly involve themselves in making community life work within the new parameters. Europeans will experience less panic when facing survival issues than North Americans. They will quickly adjust as necessary and be ready to assist others, including those outside of Europe, even when money and food are short. Europeans, though, absolutely do not want a flood of economic or environmental refugees making chaos out of what they have so painstakingly put together and will do their best to protect themselves from any such onslaught. While they might like to fix the world, they know realistically that they cannot.

One shortsighted European tendency, over the centuries, has been to ignore Russia. Russia looms so large and feels so foreign, so incomprehensible, that Europeans turn their minds from it, wish it away. This has created many problems in the past. It appears to us that it would be wise for Europe to quickly put energy, money, vision, and political and business know how into Russia, just as it does into Eastern Europe.

Ethnic ties and mature soul morality pushed Germans toward reunification. Economic and social costs have been high but seem worth it, even to the suddenly less-rich West Germans faced with their thankless cousins. The underlying conviction is that whatever the burdens, and however intense the changes, it was the one right thing to do. Germany now greatly needs to tackle, head-on, its current batch of ethnic issues. If it does not defuse the hatred and vengeance being aimed at immigrant groups, hostility and the urge to blame others, to scapegoat, will once again sap the country's economic and moral strength.

Nations with strong agricultural components, like Britain and France, will be in better shape than those that must import food, like Belgium and Holland (although those two get through the decade not too badly scathed). The Scandinavian countries look unusually cold for several of the mid-decade years which interferes greatly with food production. While Scandinavia has the worst problems with extreme cold weather, much of Europe will be lashed by fierce rain and snowstorms, with a good portion of the flooding damage from these storms provoked by extensive deforestation.

Spain and Greece are apt to be hotter and short on water. Spain falls back into poverty, but having only recently come out of extreme poverty, it is a familiar problem. Mid-decade Italy looks shaken by volcanic eruptions. Etna, Vesuvius, and several underwater volcanos will be active. Quakes of a very serious nature will occur in Italy, Greece, Cyprus, and Macedonia. Some of these quakes will be felt over much of the continent. Nature will be intense in Southern European countries, causing economic and social difficulties and extreme food shortages. Italy becomes very chaotic and is likely to be the most uncomfortable place in Europe.

Overall though, Western European weather looks generally benign and growing seasons usually manage to reap fair harvests. Decent weather helps most European countries hold together fairly well during these trying years. Economics aren't great, and there are food shortages and epidemics, but still Europe looks more comfortable than most places on the globe.

All of Europe, including Russia, enjoys sustenance and succor from the infinite soul energy present in a young woman in Germany.[8] She increases light and brings a higher level of clarity and openness to average people, supporting them to feel more comfortable with change. This strong new light also soaks into the land and raises its vibration by clearing away the dark energetic residue of centuries of battles and pain.

EASTERN EUROPE

This is the largest, most obvious place where (young soul) dirty habits are coming face to face with new (mature soul) consciousness. Environmental concerns were what first rallied people together in many Eastern European countries and inadvertently created the power bases from which the dictators were later toppled. Eastern Europe is still dreadfully polluted and fairly poor. Though the post-revolution present is harsher than most imagined possible, and western capitalism and materialism more difficult and less satisfying than hoped, many in these countries nevertheless feel positive about the future.

Rebuilding after the dictatorships is not easy. Redoing your foundations, whether after a mud-slide, fire, war, or governmental collapse is rarely a favored, first-choice activity. But, it is exciting and involving as it forces you to let go of your past and to think carefully about what you want to build. Will you join forces, syn-

---

[8] Her name is Mother Meera and, like all great beings, benefits the entire planet.

ergize, and create harmony to move through grim times strengthened? Or will you brawl and argue, fall into anarchy, wars and devastation? One way you fly; the other is a grim path leading to increasing impoverishment on every level.

In Czechoslovakia, Poland, and Hungary, creativity and a goodly portion of outside help are producing rich potentials and wide-open futures. In Rumania, Bulgaria, and Albania, all heavily weighted with traditionalist baby souls (and the tenacious ambitions of former communist officials), governments will remain authoritarian. Mature consciousness is not strong enough to get these three moving in new, exciting ways. There isn't the people power to make large scale change and the old communist officials are getting voted right back in. However, a communist system based on state ownership, guaranteed jobs and social protections without the old repression of ideas can feel more comfortable than the mad scramble free-for-all that fast market reforms and capitalism can cause.

When a country draws tight ethnic boundaries or lets old resentments rise up and rule, its economy and infrastructure go to hell as wars start, people die, and life grows intense and uncomfortable. For Eastern European countries this would represent a regressive descent. Fighting viciously for a bigger piece of the pie is clearly not a winning situation. In Rumania and Yugoslavia, the only uniting factor for most groups of people was opposition to old leaders, not a vision of improved life for all. These are the two countries most likely to indulge in ethnic warring, and downhill skids.

Yugoslavia has already taken the downhill path and serves as a laboratory where the Western world, most especially the former Soviet republics, can see by blatant, horrific example what happens when people allow this plunge into ethnic rivalry and internal fighting. Other countries in Eastern Europe also model for the world what creativity, goodwill and hard work can create — with the perseverance of Job and some support and investment from the rest of the world.

What was Yugoslavia for a moment in history is now once again in pieces. Ancient animosities and the desire to "even" old scores are fueling a war between neighbors. Serbs succumbed to their baser instincts and allowed a tough, hard-minded (young soul) leader to rise to the top. His mind does not encompass win/win solutions. But, as sour and mired as the Bosnia, Serbia, Herzegovina, Croatia, Slovakia situation is, we do see the area taking in light. Gradually it is gaining possibilities for the future, even as it seemingly shreds that future. This area reads more like a boil than a black hole. After centuries of blood wars, many in the Balkans now have the sense that it was stupid to regress back into conflict after decades of neighborliness. For many, the realization has hit that whatever can be won is certainly not worth the price, and that this war will not regain honor but is a dishonor and a betrayal of self and other. The problem is how to stop mid-stream.

Volatile ethnic disputes are the social downside of mature soul existence, but they do bring up for examination, in grueling detail, what happens when two peoples refuse to let go of the past in order to find common sense compromise and compassion for each other.

One reason for an infinite soul's presence in Europe is to clean up and purify the psychic and emotional debris of centuries of pain and conflict. Britain, Germany, France, and Italy now look much cleaner and lighter than they did a decade ago. In Poland and Czechoslovakia, too, many of the scars of wars have lifted. The light is beginning to soak into Austria, Belgium, Hungary, and Bosnia. Light may not instantaneously change a person's way of being or a country's direction, but over time it will.

What we find perilous in the meantime is that it is Muslims who are losing lives and property. Europe and Russia allow the Serbs to continue the killing because they too have old grievances with (and new fears of) Muslims. And this despite the fact that Serbian Christians are very clearly the bad-guy aggressors here. Muslims around the world can't help but notice that European

Christians are again allowing genocide. The West's hands-off policy reads particularly poorly in the close-by Muslim nations of Albania, Macedonia and Turkey. Europe is unfortunately adding extra emotional force to Muslim fundamentalist arguments that call to even the score with the West.

The Muslim World

Hamas considers the unveiled as collaborators of a kind.
It is our religious duty to execute collaborators.
—Hamas Graffiti, Gaza

To search for knowledge is a sacred duty imposed
upon every Muslim.
—The Hadith

MIDDLE EAST HOT ZONE

The Middle East has the most unsettled, ominous feel to it of any area on the globe. Overall, it looks much worse now than five years ago, despite ongoing and productive peacemaking efforts. Religion, politics, wild rates of population growth, huge proportions of young people, marginal water and food supplies, worsening economic conditions, and the increasing marginalization of women all act together to undermine stability in the entire area. Add in the many in the Middle East who have been disgruntled for centuries, upset that history somehow took a wrong turn after the Crusades, and you have really spiced the stew.

Muslims long for their former greatness: vindication can seem worth any price. These are not forgiving cultures. People may not know the year they were born, but they have linear memories going back centuries, memories which propel them to even out old insults and humiliations. Desert tribal ethics still run in the veins of the Middle East. Pride, individual strength, willfulness, blood loyalty, righting wrongs with revenge, glory through the fight — these values predate Islam but do not work well in crowded, complicated (mature soul) times, when communication, compromise and cooperation are inevitably important. Islam is by design simple, pure, austere. It is not at all a material religion. People are not easily won over by Western material goods, which they may want but resist as symbols of moral bankruptcy and decay in the West.

Arabs rather purposely isolated themselves from Western culture long ago, preferring separate, independent development. Foreigners, foreign ideas and western linear logic could simply stay away. Typical labyrinthine street design and town planning purposefully assured that outsiders would become confused, lost, and easily cornered. The resurgent fundamentalist call is for a return to the roots of Islam and the creation of pure Islamic theocracies. The battle-cry is: reject (or destroy) the West and then all will be well.

UNASSIMILATED LIGHT

The new energy and light coming to the planet to support evolution are more poorly absorbed in the Middle East than any other place on the globe, including Bosnia, Rwanda, and Haiti. When this high-frequency energy is resisted, it tends to agitate and frazzle even ordinarily calm nervous systems. Unassimilated, higher-centered energy can be extremely upsetting and can provoke emotional outbursts — which easily transfer into politics. Many in the U.S.. are also ill-at-ease with these strong new inputs and are upset, blaming, hostile, and unaware that growth is what is actually being asked of them. Because the U.S.. traditionally has a stable political structure with lots of checks and balances, citizens can get angry and agitate for change without amping-up into hot-headed destruction. If in two years the new fellows haven't solved the problems, vote again and get them out. Change, this way, is relatively safe and enjoyable, and gives time to watch, think, and adjust.

In the Middle East, however, people are much more deeply perturbed than in America — bred into chaos through numbers, poverty, lack of work, and old animosities whipped up by a thousand Rush Limbaughs, now all amplified by this new light. What is it going to be, cooperation or anarchy? Compromise or upheaval? In the Middle East there is no political structure to rely on, no easy electoral change, only authoritarian traditions. Life is fast becoming a disheartening and precarious proposition especially for those (often middle-class) citizens who can absorb and grow with these energies. Despite whatever stability they might add, their world is fracturing and factionalizing, jeopardizing everybody's future more each day.

Moderate governments throughout the Middle East now must cling tenaciously to power and battle it out on a very wide front with disgruntled radicalized citizens, so hopeless and angry that many care not if everything topples. The Islamics kill, the governments kill, and each side blames the worsening crescendo of violence on the tactics of the other. Left dodging bullets on the way to the market, the middle class is afraid to speak for moderation for fear they will become the next targets.

When emotions run strong, thinking becomes entangled. Many Arabs feel sorry for themselves, martyred and victimized by the West which paid them little respect and then pushed Israel down their throats. As a proud people, they feel anguish about being by-passed by the world, unsuccessful in any worldly way. Flaunting your piety does little to soothe the pain or fix the problems. The severely disgruntled have a penchant for overnight solutions. In the Middle East this does not mean robbing a 7-Eleven, but messianic leaders with promises of renewed Arab vigor.

This area is ripe for conflagration, something to symbolically blow out all the humiliation and societal dead-ends. And supposedly open the door to a better future. Without a spirit of cooperative support from the rest of the world, this area has potential to self-destruct, harming much more than just its own territory. In

97 or 98, a leader more savvy and charismatic than Saddam Hussein or Ayatollah Khomeini, and more terrifying to the rest of the world, will come into public view. He will be widely felt to have the answer for all the ills and resentments of the Arab world. Even destruction may look glorious, especially while imagining you'll be sitting on top of the rubble. This leader's aim to unite all Muslim nations under one banner and upend the West for good won't manifest, but the possibilities are there for an incredible amount of chaos, pain, and destruction along the way. If this goes nuclear with a warhead targeting New York City, which could happen, it looks that retaliation from the West would quickly decimate the entire area, North Africa to Pakistan, totally changing the world as you know it and causing unthinkable problems for decades to come.

A FAIR SHAKE

One possible way to lighten the disaster scenario is for the West to work more carefully and evenhandedly with Arab areas, beginning now. The irritation Israel causes needs to be defused, both by putting constraints on its behavior and by the pursuit of more equitable policies in the area by Western nations. With the Clinton Administration, this is finally beginning to happen. Chechnya and Bosnia, with their heavy-handed policies towards Muslims, have unfortunately become the newest causes of Islamic alarm, despair, and resentment. Europe fears having an Islamic state within its borders. Russia is wary of having a Muslim nation it can't control bordering its important corn growing region on one side and Iraq or Turkey on the other. And so the killing goes on.

Even without Israel, Chechnya, and Bosnia, the West carries some blame for the current tinderbox situation. Western countries covertly worked to undermine the Middle East, to keep it off-balance and functioning poorly. With life growing increasingly frustrating, ordinary people came to realize that their playing field was tilted. Covert actions certainly kept these countries from being as free or powerful or menacing to the West as they might have been, but underhanded activity is very costly in the long run, creating dangerous levels of anger, and more ricochets and intensity than positive results. The more upset people become, the more alluring are the appeals of a leader with an easy, all-encompassing solution. Clandestine activity aimed at rendering certain groups, governments, or countries powerless is one more (young-soul influenced) activity the new (mature soul) majority will be coming to grips with, as they examine old ways of being with new eyes and values.

Before car bombs and scare tactics, the fundamentalist first cure for injured Arab pride is to put women in their place — restrict and veil them, and promote polygamy. In many areas of this region, for a fully covered woman to ride a bicycle, or even walk with vigor, would be to risk stoning for being too sexual and too independent. The extremist call all over the Middle East is for the removal of women from daily life. When the female sex is devalued, softness, kindness, love, and life itself also become devalued. It would be well to carefully address the steadily worsening position of women in the Middle East. As the rest of the world moves towards sexual equality, the increasingly contemptuous disregard and abuse of Middle Eastern girls and women increases the psychological isolation of Muslims and dangerously adds to radicalism, paranoia, and volatility.

This long-seething, now short-tempered part of the world is clearly exasperated at not being given a fair shake by the West. A demoralized, but angry population, hyped-up by a powerful leader itching for a glorious holy war against Christians, Jews, and the West could mean much devastation. The greatest challenge for world politics is to include and integrate this cantankerous group of countries into world consciousness and commerce, thereby defusing some potentially fierce problems.

The mature soul has a knack for discerning what will support people, motivate them and bring out their best. It would be wise to apply that knack in every imaginable way to the nations and peoples of the Middle East. This is a tall order, but could bring some needed grace. Evolution is gradual; usually it is small, incremental movements that get life heading in better directions. It would also help if the West were to engage in a little self-examination to errors in judgment and values that have painted the world into a corner.

The peace process is helping to get consciousness moving, with some leaders and some citizens being able to move off monumentally stuck and stubborn positions. (Remember those hesitant handshakes between Yassar Arafat and Yitzhak Rabin, Arab and Jew, as if they might implode by touching?) With continuing rounds of diplomatic negotiations, leaders feel more included by the West and gradually more cooperative and trusting of each other. As leaders break down their resistance to working with each other, a good example is set for their people. Shadow leaders, though, are a big hindrance in the creation of a peaceful environment. Islamic radicals, pulling the other way, are calling on men to indulge their dark sides, fight, resist, and undermine the search for cooperation and light.

EARTH CHANGE

Earthquake activity will be strong and tragic in many countries in this region. Iran and Iraq will be shaken considerably; Turkey, Afghanistan, Georgia, Armenia, Azerbaijan, Syria, and Egypt seem to be the other areas for strong activity. Quakes oddly tend to calm life down by shaking people up and leaving them instinctive and humbled for a while. By decimating infrastructure and day to day life, large quakes force people to work together to rebuild.

On the other hand, hot weather, water and food shortages tend to cause violence and rioting. Weather in most of the Middle East is due to be more extreme, more intensely hot and cold, with less frequent and more erratic rainfall.

IRAN AND IRAQ

With many political and religious leaders fomenting rancorous feelings as an antidote for poverty and humiliation, much of the Middle East is vibrating with emotion. Khomeini, who could be called the founder of this movement, is still revered as a saint by a large portion of his countrymen because he made Iranians feel extraordinarily noble and pure at heart in their battles with devil America and wayward Iraq. Saddam, to the amazement of the Western world, reached again into that (primarily baby soul) need for ironclad righteousness and pied-piper leaders. His path seemed to go against logic, self-interest, and even self-preservation. But, losing lives and property may seem worth the cost when it promises to ennoble you and honor your correct principles.

Even though economic and military reconstruction is taking focus and energy in Iran and Iraq, both are likely to remain tinderboxes of emotion flaring at the toes of moderate Arab leaders who fear their own impoverished citizenry being infected by the fundamentalist fever.

Iran is disillusioned, sobering up and rebuilding, its people suffering the economic devastation caused by pulling away from the rest of the world. It did not win its war with Iraq. "Devil America" is as bad as ever but doing fine. The Soviets cut off funds. A catastrophic earthquake in 1990 was a crushing blow; the general populace suddenly had the sinking suspicion it had somehow gone wrong. People were pushed inward, and in Iran much internalized contemplation is still going on: God causes earthquakes, but why not to America or Iraq? Why such hard times here? Wherever they strike, earthquakes shake up more than the ground. They shake up smug self-satisfaction and all that is rigid, including thinking. Iranians are now more thoughtful, more reflective, and the country is calming down, becoming mindful again of the rules of civilized behavior. Being an island unto themselves was not as satisfying an experience as expected. Nevertheless, power issues still abound and nukes are badly desired.

Rafsanjani, Iran's present leader (an early young soul) is exponentially more pragmatic than Khomeini, and a fairly effective manager of the country's economy. With the help of the U.S., China, North Korea, Russian, Argentina, Germany, Italy and

France, he has built his military into a husky, sophisticated machine. It will not go unused. (Before too very long, new consciousness will make these lucrative, shady weapons deals much more difficult and offensive.) Iran may try expanding into one or more of the newly unleashed, primarily Muslim republics of the former Soviet Union. Turkmenistan (bordering Afghanistan and Iran) and Tajikistan (which shares the Farsi language with Iran) are both likely to be wooed, seduced, or overpowered. Iran may bully the whole area with dark threats of devastation. Hope is so small and resentment so great for many in the Middle East, that the appeal of religious, civil, or military leaders who promise grandeur through destruction (Often of a grandiose target: The Pyramids? Rich Kuwaitis? The West?) is hard to brush off.

After the fantasy push into Kuwait, the Persian Gulf War consisted primarily of the hell being bombed out of Iraq, which actually helped to siphon off some craziness and delusions of grandeur. The war served as a reality check: Iraqis are back to their everyday lives, sobered. On the other hand, the bombing left huge reservoirs of humiliation and pain which await the next moment with promises of victory. Everything has repercussions: war, bullying, and covert activity, as well as diplomacy and a positive sense of possibilities.

Iraq is still posturing. The boundless, smug stubbornness of a certain head-of-state jeopardizes normal life. Nuclear devices are being sought and bought, and concentrated biological poisons manufactured in stupendous amounts. Though people feel worn and defeated, they could take their minds off suffering and be rallied again in a bid to save face. Overall, though, visions of military glory are fading, being replaced by simple desires for food, normal commerce, and stability. But still, there may be flare-ups. Wounded pride doesn't disappear quickly, especially in this area of the globe.

Khomeini was an exceedingly karmic leader whose (baby soul) vision centered on purity and righteousness. Saddam's (young soul) vision is more about personal power expansion. Though Iran now has young leadership, it is a basic baby soul country with a fair proportion of infant souls. They want strong leaders to tell them what to do and when to do it. Though Iraq also has a preponderance of baby souls, it has a strong young and mature soul element. Economic sanctions made the plight of average citizens so demoralizing and precarious that any stray thought of improving their lot by uprooting Saddam dissipates quickly into the air. There's hardly an extra calorie to get rowdy with anyhow. Day-to-day political and nutritional survival is the issue.

THE GULF STATES

Saudi Arabia, Kuwait, Oman, Bahrain, and the United Arab Emirates are all major young soul hangouts. Gulf Arabs certainly enjoy their great oil wealth, but are forced into minding their manners by a powerful group of exceedingly pious men of religion — especially in Saudi Arabia, which is growing more tightly conservative by the minute. Underpinning each of these now hyper-materialistic countries is a puritanical, rigidly-practiced form of Islam which pervades every aspect of life. Any movement towards increased social freedom must be made cautiously, with fear of grave consequences. For example, the opening of Saudi Arabia to a highly censored form of television required a major diplomatic effort with the keepers-of-Islam, ever suspicious of anything not explicitly pre-approved in the Koran 1370 years ago. Nevertheless, first oil and business, then the affordability and seduction of Western goods, and several years ago the presence of foreign soldiers fighting off Iraq, helped dislodge these Arabian countries, one millimeter at a time, from their rigid ways and xenophobic fears of foreign influences.

The ruling kings and princes tend to be young and mature souls. They must contend with the mullahs, who tend to be baby and young and conservative. The royal rulers have reality-based fears of disturbing even one hair on the head of the mullahs. This makes it extremely difficult to liberalize any aspect of social or cultural life in these societies.

When royals from the Gulf States travel they take off the

muzzles and break all the rules, from imbibing alcohol to allowing their wives to be seen in Parisian street clothes, but for now it feels correct and comfortable enough to come home to the orthodoxy under which they were raised. Total power is kept in the hands of the male sex, total power which is always a corrupting influence and always difficult to release, even when you know you should. The occasional woman is impatient to make changes, but would risk her life if she agitated directly, and, at any rate, has little power to affect outcomes in these most male of societies. The thirty or so women who dared to drive cars at the close of the Gulf War, were all severely punished, some with their jobs, some with their freedom and lives. If you are a young soul or mature or old, and female, and have chosen to be born into one of these very restrictive societies, it is most likely that it was to get the experience and thereby balance out some karma, not to take on the cultural dominance of men.

The Saudi rulers like to view themselves as the rich patriarchs and caretakers of the Muslim world. They take this image seriously, though their poorer cousins in other Arab nations find them insufferably arrogant, lightweight with their charity, and use them as another target for resentment. Young souls, especially the newly rich, give scant consideration to sharing or cooperating to help bring everyone along, unless their own strategic advantage is immediately clear. Obviously it wasn't. If these kings, princes, and emirs had dug into their treasuries and helped other Arab nations boost education, health, and industry, it would have made a huge difference in this now red-hot area. But they didn't.

The Gulf States have given considerable money to conservative political and religious groups for decades. The 90s are seeing the Saudis, especially, progressively arm-twisted for greater and greater monetary support by radical groups like Hamas, Islamic Jihad, and the Muslim Brotherhood. These groups have used hundreds of millions of support dollars to stockpile weapons, for terrorist training, for agitating against civil governments in Algeria, Egypt, Pakistan, Turkey, etc., and more recently for monthly stipends to men who force wives and daughters into covering, and for schools, disaster relief, and hospitals. Fundamentalist groups can now afford to do more for people than many governments and are gaining power and loyalty with these tactics. It appears that the Saudis are nearly breaking the bank giving what amounts to bribe money to these organizations in exchange for promises that their own monarchy and oil fields will be safe from attack. The royals are still unbelievably wealthy, but treasuries are being drained and national stability suffers. Still, it would take a foolhardy courage to stop the blackmail and refuse to capitulate now to these increasingly militant organizations.

Kuwait has a huge young soul majority, most of whom grew too arrogantly lazy to work, too lazy even to scramble to put their postwar country back in business. A disabling decadence set in here in this small feudal fiefdom, a softness which was like a perfumed calling card to Saddam Hussein. He knew they were too much into palatial plush to be in fighting shape. (And he thought George Bush his loyal friend.)

Since it usually comes with the (young soul) turf, why weren't all these Kuwaitis more alert and aggressive and on top of their world? Life was so easy it baked initiative and purpose right out of them and often competence too. Luxuriating in easy money and smug satisfactions, they didn't bother to develop themselves or their talents. Challenging lifetimes get you going; easy and sumptuous have major downsides, for countries as well as for individuals. Kuwait will be shaky for a long while. It has money, but few human resources with which to heal and rebuild. Kuwaitis will continue to feel like displaced rich people, not at home or secure anywhere, including in their own country. They had a postwar chance, which they botched, to let their thinking, habits, and institutions evolve. The new parliament has virtually no parliamentary power, women are much worse off, paranoia so great and xenophobia so high that Kuwaitis not only booted out most of their trained foreign workers but knowingly allowed indigenous Bedouin groups to starve.

UPCOMING CHANGES

SYRIA AND ISRAEL

Syria and Israel, the other young soul countries in the region, are both military powerhouses. Prior to the 70s, Syria was a mature soul enclave, secular, even slightly racy and liberal. Mid-young now and under Hafez Assad's unrelenting, iron-fisted (young soul) rule, Syria is likely to fall back further in soul age during the 90s, its gates of opportunity not open wide enough for individualistic young soul tastes. Assad could have created a much stronger and more powerful country if he had chosen to educate and develop the abilities of this most able population; instead he chose suppression and slaughter. The high road takes more vision and courage, and can always result in the toppling of any presumed leader-for-life. Though Assad is a cynical man who never puts all his cards on the table, it is excellent that he is being included by the West in diplomatic negotiations. Catering to a leader's ego, which is what the West did for so long with Saddam (and many others), is very different than the reality check that happens upon sitting down at the negotiating table.

Israel's development as a heavy duty military power helped mend the World War II shredded psyches of its citizens by proving it could at least beat Arab neighbors back onto their heels, again and again — a most satisfying young soul experience. Instead of ever making accommodations, showing compassion or respect, Israel relied on its own brand of baiting, bullying, and torture. No doubt this behavior meant survival once. Now, these same behaviors are absolutely counterproductive, a vote against longterm survival for the entire region.

The good news: Israel is edging towards a (mature) cooperative expression, kicking and screaming though it may be. The huge influx of Russian Jews has helped push it further along the soul-age scale. Soon it will find some intention of getting along with its neighbors, rather than simply flexing muscle to keep them intimidated. Remember how this behavioral shift sounded unbelievable a few years back, right up until it began happening?

With the old mind-set you believe it is fair to use all the power you can muster to control all of life; with the new, you

202

know there are actions you should not take. Israel is at that (young/mature) juncture, clinging tenaciously to the power patterns that have worked for it in the past, knowing it must let go. This is a scary transition for a person or a country to make. If you release your old ways of being to make a move forward, which a part of you is inclined to do, it looks as if you will lose control and be defenseless, unable to avoid bad situations. Any of you who have ever had to stop trying to control a relationship and let it take its own course understand what this stage feels like; a glimmer of freedom twinkles at you to take courage, wade through your fears and let go, while conservative parts of you scream, "Go for the jugular! Grab what you want; don't give an inch!"

In the Middle Eastern world, Israel is a focal point for anger against the more powerful West. It is also another excuse for Arab failure, an easy scapegoat. At any rate, with Israel moving slowly and steadily towards a more embracing perceptivity, and world pressure now on both Israel and Syria to mind their military manners, the equation in the Mid East could change for the better. Seething resentments towards Israel from its Arab neighbors won't go away, but the timing is right for some common sense cooperation among all parties. As Bill Clinton continues to pull the U.S. back from its automatic knee-jerk support of Israel, Arabs at last feel as if their side is being heard — instead of being rudely run over. This change in stance by the West is essential if there is to be a chance for healing in the Middle East.

With Moscow and Washington no longer fighting each other for an edge here, something better can evolve. The new (mature soul) world attitude coming into play, by fits and starts, insists that it is time for all the parties to sit down with each other to share concerns, shatter old rigidities, hatreds, and opinions, to somehow come to understanding, compromise, and peace. These ideas were in the end promoted by George Bush and Mikhail Gorbachev, who had formerly both egged on Middle Eastern hostilities.

PALESTINE AND JORDAN

Jordan is small and vulnerable, particularly given its hotbed location flanking Israel, Syria, Saudi Arabia, and Iraq. King Hussein is a moderate, reasonable ruler, stretched and pulled by all sides. This country must negotiate, and negotiate with all sides rather continually to survive. Though it wears on him, King Hussein manages this razor's edge act rather well. Jordan was the only country to offer citizenship to Palestinians, at least until they were found to be plotting a takeover of Jordan. Recent free elections have placed many militant Islamics in Parliament, but the country has enough freedom to handle a healthy exchange of ideas. With calm leadership and high proportions of baby and mature souls, Jordan is not a particularly activist or volatile place, though as always, the fundamentalist undercurrent exists.

What looks problematic here is water: water drying up, water running out, desperation for water within a few years. Many countries will be hit by droughts and water shortages, but Jordan and Palestine will be particularly stricken. Lack of water can cause crop failures and food shortages, but also rapid price increases, food riots, and famine.

Palestinians, even as they get a better break from Israel, are unlikely to calm down or make much headway or advancement. People have been too radicalized already, too angered by Israel; too tortured, humiliated and impoverished by it to forgive and move on. Continuing disorder looks exceedingly likely, not balance, commerce, or self-possession. While Arafat and the Palestine Liberation Organization are willing to make peace, Hamas is busy, undermining the peace process. One essential for Hamas is the destruction of Israel. Another essential is that Hamas control the area itself. When Israel lets go of the West Bank, a civil war will likely erupt between factions who wish to control it.

EGYPT, TUNISIA, MOROCCO, AND LEBANON

Lebanon was a comfortable (mature soul) country not so many years ago, full of cafés, culture, natural beauty, and vacationing Europeans. Now it is shattered, an abysmal pile of rubble, another monument to anarchy. Its cedars are dead and dying, its citizens unproductive, exhausted with partisan warfare with no escape from intense, wrenching experience. Like Yugoslavia for Eastern Europe, Lebanon served as a warning for all Arab nations, exemplifying what happens when citizens stubbornly keep factionalizing instead of compromising, cooperating, and working towards a greater good. Afghanistan, Sudan, Somalia, and Ethiopia, though never as rich or cultured, are on the same sorry (but oh, so intense and interesting) warlord strewn path and Algeria may not be far behind.

Morocco has done an unusual experiment with its soul age mixture, having roughly 25% each, infant, baby, young, and mature, with a few old soul healers, teachers, and storytellers tossed in. Despite pervasive poverty, the evenness among the four soul ages helps create balance, stability, and a fair amount of tolerance for differing points of view. However, the rate of population growth in Morocco, like many Muslim nations, is so high as to be destabilizing. There is no resource base to absorb so many into the economy. Europe no longer serves as a reliable safety valve; it does not want more immigrants. Morocco and King Hassan are comfortable enough for the moment, but when the elderly King dies, power will be up for grabs. Islamic extremists could create havoc whenever they choose in Morocco.

Tunisia has roughly the same even soul age spread as Morocco, but it is in a better position with food and economic security (and therefore political stability) because of an excellent population policy which encourages small families and female literacy. Like Jordan, though, Tunisia is just a small, vulnerable country however rationally it is ruled, and will be subject to the waves of activism and drought that will roll through the Middle East.

Egypt's strong intellectual, free-thinking tradition has helped maintain a modicum of political equilibrium and made it less prone to the groundswell of passionate fundamentalism sweeping the region. However, unbridled population growth, worsening climate, and massive poverty sabotage it considerably by giving revolutionary talk more appeal.

Egyptian temperament along with its very small number of young souls makes efficiency and rational planning elusive. (It is primarily mature and baby.) The infrastructure remains shabby and the bureaucracy thick, mind-boggling, and incredibly wasteful of time and money. Its population grows unchecked, a million more mouths every nine months. During the difficult years to come, Egypt, with too many people on its limb, will find itself in a catastrophically worsened position as to food, sanitation, and rudimentary healthcare. We expect much death and disease to come this way, along with sadness and despair. Emotional suffering oftentimes reaches wrenching peaks in mature soul areas because misfortune and hardship in a community make for intense life experiences. Again, this is no one's idea of a good or interesting time while suffering through it.

LIBYA AND YEMEN

The populations of Libya and Yemen are not too far along the soul age scale, being primarily baby and infant. Libya, however, has lots of petrodollars and a fair-sized technological-minded young soul cast. Without military or monetary support from the Soviets, Libya is slightly less arrogant and dangerous in the Middle Eastern equation, but its ruling politics are likely to stay right wing radical with plenty of plots and terrorist activity remaining part of the scene even upon Khadafy's death.

Yemen has a fair-sized contingent of mature souls who join everybody else each afternoon to relax and chew qat, a mild leafy narcotic. Yemen now has so few business-minded (young soul) men that much of the land previously devoted to cultivating their famous mocha coffee bean has been dug up to grow qat, which interestingly not only brings no money into the country but severely cuts into everybody's productivity. Nothing like a good stagnation lifetime in the middle of a late twentieth century hot zone! Humans love creating endless varieties of experience for themselves.

POLITICAL CHANGE / EARTH CHANGE

ALGERIA

In the early 60s, Algerians found the (young soul) strength to battle out from under very determined French domination. But, like many countries that slipped out of the colonial noose, an equally authoritarian home rule was put in place. Algeria is still working on creating a new manifestation. About half of the citizenry want secularization and to surge forward into the twentieth century; the other half is made exceedingly nervous at that prospect. Few loved the ruling military elite. When an election was forced in the early 90s, there appeared to be a radical fundamentalist win in the offing. If elected, the Islamics were ready to cancel future elections and begin a theocracy. The military therefore refused to relinquish its reins and canceled the election, with nary an objection from Western democracies.

Because the current of consciousness in Algeria is heading towards a strong young soul future, the military will likely get away with their coup and remain in power using whatever force it takes to quash the radical religious right. That's what we saw five years ago. But the tactics police are using to root out radical fundamentalists have become so harsh and their net so broad that ordinary people are wanting to throw off what has become an intolerable, repressive dictatorship. Though resentment of police tactics grows almost daily, there is also fear of the fundamentalists, and the hopeless feeling that life under them would not be one iota better.

This potentially powerful nation is not moving towards a stable climate in which to do business, the least harmful of young soul outlets. Day-to-day carnage between Islamic extremists and government hit squads may ulcerate into civil war. Daily life has been brought to ruin. The very poor side with the fundamentalists, feeling that nothing could be worse than the present. Chaos increases as people no longer care what they destroy to fling this government off their backs. Foreigners, diplomats, journalists, and anyone daring enough to voice concern over what is occurring is methodically killed. Extremists are now setting out to ruin the infrastructure of the country, telephone poles and government buildings being the favored targets. Obviously, life won't suddenly improve if the Islamics gain control. Furthermore, factions now working together to overthrow the government would certainly later vie with each other for power.

We see this North African nation as likely to become the hot spot and major source of trouble in the Middle East. Appearing on the scene before the passage of too many years will be a young charismatic leader, likely to fire up the country and region, creating a great deal of trouble on the world scene. This is a bad-news leader who could gleefully instigate widespread terror. If in a few years the Middle East is as hard hit as we expect by food and water shortages, and Europe and North America need their grain at home, aiming weapons at other continents or poisoning the water in Paris or New York may look more glorious than simply starving.

The nuclear threat is greatest in the Muslim areas of the world: Iran, Iraq, India, Pakistan, Algeria, Libya, and the Central Asian republics of the former Soviet Union are within our red-alert danger zone. Although any use of nuclear weapons is likely to be somewhat localized, this is still not healthy for the planet. Because of average soul age (baby and young) and fatalistic Islamic attitudes (shrug: whatever Allah wills), and a passion for the glory of a holy war, neither destruction nor environmental degradation are terribly worrying issues for many in the Mid East. Religious righteousness, resentful anger, and desires for revenge rarely create moderate behaviors or deep, ecological thinking.

TURKEY

Just a few decades ago, Turkey's Ottoman Republic was about as large as an empire has ever been. After two world wars, the country was left with little territory, glory, or money. With this recent past history, Turks are suspicious of wars and expansionism but aren't about to let go of territory to the Kurds or anyone else.

A majority of Turks would like to further industrialize their country, make money, and get out of those 1940s brown suits.

Joining the European Union, which would aid Turkey considerably, is an open possibility if it can maintain political stability over the next five years. Political stability shouldn't be hard for Turkey but, given the times, will be tricky.

There is a conservative, traditionalist strata in Turkish society that finds the promise of a newly conservative Islamic society attractive. Already made uneasy by modernization and changes in their culture, and wary of the excesses and decadence of the West, they want to keep life as it was or make it more conservative. As Muslims in nearby Bosnia and Chechnya are being slaughtered, a pure Islamic society which outlaws western influences begins to sound good or interesting to a third of all Turks. The killing of innocent Muslims in Bosnia and Chechnya adds considerable fuel to fundamentalist separatist arguments.

Turkey is being targeted by expansionist fundamentalists to join the revolution and choose their side. Tactics include picking away at governmental power, undermining and destabilizing it. Turkey is in a toss-up situation with very diverse scenarios possible. While a majority are prepared to join with Europe and erase poverty and become twenty-first century citizens, those promoting an Islamic state have mounting emotion on their side and may be able to close the door to the West. Sending light to this area will absolutely help the situation move in the most positive directions.[9]

AFGHANISTAN

Ripped apart by its war with Moscow, Afghanistan amazingly fractured even further after the Soviet retreat. A dozen warring tribal factions vying for control of the country left the capital city, Kabul, in a ruinous state. The world now has another Beirut. Young soul warriors with a love of fighting, excellent supplies of modern weapons, and a lack of intention to get along have impoverished the future for all.

---

[9] See final chapter, The Mending, for more on this.

UPCOMING CHANGES

PAKISTAN AND BANGLADESH

These two nations exist on territory India relinquished to Muslim minorities several decades ago when the polarization of Hindu and Muslim broke India apart. Both nations are populous and growing fast; Bangladesh is heartbreakingly poor, Pakistan only a little less so. The new fundamentalism has taken root in both countries, factionalizing Pakistan, in particular, and making it more difficult and unruly to govern.

The population of Bangladesh is overwhelmingly baby, with many infant and mature souls in the mix. More anti-woman each year, life is becoming increasingly precarious for women. A telling story: Village women obtained small business loans to buy mulberry trees in order to nurture silkworms and add to the family income, i.e., feed and possibly educate their children. Incensed about women gaining any power, village men went on a rampage and chopped the trees down.

Bangladesh, always subject to monsoon flooding and damaging water-borne storms, is in an increasingly perilous position because of extensive upriver deforestation in Nepal and India. Monsoon floods are now commonly two or three times as devastating as in the recent past. This crowded nation loses many gaunt citizens each year to weather events, preventable diseases, and malnutrition. The ante will go up.

Pakistan, with its young soul majority, is more ambitious, more industrial, and more angry. Especially at India. A small war is now going on over the state of Kashmir which India has and Pakistan wants. Each of these countries has nuclear devices and (newly young) majorities proud of any muscle they can muster. With Pakistan's government in Benazir Bhutto's capable hands, the chance of nukes being used has lessened considerably. But should a militant Islamic group gain power through elections or terroristic destabilization, then the probability of use goes higher.

Pakistan, with about one percent of its natural forest still standing, is so often exposed to disastrous flooding now that it is attempting reforestation, near-impossible with so many people making claims on the land for living space, agriculture and firewood. Suffering in Pakistan will be great in coming years because of weather, overpopulation, food shortages, and disease.

SOMALIA, ETHIOPIA, THE SUDAN

All are increasingly under Muslim influence with black Christians and animists having been beaten back from power. With that struggle over, however, up comes the next: Which faction or tribe is strong enough to dominate the others and to rule. Again, we find a lack of agreement to work together and build a future. These are difficult areas for food production in good years, but now agriculture has gone by the wayside. These countries now are dependent on world grain donations. Early in 95, the U.S.., the world's major food donor, quietly cut in half the tons of grain it annually promises to the world (possibly to increase grain storage capacity beyond the current two to four months of food). This is bound to create deeper hardships in these countries that put food for their people last. Somalia, given even an expensive chance to build a coalition government, did not grab it and neither the U.S. nor the U.N. could force it. These nations are not absorbing the new light coming to them and will likely continue on their way, harming, killing, and starving themselves.

MUSLIM ASIA — INDONESIA & MALAYSIA

Indonesia, spread over dozens of islands, is the fourth most populous country in the world, coming right after the U.S. It is overpopulated but has put population policies in place which strongly promote the two child family. When a country consciously handles some of its issues, life tends to go a little easier for everyone.

Though primarily a baby soul nation, Indonesia has areas that are moving towards a more active young soul mode of being and enclaves of mature souls exist on many of the islands. Bali, the only Hindu island, has a base of baby souls, but is primarily mature and exudes a strong old soul influence. It looks very lucky and stable. There are numerous young souls in major cities and as in the politically repressed, agitated areas of Timor and Sumatra. Harsher economic times (or possibly the death of longterm President Suharto) could provoke rebellions to throw off oppression and layers of corruption, to get land reform and gain other opportunities. Political upheaval here could lead to pandemonium and much destruction, particularly on the main island of Java.

The huge majority of Indonesia is Muslim. Some island outbacks retain animist religions or use those with an overlay of Islam. The Islamic fundamentalist influence has arrived, but on top of a culture that does not share the same old-time resentments for Christians and the Western world. But, a strong Islamic society is perceived to be useful by many because it helps fend off the vices of the West. Western cultural and material influences have noticeably cut into old values. The allure of fundamentalism in Indonesia is not strong enough, given this country's cultural base, to cause chaos on its own. If political stability does not hold, then the fundamentalist claim to be able to make a better society and keep life stable will have more coin.

Malaysia's population is also primarily baby, but moving towards a young expression. Adjoining Malaysia at the tip of the Malay Peninsula is Singapore. With its similar British colonial background, and strong monetary success, famous rational policies and planning and lack of corruption, Singapore is a powerful attractive model of what can be for Malaysians. Both nations are strongly multi-ethnic, though Malaysia is an Islamic country. Because of Singapore's impact on consciousness, and Malaysia's multi-ethnic business know-how (and lower levels of governmental corruption than Indonesia), Malaysia appears likely to remain politically stable.

The hot seasons in Southeast Asia get hotter and longer, the wet season storms more ferocious and damaging. Volcanic activity in Indonesia is already on the upswing and will increase dramatically. Earthquakes in the area will be frequent, many quite strong, but the rice crops continue to be brought in — most of the time.

SEVEN

Placing Yourself
Staying Put or Moving On

Altogether elsewhere, vast
Herds of reindeer move across
Miles and miles of golden moss,
Silently and very fast.
—W.H. Auden

To be rooted is perhaps the most important
and the least recognized need of the
human soul.
—Simone Weil

THE ADVANTAGE OF FLEXIBILITY

There is both skill and art to placing yourself so that, come what may, you feel "sourced," nurtured and energized by the locale you have chosen. Here you can more easily maintain your center and do the work you are intending to do. With this chapter, we want to set you in motion, sorting through your present situation, your desires and fears, in order to get you into the right place with the right people in these most interesting times.

Paradoxically, there is little chance of finding yourself in the "wrong" place! By doing your homework, though, you can know that you have chosen, and are not stuck. Whether you ultimately stay where you are or move on, it is helpful to look at alternatives and to be led by your deepest desires and instincts. Each of you will sort this material through in your own way, until you latch on to the set of options which feels aligned with the flow of your own life.

Baby souls usually won't have the nerve to pick up and go, unless everyone else already has, as in the wake of a severely deteriorating situation. While young souls tend to have a fair amount of money, which simplifies changing locale, they are more likely to be tightly plugged into making it just where they are, being inclined to stick with their rational life plan unless they see a financial advantage in changing course.

Old souls generally have the greatest overall flexibility. While they may not have the investments or savings that make moving less of a financial crunch, they do have the psychological pliancy to re-think their lives and adjust to changes in place, relationships, or lifestyles. While mature souls are certainly perceptive enough to realize trouble is brewing, they are most likely committed to existing friendships, support groups and so on, and would feel the most grief upon separation. However, they are willing to experiment and be adventuresome. Not surprisingly, it was mature and old souls who formed the greatest proportion of the Jews who left Germany — and Europe — pre-1940, before life got intensely dangerous. There were many years of warnings and foreshadowing of what was to come, but many Jews waited until they could escape only by leaving all material things behind or until they could not escape at all.

Regardless of soul age, when individuals are first jolted awake with the realization that their geographical area may not be safe, many emotions and feelings arise. When survival fears kick in, anger, frustration, panic, apathy, denial, helplessness, franticness and so on are not usually far behind, making change seem urgent, yet overwhelming. Whether you are caught with an urge to flee or an urge to deny, you are also caught with fear. There is, of course, no escape from fear. Whether you run or stick your head in the ground, life tends to get worse. The first item on the agenda, therefore, is to face down your basic fears about life and change and death.

Some of you will find it useful to let your imagination play itself out by writing down your own worst-case scenarios, aiming to do this with a Buddha-like sense of detachment. Later you can dissolve those mental pictures and bring in your humor, but, first, it is good to know exactly what internal messages you are dealing with. No place in the world is perfectly safe and secure. Bolting for Kansas or New Zealand won't necessarily guarantee safety — you can always get hit by a tornado or truck, or a faulty prediction! Furthermore, maybe you'd regret not being a major player in the exciting adventures likely to occur in the more hard-hit areas of the world.

MORE THAN SAFETY, HOME

What we want to examine here is how you can find the place where you most belong, where you could put down roots and feel at ease and at home. If you are content where you live now, chances are good that you may already be ideally situated. Interestingly, many people in just those areas most prone to serious problems are restless, but have no clear understanding as to why or what to do, much less where to go. Sometimes, this inner push for change comes as a peculiar boredom with work, work which was previously gratifying. Maybe it is a longing for birdsong and green vistas. Perhaps it is experienced as a sense of completion or apathy about friends and neighbors. Sometimes it's a pervasive anger about pollution in your area or the increasing number of people, cars, and hassles. Sometimes a dream (or a child's dream) leaves a lingering sense of uneasiness with your current life. Dreams, longings, and feelings can very well be messages from your essence saying it is time to move on.

It is most joyful to be living in a place and situation that gives a sense of comfort, inspiration and easy, deep connections with people. When settled, you want a source place, a healing place, come what may. Optimally, you want to be able to say to yourself: I have made my peace here. Though I feel protected here, I am willing to go if this goes. I know I have work to do here, and I'm not going to continuously worry about the future.

You all need to answer this where-to-be question, individually as well as on a family/relationship basis. Notice the degree of comfort where you currently live. Does your body feel secure? How are you enjoying day-to-day life? Are you connecting with nature and feeling in touch with the Earth below your feet? Do you feel supported by your relationships, by the people you meet, by your community's vision and ability to resolve its problems and issues? Is your growth assisted in a beneficial way by events in your area, or do you notice life progressively grating on you?

For some, perhaps it no longer feels right to be on the East coast, or in a big city. Maybe you have been longing for a simpler, greener life anyhow. If you remain in San Francisco only because you can make a bundle, but hate the fog, the noise, the traffic, and you are no longer cheerful enough to relish the views, charm, and culture, it is probably wise to move on, whether the thought of a stronger seismic event rattles your Richter scale or not. If the hook is money, but all the rest of you is uncomfortable, it is time to do some serious reevaluating and clarifying of values. Generally, old and mature souls will come solidly down on the side of quality of life, of which money is a part but far from all.

DISCOMFORT MEANS FIX SOMETHING
Some people will immediately recognize feelings of discomfort in their current location. Californians, for example, are in such exodus that the numbers leaving now surpass high immigration and very high birthrates. Most report they are leaving because of the economy and crime, but at a higher level, intuition and essence are at work.

While many feel uneasy about the potential for unwelcome

events, they may still feel attached to their current area because they have always been there, because parents, relatives, every friend, and an alive-and-thriving support group is right there. If this is you, intensely involved where you are, but with a worrying ear cocked towards the future, you may want to start talking with friends about what you are sensing. Put out feelers and see who responds. You may be surprised to find others with similar concerns and leanings. Make the potential for great change in the 90s a high priority for discussion. It may be that the part of your group which actually means the most to you has been aware of prospective changes and problems. These friends may have toyed with the idea of making changes, but never really allowed the thoughts much room because of the seeming impossibility of moving bodies and lives somewhere else. Now you have created fresh openings and possibilities, for yourself and for the people who are so much in your heart.

At the very least, discuss potentials like food or energy shortages, rough economic situations which may make mortgages or nursing homes or college suddenly too expensive to manage. Begin to think about how you all might be able to support each other. Be creative in looking for options. Preparing in the manner which makes sense for you — whether it is finding gas shut-off valves, storing survival food and water, learning to garden organically, or taking a Red Cross or herbal medicine class — may help make you more comfortable in remaining where you now live.

YOUR CROWD, YOUR KARMA

It is not wrong to get hints, outer or inner, that there may be trouble in your city or geographic area and still choose not to move. Involvement with people is crucial to nearly everyone. People nurture and love you, and you them. They can also drive you crazy and be part of your karma, another reason you may not want to leave.

Karma allows humans to experience both sides of every behavior equation. It means cause and effect, so, for example, if you once abandoned your wife and three young children for a life of adventure, you are sure to be at the opposite end of that scenario, with that very person leaving you to nurse your pain and pride and to fend for yourself and the children. Karmic relationships allow you to experience the intensity and discomfort of being treated in just the way you once treated that person. Now, locked into an intricate tango, you balance out the equations. Relationship karma is the major growth formula on the Earth.

Typically, an experience that took ten years at its inception will take ten years to wind up in a later lifetime. Then both parties will feel complete in Earth information, intensity, and time. Living on the shortest end of the karmic stick, which is the side the old or mature soul is usually on, doesn't make your personality feel full of oats or bounteous free will, but karmas do tend to be compelling, intense, and interesting. While karma is ongoing, you may knock your head against a wall, angry at yourself that you don't have the guts to leave an unpleasant or abusive relationship, but the truth is that you probably can't abandon the ship and be complete. So, your essence keeps you there. You stay, but start to hate your supposed weakness. People who are ready to move generally don't leave unfinished karmic relationships behind! On an essence level, you want to get those relationships wrapped up no matter what it takes. So, you stick around — or you take them with you.

However, we sometimes find mature and old souls in uncomfortable, downright awful relationships long after the karma has been wrapped up. Many have sensed they must have been completing karma and felt they must "owe" their partners for something. With duty and completion at the forefront of their mind, they fail to sense the shift that occurs when karma is complete.

How do you know karma is over? The intensity suddenly drops away and the situation no longer eats away at you. The relationship seems more manageable or more boring. When a karma is done, some people literally hear it go "clunk." Often, one partner is out the door fast. People also choose to stay to-gether once karma is done because life is more comfortable then and they can arrive at a sense of peace with each other. But when a relationship (or a job) pinches badly, overstaying out of a sense of moral duty, ingrained habit, or fear of what anyone will think, can cause more misery and create more karma.

Interacting with the group of people gathered around you is usually one of the primary reasons you find yourself on the planet. If you want to remain where you are in order to be with them, you have a much sounder reason to stay put than money or a fear of the unknown. Should you feel free to leave your current area, you will be drawn to a new area which holds many "old" friends for you, similarly for the partners and children you bring along.

SKEPTICAL?

Most regions in the United States, Canada, and Australia have been so protected and lucky for so long that it is hard for the average citizen to imagine that life could rapidly change and grow very tough. Europeans, with a lot more living history be-hind them and two recent wars on their territory, know in their bones that security can go out the window, overnight.

Thus, it is not surprising that there are many people who can't comprehend that a serious problem could present itself. Some get angry at anyone who dares to stir up their feelings, but the anger is really at their own sense of vulnerability and helpless-ness. The old souls in this group may quickly assert that they are protected if there should be difficulties. If this is you, it is good to check in with yourself to see if you actually feel well protected where you are, or might you be playing ostrich? If denial comes up fast for you, we suggest looking a bit more deeply for buried fears, resignation, or can't-do attitudes. It doesn't matter so much what you decide to do, but getting conscious lays the best groundwork for good decisions. Fortitude and dispassion have a place in the 90s, but feeling resigned or angrily in denial are not optimal attitudes or opulent states of mind and are therefore best examined.

Many rational thinkers react to the potentials of the 90s with total denial. The end of the millennium makes people superstitious, they advise. No unusual, predictable events are lurking, period. Furthermore, they assert, the economy always goes up and down, the environment is fine, and the Earth and the weather always act up periodically. Talk their ear off or appeal to their intuition to no avail. They set their chins and pull their necks in. If still feeling communicative, they may inform you of a person who got scared ten years ago and sold her close-to-the-fault property and for what? Property values soared and no live action on the fault line yet. Reader's of this book likely realized long ago that some people's opinions won't change no matter what persuasive tactics are taken.

TIMING VS. LOGIC

Sometimes people are lucky; timing is easy and perfect. You realize you want to go, the new place which draws you is obvious, work opens up easily, good-byes are simple, and off you go.

In timing a move, you manage that best by being aware of feelings as well as what you perceive as logical options. First fear tells you to get out fast, and then it tells you fast is impossible. Logic will often tell you to take two or three years to plan and prepare for a transition of this magnitude. Get a job, move your business, wait for the market to improve, sell your house, build another, save more money, the kids should graduate first. The list is endless. Make your transition as painless and guided by common sense as possible; but also watch your body and feelings for timing clues. Have confidence in your decision making skills.

When the area you live in feels dense, when it feels less life-supportive than it once did, you are getting an alert. Do you notice anxiety leaves when you are out of town, or that you grow noticeably heavy or depressed coming back into town? These are signals. Acknowledge these messages, and don't ignore them.

PLACING YOURSELF

Bury these signals, because they are inconvenient to your current plans, and you bury your sensitivity. Soon you stop enjoying the sunlight as it flickers through tree leaves, but you've grayed down so much you don't miss it. Your early warning system closes down. You become dense. Your body may get heavy or depressed. Soon its immune responses have diminished too. The price paid for not following your intuitions is higher in times like these.

WHERE TO?

Often you know already what area to put yourself into. Perhaps you have always wanted to go to Florida, or back to Vermont, or are being drawn to the cowboy thing — or a spiritual group — in Montana. Perhaps your parents are still in Iowa, which feels more charming every time you visit. Maybe New Mexico has always enchanted you. Many of you will already have openings to walk through into your new lives, places you think about that feel magic or special or light — despite your logic which says Iowa is a snore, Montana too dismal, and Colorado and New Mexico too expensive or too redneck.

Special feelings often linger for places where you have had pleasant past lives; your body even now feels especially peaceful in those locations. Also you will be drawn to climates which are your favorites from past lives and which agree with your constitution now. You may be drawn by the sacredness of a particular piece of land, whether in Hawaii, near the Rockies, or down by the old mill stream. And you may be drawn to places because you have business there, or a person you need to meet. Sometimes it is the old gang awaiting, a very nice scenario.

What if you are sick-and-tired, itchy-footed, and otherwise complete where you currently live, but don't have a clue about where to go next? And you can't imagine any place in the country as fabulous or even very interesting. Perhaps you imagine nothing is affordable? If this is the stuff of your mind, it is important to open all its windows and doors to new possibilities. Do not limit yourself by what you now think you know.

For instance, many Californians believe that no other locale could be as good because of consciousness, scenery, or weather. People on the East Coast indulge a more intellectual snobbery, believing that no other places could be as stimulating or cultured. These are valid lifestyle concerns. However, looking deeper, you may find provincialism, illusion, and ego lurking in these ports. Also, be aware that the quality of life on both coasts has changed greatly, generally to life's detriment, over the last decade. Many inland areas which formerly were dull, stagnant, and small-minded have new energy and life seeping into them, both from people and from nature itself, while the coastal areas look worn, tarnished, and without their old energetic vitality.

When truly ready to change locales, people are willing to make tradeoffs. Exchanging year-round warmth of climate for year-round warmth of community may suddenly feel like trading up, not down. Lamenting the loss of an excellent daily newspaper and a cutting edge culinary scene may taper off when nature, safety, and kindness surround you.

When you begin casting about for where you belong, ask for dreams, for chance, for luck, for guidance, for inspiration from your wiser friends on the astral, your guides, angels, Jesus, or Gaia. And then listen. Be receptive to what information and synchronicity comes your way. And, check it out. Validate for yourself what rings true, what seems exciting and right — and what seems off-the-wall nuts.

Many of you are sensitive enough to clear your minds, close your eyes and, then, with the idea of opening some perfect possibilities for you, put your fingers to a map and see where it "feels" alive and good. You may be embarrassed doing this, but just notice what your sensations are. What stands out? Does your heart feel good over the Rockies or near the Mississippi? Do your fingers tingle over the Southwest? More than throwing darts at the map, this process will help you hone intuitive skills.

HOW TO?

If you feel strongly drawn to Tibet, and always have, we'd say call it pleasant past life memories. Read books, look at photographs, do some past life regressions, but don't spend much time considering how to make it your next domicile. Sort through your possibilities with common sense, research, inner-voyaging, and some strategic trips.

If you are considering North Carolina and Virginia as potential new centers for your life, but don't know which or why, do research. Check out specific books on those states as well as more general books like *Places Rated Almanac* and *Retirement Places Rated*. As you browse through these resources, be aware of intuitions and feelings. It is easier to focus yourself in this way than it is to travel all over these states.

In addition to the bookish route, start talking with friends and acquaintances about their experience of those states. A town loved by somebody you love may be right for you as well. Listen to people's voices as they describe places. When a person really likes a certain location, his voice will glow, as may his words while he shares the memory of it with you. Then notice if you are being touched. Are you being nourished by the energetics of that spot, even through someone else's memory? By following those rays of affinity for a particular place, you end up where you want. Let inner guidance lead you. If every time Boulder or British Columbia are mentioned, you sense magic, you owe it to yourself to check it out. See how it feels — in person with your feet on its ground.

It isn't wise to move to Nebraska because you think it will be safe, if when you are there it feels terminally boring, depressing and your body seems to weigh thousands of pounds. Safety isn't enough reason to go through that, and you can bet with feelings like this, Nebraska is not where your old gang is either!

When searching out a destination, keep your mind very open. Anything is possible. By staying open to all possibilities you don't limit yourself. If you love Santa Fe, or Hilo, more than anywhere on Earth, but dismiss both as places with poor employment opportunities, maybe you have just lost the most wonderful locale and lots of wonderful people. If the location is right, you can find a way to be there. On the other hand, perhaps there is a "better" place for you; you have to use your intuition to feel this through. Don't get limited by the first thoughts or first objections of your rational mind.

It is smart to gather statistics for an area. Check out the soil fertility and growing season, the levels of air and water and crime pollution. How is the health of the educational system? Check on what the weather has been doing, and the economy, but remember it is difficult to predict with perfection what will be happening five years from now, what climatic changes or increased economic difficulties will bring to any particular area. You can't totally protect or insulate yourself from these changes, though you can make some educated guesses, such as that small will be more comfortable than large. The idea is to go with your instincts, heart, and mind.

If you adore the area around Tucson and feel pulled to be there, but your mind says, "terrible water problems and too hot," we'd say think about it, feel it through for yourself, listen to your deepest intuition. It could be the Tucson climate will change and get better, not worse. Or, maybe you go there, meet a gang of old pals and head for Manitoba together. It is all individual, and you are smartest and luckiest when led by your deepest guidance. That doesn't mean throw your supposedly rational mind out, but put it in perspective by giving your intuitions, feelings, and desires a good hearing. Stay open to any area you might want to be in.

ASK FOR INSPIRATION

Work with divination. During meditation, take an inner voyage to "try on" various locales. Pray, ask for guidance. Ask for clear signs about what to do or where to go. Consult the I Ching. Have a tarot reading. Get some channeling. Go to bed asking for clear, inspired dreams which show you what to do.

We are often asked to rate how much a person or family are in affinity with particular areas. We usually look for overall affinity, but emotional, physical, spiritual, and financial affinity can also be rated separately. Rating a town for its mate-finding potential is not an uncommon request either. You can do this intuitively for yourself. Imagine a one-to-ten scale in your mind's eye and pose your question. Where does the pointer go? What number lights up? Some of you might enjoy learning to use a pendulum or muscle testing (Applied Kinesiology) to track down specific information. Both are good ways to get past your mind and access your body's innate wisdom. Hone your intuitive skills with the methods that appeal to you.

It is always important to validate channeling or any information you divine for yourself with your inner knowingness; information will resonate with your core energy when it's correct. You feel the "click". An advantage of channeling is that it can more easily open you up to possibilities you wouldn't ordinarily consider or ideas that represent a whole new way of thinking about your life. An advantage to working with ritual, guides, dreams, the pendulum, or muscle testing, etc., is that your intuition quickens and grows as you learn to read yourself.

CHECKING OUT THE NEW LOCALE

A certain active breed of people are inclined to sell most worldly objects, jump into a large motor vehicle, and start driving around the country trying to figure out just where they want to live or "retire". Usually this ends up quite confusing since there is so much input and so little focus. That is why we push doing homework first, and getting guidance. Wait until something clicks; then do the field work.

In addition to all the ways you would normally size up an area, we suggest paying particular attention to your body and to your interactions with the locals. Your body will tell you if it is happy in an area by how it feels. Is it suddenly thrilled to be breathing? Is it sparkling, more upbeat than usual? Is it relaxing easily, is your first chakra content and quiet? Are you feeling nurtured by the scenery, whether natural or man-made? When the landscape looks beautiful to you and your body feels well, usually you are in a benign spot, one with healing energies for you. If everything seems all right but your body feels edgy and details are not coming together easily, you are probably not yet in an optimum place.

Notice the local people, because you will want a group of them to fill your life with all that humans can. Survey the newspapers, the bulletin boards and the yellow pages. Explore the bookstores, the health practitioners, the natural food stores, the art and music scene, the restaurants, and whatever else interests you. Tell people you are interested in the area and are checking it out, trying to figure if it is where you want to be. Let them tell you how it is for them. Talk to the old-timers; talk to the supermarket clerks. Are you connecting?

When you are in a good area for you, you will find yourself looking into many people's eyes and enjoying their energy. That is one clue that you have old friends there, which always means more comfort and familiarity.

OLD & MATURE SOUL ENCLAVES

Many of you will be drawn to areas where old and mature souls are collecting, for having a generous number of like-minded individuals around helps smooth your life, makes socializing and feeling part of the new community easier.

You want to feel inspired with this move, not like a miserable wet dog with its tail tucked in. It is crucial to feel positive about where you are going (or where you are), so even if an area is loaded with people of similar consciousness, pay attention to how you are actually feeling and how well you connect with the individuals you meet.

There are a number of fairly secure areas in the U.S. and Canada drawing fair numbers of mature and old souls. The Southwest has become a major magnet. New Mexico, Colorado,

Arizona, and parts of Utah are all strongly drawing newcomers. Portions of Oklahoma and Arkansas are also attracting many new people, as are certain areas in the Virginias, the Carolinas, and Kentucky. Vermont and New Hampshire are again drawing old soul attention, and seem comfortable havens. Montana, Idaho, Minnesota, and Wisconsin are having old and mature soul influxes also. Along with the interior valleys of British Columbia and, before much longer, Alberta, these are the places in North America we see with the most mature/old soul attention focused on them, which are also likely to remain comfortable locations.

While there are many other places in the U.S. which are also safe and stable and have interesting populations, we've only listed here the areas which are now both drawing large numbers of conscious people and have a settled, balanced feel to the land.

THE FAMILY PACKAGE

If you have children, we suggest considering school systems, community crime levels, transportation, etc., as well as their input, to the level which seems appropriate to you. Your kids will instinctively be directing you away from places wrong for them and towards locales where they will be comfortable. They do not do this consciously, or even by their grumpiness or excitement, but they do it on an energy level, in a manner quite difficult to pin down and describe precisely.

It is not necessarily their objections that will tell you where to go or not go, because on a conscious level they do not know. Often they will object to any change, except maybe those that sound glamorous, like Malibu — or Paris. If a location is absolutely one hundred percent wrong for them, you probably won't be considering it for long. Their unspoken energy will close the door.

The family is a unit which moves through life together as a package. Tightly wrapped or fraying at the edges, blood keeps even oddly composed families at least tracking each other. Your children knew it was a package deal, that they got you, your mate or mates, your lifestyle, foibles and strengths, and your potential for change when they signed on and climbed aboard. They knew the parameters within which they would be working. By carefully and consciously choosing what your family will do, you can trust your choices however loudly the children grumble.

YOUR KIDS PICK YOU

Generally, "child agreements," the agreement to bring certain essences to the planet, are made only when everything jells on a deep level so that each essence, parent and child, gains. By that we mean that each gets the lessons it wants for growth, the opportunity to complete karmas and meet the people it needs in order to have the sets of experiences it desires. This can mean a childhood where the musical talent you want to explore gets nurtured by dad who is with the symphony and by mom who plays drums in a women's rock band. It can mean a warm, supportive family, or a favored older brother who tortures and easily one-ups you. It can mean always having good old friends around you, or it can mean feeling so much like a stranger in a strange land that you are forced to explore your inner world and miss out on street-corner fun.

We can tell you that because of the complex bonds with your children, you are unlikely to give deep consideration to a location that will ultimately not work out well for them. Your child picks you for exactly who you are, and aren't, and for what you are likely to offer, and for the way you are likely to impact them. All this is orchestrated on the astral plane to allow each essence to accomplish chosen life tasks. Again, we are not talking about idealized, trouble-free existence, but real life with warts and challenges. Generally, old souls are wrapping up karmas in many of their relationships including those with children, and rarely instigating new karmas. This does not mean that if you have a temper and a tendency to hit and be nasty that that is the level you are "supposed" to parent from. If your behavior bothers you, or drives others up the wall, it is always best to work on clarifying it. Nevertheless, it is basically guaranteed that your child will not be thrilled with you and your package all the time, nor will you always enjoy and be proud of your offspring's personality or behaviors.

Families are intricately bound units, bound by love, by duty, by guilt, and by many forces from the past. Children will have all sorts of overt and covert ways to control you and will try to control the moving question itself. Teenagers, especially, are not going to be pleased about a change of locale. Nearly always they will act mortified and martyred, feel depressed and angry, and do their best to make sure you feel guilty and miserable for forcing them into something they don't see as their choice. And, to be fair, moving is particularly wrenching at puberty. Adolescents, because they are beginning to deepen relationships, feel discomposed and distraught when ripped from newly budding friendships.

A child knows quite well, on an energetic level, where it belongs and is much more powerful in controlling outcomes than you could imagine. What this means is that when you sort through for yourself where you want to be, considering your children as much as is practical, that your choices, your heart and gut choices, are likely to work quite well for your children too — even though they complain all the way. They gripe because of inconvenience and fear of the unknown, not realizing they have also chosen, on deep, energetic levels, to go where you are going.

SACRED SPOTS

As we see it, the next eight or ten years will be most comfortable spent in an area where you feel nurtured by the land and the community of people. It is not necessarily better to be situated where there are substantial new age communities, as in Boulder or Santa Fe, or big vortices of energy as in, Sedona or Mt. Shasta. Being in a location where energy is continually stirred provokes growth and change, but can be hard on the body, not restful at all. You are the one to decide which qualities you want, what is most important for you and yours at this time. Living in a location which feels right to you has everything to be said for it.

Wherever you "land", periodically you may want to make treks to the Earth's special places, the places which absorb your negative energies and cleanse your body, mind and spirit. The Earth recharges your life force most powerfully in these special power places, which may be known to you alone, or be as famous as Yosemite, as grand as Grand Canyon, or as well traveled as Hawaii, the Greek Islands and the English countryside. It makes little difference where, as long as you allow nature to alter and purify your consciousness. You know an area is sacred by its power to move you.

Sacred spots help awaken your innate capacity to be in an intimate, personal relationship with nature. As you open yourself, nature will reawaken your sense of wonder and give back boundless love. Be open to what attracts you out of the corner of your eye, for this is one way to become tuned to nature's ephemeral energies. Of course, the trick is to let that activity remain peripheral and not attempt to bring those energies into the center of your vision where you will immediately lose all sight and sense of them. You can't use logic or your will here; rather, you must remain quiet and receptive. See what happens.

FENG SHUI

Once you have placed yourself — whether you have moved or not — do whatever you can to make your space and land feel clear and sacred. It is fun to gather up some friends and do "house cleanings" for each other, the idea being to rid your living space of all old, rigid, stuck energy. This old stuff may belong to you or to previous dwellers in the house. Purification is easiest to do in a physically clean house, one with cobwebs off the ceiling, dusted bookcases, and clean windows. Old, dead energy often clings to neglected spaces.

There is no perfect way to cleanse a house since basically it is done by intention anyhow. Nevertheless, it is richer and more fun to ritualize it. Use candles, directing the fire spirits to purify your space by letting all darkness be dissolved in the golden light of the candle. Burn sage or lavender, dry, bundled together and tied, letting its smoke and smell burn out heavy energy in your rooms. Open your windows to push old energy out. Throw salt into the corners of rooms, and herbs like lavender or rosemary.

Be aware which of your rooms feel clean and light after you have finished and which still feel heavy. Perhaps a room feels better except for one particular area which might feel cold or dim, gray or sad. Often the corners of a room pile up old energy and take extra effort to clean.. Feel your space, walk it and take charge. You can put quartz crystals, point up in the corners of a room to energize an area which feels flat. Keep purifying until your living spaces feel sparkly and alive to you.

Also walk the perimeter of your house, creating a sense of light around it as you go. Let the light penetrate the ground many feet down. Feel as if your house is protected; ask for protection and love to surround your house. Get a sense that you and loving unseen energies are together creating a nurturing, safe haven.

Walk your land. Be aware of where the ground is happy and healthy and where it is not. The vegetation will offer clues. What could you do to energize the sluggish spots? What could you do to make the area more special, more sacred and more beautiful? As you put conscious energy into your land, it repays you ten fold by nurturing and supporting you.

Feng Shui is the ancient Chinese art of placing yourself in nature and housing so that the surrounding physical energy will be beneficial and life-supporting. Investigating these eye-opening, useful concepts is worthwhile.[1] As you know, the Chinese were long ago able to see how energy ran through the body (upon meridians) and see how to manipulate and balance that energy (with acupuncture) to create greater harmony and health. Feng Shui is the study of how this energy runs through nature and through man-made structures, like your house. Feng Shui also in-

---

[1] The Sarah Rossbach books, *Feng Shui* and *Interior Design with Feng Shui*, are the best so far.

cludes "fixes" for energy when it isn't sufficient or vital or harmonious. In tricky times, it only makes sense to keep your environment as perfectly life-supporting as possible.

EXERCISE

This is simply a list of questions to help you get in touch with how you feel about staying put or leaving. Rate your answers, if you wish, on a scale of 1 to 10, with the low numbers meaning no, not really, not much, and the high numbers meaning yes, very much. This will help you weigh your answers and see what is most important.

1. How important is it to you to feel connected with nature?
2. How much do you enjoy breathing the air where you now live?
3. In general, how committed are you to follow through once you see a change is needed.
4. How strong is your tendency to rethink periodically what you are doing?
5. If you have felt you would like to move, rate that desire or urge.
6. Are you annoyed with waste in your current lifestyle?
7. How strongly do you believe that where there is a will there is a way?
8. Would you like more time available for your spiritual life?
9. Rate your spirit of adventure.

10. Rate your courage.
11. Do you find a particular part of the country or the world "calling" to you?
12. How important is quiet to you? How much do you enjoy solitude?
13. In your present location, how *currently* important are your friends to you? (Have your connections loosened over the past year or so?)
14. How important is money to you?
15. Are you attracted to living more simply?
16. How much do you enjoy your children's friends?.
17. Rate your joy in being alive on an average day now.
18. How important is it to live close to parents, children, or other relatives?
19. Rate your attachment to your current locale.
20. How connected to nature are you in your current location?
21. How much do you enjoy the ambiance of your town or city?
22. How involved are you in what your town offers?
22. How important do you believe it is for your children to remain in the same schools and neighborhood?
23. Rate your children's schools.
24. Rate your daily dance with cars and traffic.
25. Rate your fear of living where you do.

EIGHT

Emotional Punch
Self-Care during Rapid Change

I've had a lot of problems in my day — most of which
never happened.
—Mark Twain

Be a light unto yourself.
—Buddha's last words

STATE OF MIND VS. STATE OF PLANET

To have your personal state of mind dependent on the state of
the world is not the way to be happy — especially during the next
dozen years. If you explore and nurture your psychological and
spiritual nature, you will experience tremendous growth and transformation. In hard times, emotions tumble out more easily. Let
them roll and you will be enlivened; stifle them and you'll be depressed; do nothing but hang out with them and you'll be exhausted. It is just that simple and that difficult.

Fear will be uncoiling. Change being change, it can bring
panic right along with excitement. And what is being discussed
here is not small change, but events that will require major goal
and value reevaluations from you all, as well as creative responses
from society as a whole.

FEAR & COMPANY

If you are living in Kansas and the weather is fine and life is stable, you might experience little concern should California suffer another devastation. "Well, that is just California and it doesn't have anything to do with me." It might as well have been one more problem in Bangladesh. Perhaps the event stirs your compassion, but unless you think it will hurt you economically, you don't feel anxious.

However, the events of the 90s are going to be so pervasive and require such major social and economic readjustments that everyone is likely to feel personally involved, or vulnerable. Suddenly it won't only be casual comments about June's strange cold wave, but real concern about the pace of change and the out-of-control feel of nature. Science clearly can't stop Mother Nature or fix out-of-kilter weather and ecological systems — or the insects gleefully taking advantage of new situations. Almost everybody will feel instinctive at times, Kansas included.[1]

There will be people who are loudly saying: Look, we can hold this together, don't fall into panic. Many elected officials, local, state and national, will rise to the occasion. Because of the responsibility of their positions, these officials will manage to process their own personal fears, or set them aside, in order to keep their part of the structure running as smoothly as possible.

OLD SOUL EQUILIBRIUM

As a conscious soul, your job is similar: handle your fears so that you too can be helpful. Once you've collected yourself, your steady vibration absolutely provides balance for others. Old souls, in particular, know that it is not useful to live with fear. Life is experience. Enjoy its interesting drama. To get terribly excited or agitated throws you off center. Staying on center becomes important to most old souls; in fact, it is often at the cutting edge for spiritual growth. Firewalks have achieved popularity because they

---

[1] Michael uses instinctive to refer to behavior based on first chakra fears and instincts, which makes access to the reasoning intellect or to feelings of love and connection with others more difficult.

are a dramatic, highly graphic demonstration of the power of over-coming fear. Many of you learned that by keeping your cool you can cross hot coals without charred feet. To stay joyful and shin-ing in times like the 90s, you will need more than a little reminder — or a firewalk experience — to remember to be detached or be-mused, and to keep working through your fears. Practicing a spiri-tual discipline always, always helps.

Old souls explore their spiritual natures, often with a scatter-shot approach, developing unique philosophical viewpoints, per-sonal rituals and practices. In order to remain centered, with heart and feelings open, you need to get your spiritual practices off the shelf and into action. The times will lean on everyone to integrate spiritual philosophy with life.

A person who has lived many lifetimes has an advantage in rough times. Having gone through disasters, crazy karmas, food shortages and famines, political upsets, intrigues and wars gives you flexibility, a backlog of experience that is not conscious, but nevertheless affects your perceptions. On an essence level you know a life can get backed into a corner and then, Boom! a door opens, and suddenly you are once again swimming with options. And should no door open, you know you can survive that too — after all, here you are now. The body isn't everything.

If you become shaken because of some event, notice how fear feels in your body, get conscious and do some processing. Ground and calm yourself and you'll feel whole and ready to be helpful to others again, faster than you might imagine. And process tomor-row's fears tomorrow.

Whenever the world unravels, something inside you is ready to go too. Better to let go, and take the path that opens, rather than to hang on to old ideas or ways of being that no longer serve you. When you live in the now and it changes, you have a new now. Be gentle with the scared parts of you that resist change and you will relax more easily into the now. No one person can control or stop these changes. Roll with the new energy, let go of the old.

SEIZE THE DAY

The 90s present extraordinary openings for working consciously in the world. You won't want to miss these windows of opportunity by getting stuck in the muck. This shift will allow you to bring out your best while assisting a wavering society to move forward, instead of falling backwards into a sea of chaos.

As the old approaches to life stop working, fresh solutions are begging to be found. Most people already know many social blind alleys they would like to see changed, whether civil rights, women's rights, animal rights, environmental rights, education, medicine, agriculture, the judicial system, tax policies, television programming or government itself. Many of you will be choosing to put your time, energy, and creativity into exactly those areas of society which have already drawn your attention. Your unique life task will often be tied squarely to what you have already had annoyance with or (secret) dreams of changing. The late 90s are a perfect time to galvanize change, especially on local levels.

If the form of society is to evolve easily (with your vision blooming), you must handle the part of you that is apprehensive about change. Master your fear and you are more than free, you are a plus for everyone. No matter how it feels, life is moving towards balance.

FALLING BACK IN CONSCIOUSNESS

When panic buttons screech, it is normal, but not optimal, to devolve or regress in consciousness. Falling back into a primitive scared-to-death (infant soul) place, you feel shaky and panicked, with no sense of what to do first. This is about as bad as it gets. Actions from this level of awareness won't often make practical sense.[2] This regression can happen to anyone. During wars, soldiers and civilians both occasionally get snagged by this thick level of fear because no one has any idea what is going to happen next or how bad it will be. An ordinarily courageous person can be-

---

2 Many residents of Oakland, California, watched the neighborhood firestorm on television until it was too near to think clearly about what objects and papers to pack in their getaway cars.

come immobilized, or a quiet one, hotheaded and dangerous.

When fears are provoked, people typically regress to a level of consciousness where they draw comfort from a rigid right/wrong system of evaluations. "What's mine is mine. What happened to them, happened to them because of the sinful way they were living. Too bad, but not my problem." Acting from this (baby soul) consciousness, an individual finds little reason to look past family or small community group. Judgments move in with this level of perception. Recognizing fear-based judgments spewing out of another person's mouth (or your own) is the best way to bring heart and compassion back into play.

When fear carries someone away into a yang (young soul) place, he may grab a gun — not necessarily to shoot people, but to be sure he can protect himself, his house, garden, wife, and so on. The men in an area might form a militia to keep everybody else out, especially those devastated by a nearby flood or earthquake. If a person becomes fearful enough at this level, he'll be agitated, restless, angry, and may feel compelled to act (usually not in a logical or helpful way). Remind that person, or yourself, that it's best to find your composure and act carefully in order to avoid unwanted consequences.

Becoming excitable, shaky, or perhaps hysterically talkative, attentive to every horror story, and, in general, stuck in drama, very emotional drama, is to fall into fear (at the mature soul level of consciousness). While it is healthy to acknowledge feelings, to share and cathart, when trapped at this level a person raises her degree of pain and that of everyone around her. Walk the dog, relate to nature, talk to your cat, listen to an inspirational tape, dance and shake, write affirmations, make music, chant, take flower remedies.[3] Do whatever it takes to get yourself calmed down.

When under stress, people retreat into the old family patterns they were imprinted with. For example, the child of baby soul parents will more likely fall back into a rigid, judgmental consciousness, again and again. A mature soul upbringing may find a

---

3 Rescue Remedy is a homeopathic formulation made from flowers. Available at health food stores, it is useful in countering fears and smart to keep among the first aid supplies.

(normally) calm individual yelling, gesticulating, and spouting off feelings. When the outside world seems suddenly horrifying, even the most mellow old soul is likely to slide back into an in-shock, instinctive place, for awhile. Falling into any of these levels is not bad, though because they all feel so wretched, they can't be called optimal.

The advantage of having an intellectual grasp on how consciousness slides around the soul age scale is that it allows for a quick analysis. You can see where you or the neighbors are caught and take appropriate action.

WHAT IT IS

Your sense antennas pick up a perceived threat to your well-being and suddenly you are zapped with fear and very alert. Fear makes you pay attention to what seems to be threatening you. In the body, this radar originates at the tip of your spine, in the first chakra area, but can quickly cloud your entire energy field.[4] Soon, neither you nor your world looks or feels as bright. Fear ignites all the unresolved issues you carry, from this life and others. While it always starts at the base of the spine, fear may be experienced elsewhere as flutters, a pounding heart, the tight ball in your stomach, the heaviness in your chest, a tight throat, or a blinding headache. It can make you freeze, or aggress, or run and hide.

The first chakra, your instinctive center, is a library of information dedicated to helping preserve your body and insure physical survival. This memory bank contains permanent past-life information, often stored because of trauma, as well as present-time survival information. It contains the "Watch-out!" messages picked up from your family and culture and experiences.

When anything happens now which resembles, however remotely, a traumatic event from the past, your instinctive center initiates its red alert, pumping adrenalin to make you react instan-

---

[4] Chakras are the non-physical energy vortices that act as communication links between body and essence. There are seven main chakras, all lined up along the spine from the coccyx to the crown of your head. *Wheels of Life*, by Anodea Judith, is an excellent book about the chakra system.

taneously to the perceived threat. While the first chakra keeps you from danger, it does so by releasing adrenaline which quickens your reaction time and has, at the very least, helped you to avert automobile accidents. Remembering what your body feels like after a close call will help you understand the toll these first chakra reactions take on your physical vehicle.

Living in a transforming world is exciting. Physical bodies, though, are conservative; they like predictability. If your instinctive center is pumping adrenalin, even at low levels, you'll start to feel like rubble inside. Prolonged anxiety is incredibly wearing and ultimately hurts you very much. This is one big reason why it's necessary to keep clearing fear as it comes up.

The pure vibration of fear is leaden — no light, no hope, no fun, somber, dense, and very limiting. Fear makes you feel small and insecure. How could it not drag you down? And then, adding insult to injury, it will bring up the progeny you'd rather ignore — those shoved-under-the-rug, but still pesky personal issues such as feelings of abandonment, loneliness, powerlessness or vulnerability or perhaps fear of failure or even fear of self-expression. So the good news is that as the events of the decade confront you, you will also be clearing away your underlying issues, processing the old personal stuff you have carried around for decades — or lifetimes.

GETTING THE MESSAGE

If you don't release fear you paralyze your life energy. How to let go? The first action we suggest is give this instinctive center message some respect. Thank it for warning you, for showing you something that you need to beware of. Ultimately, you want neither to resist nor dwell on these fear messages, but rather to acknowledge their value. Aim to interpret this communication as clearly as you can. Study the message. Don't just force away the negativity — or give in. And don't bottle it up either; that is asking for sickness. You want to see the truth and reality of a situation so you can deal with it optimally. Then you are empowered.

Should you be having trouble getting the message, you might want to do a short visualization. Put yourself into a relaxed, meditative state. Pull your inquisitive psychic energy inward and let go of the world. Listen to a relaxation or meditation tape if you need support in letting go of the jangles.

Become aware of your instinctive center, that energetic ball of energy at the base of your spine. Acknowledge it and then, in your imagination, bring that ball up to the level of your mind so that you can take a look at it to see what is there. You will become aware of a feeling or image, perhaps you will hear words. Stay with what is happening for a minute or so and see where it leads into your life now.

Quickly write down what happened before it becomes obscure. Getting and keeping first chakra information conscious is often tricky in the extreme. It may be easier to work with a friend who can lead you through the process, keep asking questions and keep you focused. You may feel like you made everything up or that you didn't get any help. Looking at these stored first chakra patterns and messages is always difficult. After all, this thick old sludge pool of stuff is not physical; neither is it right here, right now. On top of that, the instinctive center tends to feel taboo, like an energetic hot potato. What it stores are not your proudest moments or highest thoughts. This area feels different than hanging out at your seventh chakra all close to God, the angels and your higher self. However, on your road to wholeness, it is necessary to make friends with your first chakra too. In fact, its inescapable.

FINDING THE LIE....AND YOUR TRUTH

The next step in releasing fear is to find the lie. Fear messages are always all-out assaults to get you moving, but they aren't all-out truth. Yes, maybe you feel boxed in by new circumstances, anxious, as if you may die without job security, but actually you are in no immediate danger. It's possible that life may change tomorrow and be better than before.

Or, perhaps the fear is that you won't be able to put food on the table for your children. The truth may be that even though economic and environmental conditions are worsening, you can still provide the basics. You can grow food if need be and request help and protection from the devic world.[5] Furthermore, this is not the thirteenth century, you are not a hapless peasant whose children must beg and steal. Release your urgency.

The next step is to declare for yourself what is true. A powerful affirmative statement, one which you would dearly love to be true, is better than a negative such as, "I am not in any danger now". How about, "I handle life's changes beautifully." Or, "I trust life and grow from my challenges." [6] Affirmations are short, positive statements which boost and expand you and help you flourish. While you are in the process of change, your mind can cling to affirmations instead of becoming wild and fearful. "I am protected and soothed by angels." Write affirmations twenty to thirty times until you begin to feel peace. Alternatively, use a second piece of paper to list all the negative, can't-do, disaster chatter your mind throws up. Then write the affirmation again and listen. Does it sink in? Or is your negative mind still spewing out arguments? If so, write out all that negative alarm until their is no more and the mind relaxes again; then try the affirmation again. Repeat the process until the affirmation starts resonating through your body/mind with no fight. Write it a dozen times and enjoy. Burn or shred the negative list with an air of finality. Tomorrow, write your affirmation again and listen. If that can't-do voice is still grinding away, put it down on paper as before. It will give up more quickly on the second day. Soon you will be enjoying the expansive feel of your affirmation in your body.

LETTING GO
The last step is to let go. Give that first chakra a sense of relief. Remind yourself you can release that quaking, uncomfortable energy, instead of doing the "normal" thing, clutching tightly to it.

---

[5] See any of the various books about the Findhorn Gardens or Machelle Small Wright's about her Perelandra Gardens.

[6] Louise Hay's books are filled with affirmations.

Letting go means opening the chakra and allowing it to drain. This feels a bit like relaxing this area and letting excess energy fall down towards the center of the Earth where it can be healed.[7]

It is quite ethical to permit this negative, fear energy of yours to drain into the Earth. The Earth may be burdened to a breaking point by physical pollution, with ecosystems no longer able to clean and renew themselves, but it is wholly capable of recycling psychological energy, negative as you want to make it. When you have a body, you are inextricably linked with the Earth and can look to it for support.

GROUNDING

The final part of the fear-releasing process is to imagine a small cord with an anchor on it dropping down from your first chakra and being magnetized towards the center of the Earth. At the core of the Earth, imagine hooking this line onto rocks or energy grids, whatever you feel is there. For healing purposes, it is best to visualize the center of the Earth as cool, safe, caring and very stable (as opposed to molten red and devilish). You might like to visualize the center of the Earth as Goddess energy, powerful, good, giving, and as softly radiant as pearls. It is High Being energy, like Christ, or Buddha or Krishna, but slightly different because it comes from within the planet. This is what you want to relate to. With this anchoring cord pulled taut, you feel more secure and excess or negative energies can travel down the cord to the Earth's center.

When you are first creating a grounding cord, it is likely to feel cumbersome, and silly; hard to visualize or feel, much less keep in place. But as you work with it, the whole process becomes easier and will start to feel very right. When you have a body, which is now, keeping that cord there all the time is a highly useful habit to acquire.

An anchoring cord is actually a normal part of the healthy body's energy patterns; it is a natural occurrence, usually quite un-

---

7 See exercise at the end of this chapter.

conscious. But this energetic connection to the planet is something that tends to disappear when a culture gets overly intellectual, as in the U.S., Canada, Japan, or Northern Europe. Then, you must consciously connect. Being grounded helps keep your body healthy; it helps you relate to nature and maintain a sense of security in the world. Grounding keeps your head out of the ozone and you out of trouble. Plus, by pulling Earth energy up into your body, you help manifest the physical things that you want.

Is it going to be harder to root down into the Earth when the Earth feels untrustworthy? You bet! At those points in time, it is useful to imagine some protection around your cord so that you don't soak up the uneasiness present in the Earth's crust. The core will always feel stable; the axis could shift fifteen degrees and the core energy is still going to be secure, nurturing and comfortable.

Should you care to do some Earth healing, send loving vibrations to the Earth through your cord. When the ground feels uneasy, this is a wonderful thing to do. Instead of pulling in uncomfortable vibrations, you send out peace, love and stability. Hardly anything is more unnerving than feeling the Earth is out of control. If the Earth is suddenly not dependable you wonder what is. Sending love out to the Earth through your grounding cord will help you get beyond fear and be rebalanced more quickly.

GAIA AND GOD

Earth is an unusually beautiful planet. The brightness and diversity of nature is stunning. The spirit of the Earth, increasingly referred to as Gaia, can be perceived easily in your tuned-in moments away from the city. Gaia is the gorgeous surface of the planet you all enjoy, but also the heart of the Earth. Merging with nature and absorbing the wonder happens more often and spontaneously with a grounding cord. Having this conscious sense of connection can lead towards greater inner peace.

Keeping the energetic link open between the seventh chakra and the Tao, your guides and higher self is a piece of cake for most old souls. You do this naturally. The difficulty for older souls is that typically the upper chakras are too open and active to be in balance with the lower ones, which are often ignored, sometimes to the degree that earning a decent living becomes difficult.

It is every bit as crucial to be connected to the heart of the planet, the Earth, as it is to be connected to the heavens. Because access to the Earth is gained through the lower chakras, which have been too typically deemed low or unimportant, this link is often lost. Humans are more powerful and happy when relating to both body and spirit. Conscious lifelines down into the Earth as well as up to the Tao are recommended. Especially in difficult times, it is worth the effort to heal your instinctive center and get in good relationship with the Earth.

ONE OUNCE OR LESS

We offer another inducement for making friends with your instinctive center. It is always with you: all its unresolved issues occasionally act up, until healed in this or a future lifetime. When you die, the emotional, intellectual, and moving centers die right along with the body. But the instinctive center, as a pattern of energy, goes with you. Where essence goes, the instinctive center goes; as essence pulls out of the body at death, it pulls the instinctive center with it. The body then weighs nearly an ounce less. Your essence will plug it into your next body like a silicon chip into the memory bank of a computer, insuring that you carry on with all the issues and fears you've accumulated.

NOBLE COURSE OF ACTION

Fear is a challenge. Know that some heroism is being called for, maybe big, maybe not, but we think it heroic to keep handling your fears and moving towards positive action. You will develop courage and discipline as you dauntlessly continue to heal apprehensions.

Dropping worry or panic for even one moment is better than never getting separate from fear. It is akin to stopping mental chatter for even a few seconds as you meditate. Benefits accrue from even those small initial moments of peace. Clearing fear from the body during times of great transition can be as momentous an ongoing process as clearing chatter from the mind with meditation.

Dealing consciously with inner issues allows parents to be stabilizing factors for their children. The children then are more solid sources of support for their friends. A balanced, happy person has a ripple effect that allows others to relax their own first-chakra fear issues. Conversely, one person's anxiety can ignite the first-chakra reflexes of many. Your instinctive center (first chakra) is quick at sensing others in fear, whether they are consciously aware or in denial. Frightened people affect others greatly by their vibrations alone, but then, so do balanced, loving old souls. (One more reason to be grounded: like dogs that give you more trouble when they sense fear, humans may too, especially the young souls looking for an edge.)

SADNESS AND GRIEF

When the Earth is unsteady, your whole life can feel insecure. Sadness creeps into the body and personality when your hopes and expectations are dashed. Sadness is a sign you are attached to life being one way, your way. It makes you droop and stoop and whine. You need to let go. The late 90s will be insistently pushing you to be prepared to change everything and anything to flow with the times.

When you lose a person you love to death, you grieve; you are tremendously sad, inconsolably sad. When you feel you are losing everything — your way of life and many people in it — the finality of so many separations weighs heavily. Sadness and depression prepare the way for eventual acceptance of your losses. Grief tends to come in waves, inundating you with gloom, heaviness, sadness. Then it lifts, allowing in a little light, tentative, but present. Just when you think maybe grief has gone away, another wave comes, usually not quite so strong, but nibbling away at any ability to celebrate life.

There isn't much to do about grief but be with the experience, the sorrow and melancholy, anguish and gloom. It comes and goes, and one day it lifts and is gone. You will be changed.

Sadness and grief will be two basic responses to the surprises and blows of the next twenty years. Sadness and grief arise because you can't have it your way, because living means losses, and because you can't control the world. As you go through these emotions, you clear the air and melt the rigidity that says life must be on your own terms. Cry, sing the blues, regret life, let loose, complain, wail, and wallow. Enjoy your "tantrums" and the sadness will gradually let you go. Avoid and suppress these unhappy emotions and you'll go gray and stay depressed. As you move through sadness and grief, you come out lighter, clearer, stronger.

SELF-CARE IN DARK TIMES

Gift yourself. There are many ways to nurture yourself. Sitting in front of a fire gives peace and steadiness. The element of fire (safely contained) is exceedingly soothing to the first chakra and to a body having survival worries. Fire is like a doorway linking you with all that is ancient on the planet. Red wine and home brew nourish body and soul too. Sing, chant, dance and make music; all are healing. Invite your friends and build some wonderful fires and evenings. Put that companion animal in your lap.

Bring out your humor and put yourself in the vicinity of those who make you laugh. Value those who can disengage from misery long enough to find the funny side. Comic relief is always healing, and oftentimes it gives needed perspective.

Food and drink can give a sense of security and comfort. However if you overdo, you go unconscious and back to the discomfort of square one. Be aware of your own comfort foods and use them as consciously as you can. Some people drown themselves in pizza, while others immediately head for sweets; creamy childhood memories pull others towards ice cream, macaroni and cheese, or mashed potatoes and gravy. Be mindful. Getting comfort from substances can present problems. You've got to do your processing, your inner work, and you can't do it in oblivion. So use food and drugs with care. In fact, eating well and cleanly will maintain balance and strength most easily. Walking, cycling, jogging, dancing, yoga, tai chi, and aikido all help maintain power and centeredness in your body/mind.

Wake up early and greet the new sun and the new day. Find a good viewing spot and watch the sunset. Walk a scenic path. Bask in light of the full moon. Take time to smell the flowers, the grass, and the air. Go to the park and use the swings. Take a bath by candlelight. Burn rose incense. Bake bread. Ask a special friend to read you a story. Count your blessings and release the experience of the day as you prepare for sleep. There are many, many ways to nurture yourself, but you have to make them happen.

EATING FOR HEALTH

Bodies are very different from each other, unique in what they need and in what they don't process well. Because these times are emotionally trying and because of assaults from ultraviolet radiation, two well-known immune system downers, we think it important to mention a few things about food.

Number one: prepare and eat your food with love. Any food then becomes more agreeable to your body and more supportive for it.

Number two: the healthiest way to eat, for a large majority, low on the food chain. This means eating a variety of whole grains such as rice, barley, wheat, rye, and millet plus a variety of beans and vegetables, and the occasional bit of animal protein. Try to use daily a fermented or cultured product like yogurt, soy sauce, miso, tempeh, kombucha, sauerkraut, or pickles. Eat seasonal fruits at separate times from other foods. A diet like this does amazing things: It puts little strain on your body; gives lots of energy; gets rid of cravings fairly quickly; helps you maintain balance and calm; and keeps your immune defenses alert and strong. If you are having trouble fending off an illnesses, consider eating along these lines.

Periodic cleanses are also helpful.[8] Existing for a few days on only dilute fruit juices or an alkaline vegetable-miso broth, resting, and using a ground psyllium seed preparation to keep your bowels moving will go a long way toward getting toxic debris out of your body and help you maintain a high degree of health.

NATURE'S HELPERS

Gemstones and minerals are part of nature's bounteous gift to humans. All exert a positive, beneficial effect on a person in contact with them. Appropriate stones can make life flow more easily. You can grow faster and more comfortably under their influence.

For better or worse, your environment always affects you. Rocks and gemstones are particularly potent parts of the human environment. Stones can help you maintain balance in your life and assist you to work effectively on the parts of your personality or life that cause you trouble. The strongest effect usually comes from wearing stones, either on the skin or in a pocket. You don't need to be particular over which chakra or on what finger you place these stones. They will fill your energy field with their gift regardless of their starting point. Larger chunks of minerals placed in a room gradually fill up the space with their energies and contribute vibrationally to the room's occupants.

What follows are some generally easy to find minerals advantageous in hard times.[9] Choose the ones you are attracted to, always opting for what draws you. Sometimes it's the dazzling green gem, and sometimes the simple mottled-brown rock.

Freezing any stone (once a week if it is getting high use) will help keep it energetically fresh. Overnight in the freezer usually does it. The process doesn't disturb your food; the stone contracts with the cold and when defrosted, releases exogenous energy it may have picked up. Bathing stones in sea salt and water and leaving them outside in the sun and moonlight renews and pampers

---

8 Check with your health professional first.

9 An excellent resource book: *Michael's Gemstone Dictionary,* David and Van Hulle.

them. A gem which is on your finger or your in pocket is a thousand times more likely to become drained, clogged, or exhausted than a stone left in its natural setting. So, give your helpers a break and keep them energetically clean.

GEMSTONES

Shells of all kinds, including mother of pearl and abalone, plus bone, ivory, flint, and petrified wood are the basic calmers of anxiety, worry, and survival fears. They are grounding, and give the sense that everything will work out in the long run.

Rose quartz assists a person to stay aligned with essence. For those among you who tend to space out, this stone will gently help keep your essence in your body and your feet on the ground. It also helps heal the heart.

Leopard skin agate and black obsidian, both widely available, inexpensive, and strong in effect, are calming, healing, and very helpful for dealing with deep emotional impacts. Both help you identify your instinctive terrors so that you can conquer them. Black coral is also a major healer of anxiety and survival-oriented fears. It too can help you to see your issues clearly so that you are able to handle them with more ease.

Blue aventurine keeps the first chakra, and the feet, open and unblocked so energy can flow through unimpeded. Red calcite allows negative emotions to drain more easily from the body. Moonstone inspires you and gives the feeling that anything is possible. An ancient Wiccan full moon rite is to face the moon, humbly and receptively ask for inspiration, put a moonstone in your mouth, and open it to the moonlight for a few minutes. The stone then goes under your pillow to dream on until the next full moon.

Green jade, well-loved in Asia where lives often require some stoicism, creates a mood of tranquility and helps the wearer emanate a calm peacefulness. Gray and brown jades drain excess energy from agitated chakras, allowing them to rebalance. This is especially useful when you are feeling jammed up with a new surge of energy coming to the planet.

The lace agates — blue, white, and lavender — all create the secure, strong feeling that as new situations arise, they can be handled. Even very stubborn people are helped to be more flexible, encouraged and assured that life won't collapse into something overwhelming.

Pearls, sugilite, malachite, and granite all balance all the chakras. Pearls have the virtue of enhancing wisdom. Sugilite facilitates receptivity to higher wisdom and is an excellent channeling stone. Malachite increases loving tolerance and beautiful, balanced feelings in the body. Granite paves the way to a direct connection with heaven and Earth because it is supportive of the first chakra and the seventh.

Gemstones and minerals can't do your work for you, but they are tools which help you grow in the directions you choose. In a body, it only makes sense to take advantage of these benign helpers that give so easily and freely of their energies.

MORE GROUNDING

You ground yourself with an energetic cord which roots you into the Earth. It is also important to ground yourself physically, psychologically and spiritually.

You ground yourself physically by taking care of your body and health. You exercise, eat well, and groom yourself. You also ground yourself physically by taking care of your space, keeping it orderly and clean, and by keeping your plants and animals happy and healthy.

You gain psychological grounding through your commitment to grow, your dedication to cleaning out fears, angers, past hurts, sad stories, and unhappiness. You also gain psychological grounding by prioritizing so that all parts of life get attention and time. Life has a richer texture when work and play, time alone and relationships, entertainment and service are balanced.

Spiritual grounding comes from slowing down enough to touch in with that which is absolute. You get it many places: from reiki, yoga or tai chi, from spiritual and metaphysical books, from meditation, or from church ritual or pagan ceremony. What matters is that you take the time to find the forms that help you to touch in with the absolute and timeless.

Years like these will push you to transform yourself simply to avoid suffering relentlessly. You will do best by staying calm and releasing urgency, by noticing and letting go of attachments (stocks, weather, lifestyle), by turning inward and upward to keep your vision clear, and by making yourself useful in your community.

EARTH MEDITATION

This is a grounding exercise, for daily use until you feel yourself grounded most of the time. For many westerners, this will happen after a month or so. We are presuming that most of you know how to get quiet, relax your breathing, and alter your consciousness slightly.

To do this exercise, either lie or sit. If you are sitting, keep your back fairly straight. Since this exercise is lengthy, it is best to record it for yourself. Read the words into your machine while you are in a slightly altered state. Then, you have it to play back whenever you want.

> First of all take a few slow breaths through your nose. Enjoy the exhalations, breathing out softly through your mouth. Breathe slowly, begin to feel yourself relaxing. Let your body start to get heavy; feel your weight in the chair or against the floor.
>
> Now, become aware of the top of your head. Open your crown chakra by allowing this area to relax. The top of your head may feel warm as you relax and open. You may see light there, shimmering white, or silver and gold. Keep breathing. Allow yourself to feel the connection to your higher self, to your soul. Ask your soul to make the connection stronger. Feel the love. Bask in it.
>
> Now, move your consciousness to the first chakra at the base of your spine. Take a few breaths being aware of the first chakra and still keeping the crown chakra open. Breathe in. Feel like you are breathing in through the first chakra. When you exhale, feel your breath going right through the first chakra area and stimulating this ball of energy. You may notice the luminous red color. Breathe in again through the chakra, hold the exhalation

momentarily, and then breathe out through the chakra. Do this several times. Soon you will be able to feel the vortex of energy there. As you breathe into any chakra, its energy becomes more coherent and vital.

Keeping your consciousness on the first chakra, imagine dropping a little cord from it towards the center of the Earth. This cord is going to anchor you to the Earth's nurturing energy. Keep your chakra loose and relaxed as you let the cord sink into the center of the Earth. Let your cord quickly be pulled towards the center of the Earth. You are now vitally connected with your planet. If the cord you sent down is narrow, like the size of a pencil, experiment by expanding it to the diameter of a garden hose. See what that does to the energy. Again, secure it tightly into the center of the Earth. Be aware of the magnetism between your first chakra and the center of the Earth.

Now, if you wish to let go of all that is negative, unde-sired, or unhealthy in your body, imagine a giant vacu-um in the center of the Earth. Turn on the switch and let it cleanse you by pulling out all that is negative or outdated. Take a few deep breaths while this is happen-ing. Keep your first chakra area relaxed and open. Let all that is negative and uncomfortable be released to the center of the Earth. Thank the Earth, acknowledge it. Ask your higher self to place light into those newly empty areas of your body. Breathe in the light and let it circulate, glow and be absorbed by your body.

If you wish at this time to journey to the center of the Earth, again place your consciousness at your first chakra. Begin moving your consciousness slowly down the cord through earth, through rocks, through water, through caves of rose quartz and amethyst. Follow your cord into the center of your planet.

Be aware of how deep you you have gone, how peaceful you feel. Let yourself be nurtured by the Earth. Ask it to nurture you, to give you love, to feed you love. Keep breathing; take a minute or two to enjoy and absorb the nurturing you are receiving. The center of the Earth always feels peaceful, it is always calm and nurturing. You can renew your spirit here and your body. This energy is very good for your body. When you are ready, bring your consciousness back up your cord, through the Earth, back into your body.

Notice your cord and make sure it is still well connected to the Earth's center. You can then swim, jog, ride in cars, motorcycles or airplanes and still have your grounding cord connected. In fact, you will always be safer for it. If your cord is not pulled tight, pull it tight now. Notice how that feels. Give your cord an earthy color, green, ocher, gold, red. Make it shimmer, make it alive, it will keep your body happy and well-nourished.

If you wish, bring this light up into your abdomen. Fill your abdomen with this light. Now, bring the light up to your third chakra, your navel center, and then into your heart chakra at mid-chest level. Bring Earth energy up into your heart and let it stream out — direct it to all the people you love, to your house, your projects, the people in your town and world. It is a beautiful energy. Let more come into your body and stream out your heart. Run that Earth energy through. This is a very healing energy.

Now be aware of your crown chakra. Allow it to gently open while you keep your first chakra open also; let your entire spine be filled with the light streaming in from above and below, from both chakras. Let these energies blend in your heart. Feel yourself magnificent, glowing with light. Ask for inspiration, for clarity, for healing, for all you want. If you would like to sit and bask in this energy, take some time now.

When you are ready to come back to your day and your life, thank all your helpers. Ask that your chakras be balanced and made appropriate for daily life. Your energy has been very far out in the universe; draw it all back to you. Draw your energy to you from in front of you, behind you, above and below you. You are refreshed, back in your body and ready for life. Enjoy your wonderful day.

NINE

The Mending
Fulfilling Your Soul's Purpose

Everything that lives,
Lives not alone, nor for itself.
—William Blake

Spiritual growth may be measured
by a decrease of afflictive emotions and an
increase of love and compassion for others.
—Chagdud Tulku

WORLD SERVICE

Love is our greatest impetus for channeling information through to you on the physical plane. Sharing information about universal patterns and dynamics is also a form of service for us, one which rewards by furthering our own growth. Service to others always carries a bonus for the doer. It is your service which will help change people, the planet and yourself.

Prepared with information and awareness, you can remain more centered during these upcoming changes, giving a better chance to calm and stabilize communities and nations. As individuals you are powerful in where you choose to put your energy, in what you promote.

One intention of our work is to expand boundaries of consciousness so that you can become more active and empowered in the world, less reactive to it. Human consciousness is changing to be sure, and nearly of its own accord, but to mend the Earth and keep the best scenarios, action is required to reshape politics, economics, business and technology. The thinking of the average man, woman, and government is evolving. Life is being reshuffled: Your individual energy and contribution over the next ten years can make a tremendous difference to the outcome. Many have the internal sense that you are part of the new surge of world servers: your inner voices bid you to heal the planet. But then, the job looks overwhelming and your resources feel ridiculously small. Another reason for sharing this material is to give you the solid confidence to forge ahead into the areas of life you would like to see renewed, reformed or re-birthed, knowing they are yours "to fix."

While the business-as-usual machine is still steaming along with momentum on its side, changing course is laborious. But daily the old system grows shakier and more vulnerable. Soon, the world will be more open to your point of view, fresh insights, ideas and projects, open in a much more generous way than now. Your intent and actions can suddenly make interesting, influential differences.

Share your life. Support people, let them support you. Help heal the planet together. Associations of people with common purposes and ideals enhance each individual's energy and have a powerful (and faster) impact on the world. When you choose to work in groups, be clear about keeping your integrity intact. Remain true to your deeply held values, speaking up for them when necessary. Mature souls, especially, can be subject to intense, blinding idealism; an old soul's value may lie in staying calm and creating tolerance for diverse points of view. Push positive change forward while healing polarized, right/wrong positions. Do this with logic and clarity, do it with feeling and love, and do it with energy work and visualization. Focus on bringing forward the higher selves of all concerned.

To participate at high levels in the outside world, stay in touch with your inner world, your essence. Continue to heal your past as you heal your present. Ask your higher self to give you light; ask your spirit guides for healing, love, and strength. Sense the divine in the Earth. You have rituals to greet change in the seasons; create rituals to greet change in your life. Don't miss out on revels and good deep belly laughs. Remember the simple ways to keep yourself fresh and inspired through these times. If you grow too involved in the rush of events to be still and at one with your essence, then you lose power, effectiveness — and the beauty in your life.

INSPIRED YEARS

A sense of inspiration and emotional connectedness will be worlds easier to find during the mid-90s, especially noticeable when these times are compared to the 80s. By late 95, the ability to act to produce the change you desire should be easier. Moving and shaking won't seem so far out of your range!

A very unusual grouping of "higher-centered" years will occur between 93 and 97. As we see it, every year has a centering focus, a personality, a character, or hub around which people work, feel, and process during that particular solar energy period. At the basic level, a normal year carries either an intellectual, emotional, or moving focus (just like most people do). Everybody, no matter their personal centering, will also be experiencing life through that year's particular lens.

About four times a century there comes an instinctive centered year, a catch-up year when all the uncomfortable stuff that's usually swept under the carpet of awareness surfaces. You feel mired, stuck, uncomfortable. Finally you manage to tackle your issues, surrender, process, heal, fix, or release, whatever is appropriate. This process occurs in groups and political entities of all types too. These instinctively-centered years are usually sticky and unconscious in feel, no one's idea of a good time, except by the end, you, and your social institutions, by extension, are somehow unburdened, refreshed and clearer. The last was 1989, the next 2014.

Even more sporadic and rare than the instinctive years, are higher-centered years. The focus then moves to the higher intellect (truth, justice, knowing), higher emotions (love, unity, connectedness), or to the higher moving center (union, awe, beauty). The 90s unusual set of *five* higher-centered years in a row is aimed at supporting and boosting consciousness by giving humans higher, finer energies to work with. When life is perceived from the higher centers there is no separation; you and the flow of life are one; you and others are one. Old and mature souls especially enjoy that sense of oneness, and tend to feel uplifted, inspired, and happily expansive. Young souls tend to ignore, as best they can, these higher centers and states. They like to play with the energy of separation and thus do not particularly want to see all life as a cozy, interrelated unit.

In years so strongly influenced by higher thoughts, feelings, and actions, people, especially if they meditate or commune in some way, will more easily be lifted into expansive, beautiful states of consciousness. So for these five years, and continuing on to some extent, you may more frequently experience the beautiful feelings of idealism, love, and heartfelt compassion for others (or be so pained by the lack that you are motivated to change). At the very least, you and society will be searching for bottomline truths about how to handle life. Family values are bound to receive a boost and violence the critical analysis it deserves. You will likely find yourself cultivating and enjoying more tender connections with people. Perhaps you will be feeling a desire to add order, harmony, or beauty to your environment. You may find yourself slowing down, living more simply, and taking some new paths.

THE MENDING

PERSONAL TUNE-UPS

If these years do not feel glorious, or even easy, for you, you may be wondering why. First of all, these energies can be turbulent as they come in. This makes for wear and tear. You may feel worked over and grumpy if you are not making adjustments in your life or have been trying to keep change at bay. The price for not following your intuitional flow is a bit higher with these energies.

When you can't internally match the new energy frequencies, it is often because kernels of resentment and fear are still in your being and need to be cleared. These intense new energies have a way of drawing everything that isn't light to the surface, and into your face. What happens is that the dingy, dirty, and murky bubble to the surface for you to encounter, heal, and release. It is uncomfortable work your ego would be thrilled to sidestep, but in these high-energied years the darker parts of yourself become trickier to dodge and deny. This string of higher-centered years will push you to clean and shine your temple, within and without. Ironically, having five higher-centered years in a row makes the situation more difficult to handle, requiring, as it does, a more thorough, ongoing clean-out. Remember, for a moment, where you were mentally, emotionally, and spiritually in 92. You have since been pushed toward total transformation. Though it may take the remainder of the decade to fully absorb the light "shocks" of this period, you probably are quite transformed already!

Since these energies ebb and flow unevenly, occasionally coming in great surges, your physical body may have periodic difficulties adjusting. The nervous system takes the brunt of the changes; you can feel quite ragged as it struggles to adjust. Take the hint to detach and make space for spirit. Don't run faster: Breathe. Meditate. Garden. Ground the energy through your body into the Earth. Be willing and glad to take the light in, be receptive, but then ground it to the planet, share it with the Earth. Let the Earth absorb this light and draw it from you. That way you get to enjoy the energy, you help ground it to the planet, and you don't overcharge.

UPCOMING CHANGES

SOCIAL TUNE-UPS

While you are performing your tune-up, society will be doing the same, looking for bottomline truths, examining what justice means and how to get more of it. Healing social disorganization and violence will be major concerns, as will removing obstacles to people's self-sufficiency. What is the proper way to divide resources, whether education and health, chickens and gasoline, in a city, nation, or world? Happily these higher-center experiences allow people and societies to jump realities, see connections and possibilities, and thus break down mechanical habit patterns from the past and create policies and programs which are outside the lines of the present system.

RESPONSIBILITY

Interestingly, it was this mandate to rethink sloggy and unjust systems that brought both Bill Clinton and Newt Gingrich to the fore. Truth and pragmatism are in the air, an auspicious combination, but people still need to help the clean-outs along. Democratic process had become corrupted with neither deficit spending nor unruly policies producing results. With constituents hungry for real change, politicians are slowly beginning to think outside the lines drawn by lobbyists and tradition.

Individual rights versus individual responsibility, you won't miss hearing these arguments. The debate over property rights versus common rights, community rights and the rights of later generations will similarly escalate. But soon, the mature soul plea for recognition of common rights and the rights of future generations will be assimilated. Some citizens may gracefully release their particular entitlement, governmental gift, break, or price-support when they see others also letting go. There are no shoulds and oughts, only people, you, rethinking how society, business, and your world are governed, aiming to put life on a more just, more sustainable track so the diverse needs of all life forms can be met.

Being responsible means responding competently, tuned into a sense of what is correct and true for you in any given situation.

Being responsible entails being in integrity with yourself and following your intuitions, your inner voice. Sometimes that means surrender, but it can also mean perseverance; sometimes it means taking outward action, other times, going inward. No right, no wrong, just flowing with that inner sense of what is true for you. As you do this your guidance grows clearer, more steady and reliable.

MORE ROOM FOR SPIRIT

One common and fairly effective response people will have to the onslaught of events will be an increased sense of prudence. This need not be fear-based; it can feel like grounded commonsense. People are more frugal already, spending less, especially on frivolous consumables. Many are consciously cultivating life's simpler pleasures. Conspicuous consumption already carries less status and will more quickly than smoking succumb to social pressure. Eventually this means less Wal-Mart, not just less Neiman Marcus, and goodbye I. Magnin.

Prudence inclines you to use forethought and caution and value temperance and centeredness. This heedful, measured stance will enhance your comfort through the 90s. As you ground yourself in this way, your inner responses and actions will come from the deepest aspects of your nature.

Combine prudence with higher-centered times and you have an interesting result: people on the prowl for the heartfelt values needed to truly enjoy and sustain themselves. Young souls will still equate net worth with self-worth, but not as many will be willing to play the game with them. Once the material world has less to offer, it will be easier to relax consumerist values, a relief to let go of addictions to material trappings. And interesting to find worthy replacements.

Possessions can be exhausting; freedom from attachment to them, exhilarating. Self-centered, money-oriented living didn't bring hoped-for satisfaction or happiness. Redoing the living room didn't bring it, neither did the sexy red car with its five-year price tag. Where does one get deep, enduring satisfaction? What brings it? Now it gets down to spirit, people, love, and service; doing work you love, and doing your work with love; pitching in with the projects that call you. You make the beauty in your life. This is the perfect time to uncover what life can be about when it isn't mostly about endless consuming, accumulation, or profit maximization. As you detach from material existence, you make more room for spirit. You haven't relinquished enjoyment of life; you have set yourself free from material snares, an unorthodox move before now in Western cultures.

VALUES CLARIFICATION
Clarifying planetary values is another interesting task at hand. Prudence, along with the incoming desire for balance, creates a new imperative for governments too; don't bungle the money. As it gets perfectly clear that more products and more production aren't necessarily any better for a nation than they are for individuals, new yardsticks will be found for gauging a country's progress. Literacy. Originality. Justice. Genius. Exciting seasonal festivals. Wily use of resources. Supportable populations and birth rates. Non-polluting, sustainable technologies. Harmony. Toss in your favorites.

Right now, a nation can sell off it's forests, claim a big rise in the gross national product, thrill the accountants at the World Bank, and get loans approved, all the while ruining its weather and agriculture and impoverishing its own future. Measuring a nation's health and vitality by increases in gross national product will seem dangerously shortsighted.

Changed circumstances will force governments to prioritize expenditures and spend only on what sifts out as necessary and worthwhile in light of the times. There will be inflamed debates, but one item needing to be near the top of funding priorities will be preservation of the environment. Financing glamorous scientific projects such as billion-dollar super accelerators or space labs and shuttles will probably have to wait. Cleaning up technologies so the planet can heal cannot wait: This means lowering carbon dioxide emissions and ozone depleting chemicals, putting money into solar and wind technologies and getting them up and going. It foreshadows new kinds of cars and transport. It implies finding ways to keep forests healthy and threatened species alive. It may mean innovative immune-system enhancement programs for all living things.

Concern over reckless business practices is likely to reward people who blow the whistle on out-of-integrity industry practices. While whistle-blowers may currently have paper promises of protection and job security, reality falls far short, with their truth-telling acts of courage often causing great personal suffering. With fewer old-style hierarchically managed plants and industries and more worker responsibility and input, whistle-blowers ultimately won't be so sorely needed.

Governments may begin raising money and making moral points by consistently penalizing illegal or careless activities on the part of industry. With your vigilance, puny fines and slaps on the wrist will be fewer, politicians knowing they risk falling into very hot water themselves if they allow even small-scale world endangering behaviors.

ALTERNATIVE TEACHERS

North Americans, with their particular pride in living according to rational principles, have been sadly in denial of the entire non-physical, non-seen world. Well, except for a male god figure, who isn't expected to appear or talk, and Mary, whose sightings and messages are usually considered specious by mainstream churches. Denial of subtle realities is so pervasive that most Americans have no awareness when a recently-dead relative is trying to contact and soothe them. And this is one of the easiest unseen energies to pick up, simply because it is so familiar.

Ha, some say defending the shrunken state of their world, "Non-physical experience is simply hallucination, cheap wish-fulfillment, usually from the hotter, intellectually sloppy nations of the world. Look at the surrealistic novels coming out of Latin America; these are imaginative minds, not rational, not realistic. Like people, many countries are held back by their beliefs in spirits, angels, devils, or gods. Look at how poor, how uneducated, and non-technological they are."

Such blind pride in a limited world view has been fashionable in North America since the arrival of the Puritans. It is far from poverty-stricken hot countries where people remain in touch with the unseen world. Iceland, cultured, educated, and bracingly cold, maintains rich awareness of the spirit world. Japan, brainy, technological and certainly temperate enough to encourage logic, is tuned into dead ancestors and unseen spirit energy in the natural world. Eastern Europe remained awake to the unseen magic of life, despite the recent colorless, rational overlay of communism.

Consciousness is changing rapidly and the unseen becoming real. Glorious near-death experiences are no longer a cause of social isolation, embarrassment, or insanity. Feng Shui masters, who look at and fix the way "energy" runs, or stagnates, in your house, are roaming the country, with even stolid mid-westerners buying their services. People, not a majority, but a substantial underground, are suddenly talking to devas in their gardens and angels at their shoulders. Many want power rocks, power animals, and contact with their spirit guides. The Goddess has been pulled from her burial ground. White-skinned shamans are very present in the alternative presses. All this reflects the major consciousness shift going on as the world, including your culture, shifts away from rock solid materialism towards something fuller and freer.

NEO-PAGANISM

Two new spiritual movements we see as likely to be very impactful over the next decades are shamanism and Wicca, a Goddess centered spirituality. Interestingly, both are nature- and spirit-based to their cores, exactly what the natural world needs if it is to retain more than a token resemblance to its present self. Earth-centered needs are truly great right now. Much of the wisdom and power of Wicca has been carried by women, while much of the wisdom and power of shamanism has traditionally been carried by men. Both present wonderful, deep forms for healing self, relationships, and the Earth. Both are wise to the ways of touching into the wisdom of the unseen worlds.

Shamanism and Wicca tune into the power of nature and human oneness with it. Both powerfully employ ritual to bring balance back into life. Both present strong alternatives to the waning philosophies that teach that man (whether dominant species or sex) owes the Earth and its creatures nothing. What is evolving instead are philosophies and practices which integrate people with the planet and the land, on every level, seen and unseen.

At this point in time, shamanism is connecting with a broader strata of the population. As basic to shamanism as drumming is discovery, adventure, and inner heroic action. Do you wonder that it is more attractive to men than hanging out with a self-help book or taking a workshop on angels? Wicca suffers from bad press (hags, smelly brews, and mean spells; losers who were burned) and from the perceived weakness of being a Goddess centered spirituality. All this, of course, is rapidly changing as women gain equality and a sense of their own worth and power. Hag and crone are beginning to be embraced as powerful aspects of womanhood, instead of shameful aspects of aging. We expect that nature and Goddess-centered spirituality will be a strong part of life in the 2000s, pulling Westerners away from the unbalanced, overuse of the intellect, a blessing all the way around.

STEWARDSHIP

There are many ways to care for the Earth. Making lifestyle changes is one; voicing concerns about activities which poison air and water or shrink forests is another. Protecting rural areas and wild areas is another. Countering spiraling birthrates is basic. Educating adults and children to treasure the land is yet another way to honor the planet. Letters written to local newspapers, TV stations, or national magazines can educate many and bring constructive change. Groups which give voice to your values and concerns can be supported. These are but a few of the many helpful outer actions you could possibly take. Fix the things that irritate you, do what grabs and interests you, for that is your part to do. Release of your feelings of being a sidelined non-important person. Don't let your old soul laziness sideline you either! Ask for opportunities to make a difference; be amazed at the happenings. Your spiritual practices allow you to take in much beautiful energy, but to stay in balance, you must also give it out.

WORKING WITH ENERGY

The spiritual light coming to the planet is in the (sometimes awkward for humans) process of evolving, becoming higher and finer year by year. When you feel the shifts, the surges, the strengthening and uplifting of the fields bring these the new energies into your body willingly and happily. Instead of resisting and being pushed about by the new vibration, consciously steady yourself in it. Ground it through your feet into the center of the Earth. This helps you. As you anchor the light you help to integrate the new field with Earth energies. This helps stabilize both.

If you are one of the many old souls who enjoy working quietly in the background on energetic or meditative levels, we have a few observations and suggestions. Beaming light to those leaders who catch your attention or concern is remarkably useful, more than you might realize especially since one may never know the results exactly.

Anyone can consciously be a channel for powerful Universal light. Bring it into your body through the top of your head, then down into your heart and solar plexus. Send it out through your third eye, throat area, heart or solar plexus (whatever feels comfortable and appropriate) to the intended recipient. It works best to focus the light you send to a high purpose, for instance seeing it as protective, or to be used for courage or flexibility. Bill Clinton, for example, would benefit from light sent to steady and ground him. You can focus the light on bringing out a leader's true essence, so that the higher self can come more fully into play.

You can send light to the people in any nation or area. Beam it to the Russians and see them using the light to heal and bring forth their highest good. Beam it to Bosnia or the Vatican and focus on bringing out the qualities of flexibility and compassion. Send the light of harmony and unity to the entire globe. You do this energetic work with the desire to serve the world and to bring forth everyone's highest good, not ambitiously to stretch your power.

As more decisions are made by group process, in meetings, those of you who don't enjoy asking questions or speaking up with suggestions and opinions, may choose to participate on energetic levels. Consciously channeling light into yourself and anchoring it in the room can help lift even the most contentious atmospheres and encourage creative, enlightened planning.

On one level, these changes are a grand setup to press you into becoming more of the powerful beings you are.

YOUR OWN BACKYARD

On a very personal level, perhaps you are inspired to re-forest lawn and plant bushes the birds like. You then encourage the same cornucopian tree planting in your neighborhood or town. Perhaps you take a piece of land and nurse it back to health, making it as luscious and special as you can. Maybe you study non-chemical, life-promoting ways to garden and grow non-hybrid vegetables and flowers, discovering the beauties of devas in the process. Possibly you find yourself embellishing a particular area with stacks of rocks, shrubs with berries the birds love, and a handmade bench, making it feel like a holy retreat. Maybe you bury quartz crystals which you have blessed to hold a peaceful vibration in highly stressed locations in your town. Perhaps you start that full moon group you always longed for or give parties on the solstices. What are your ways of connecting deeply with the Earth and its peoples? You will want to find them, for therein lies the healing. Each one of you affects events all the time; our suggestion is do it as positively and consciously as you are able.

About the Author

For nearly twenty years, Joya has worked in the healing arts as a vision therapist, a life/death transitions counselor and a nutritional and psychic consultant. She has been channeling since the mid-seventies. She was introduced to Michael in 1984. The last ten years have been dedicated solely to working with Michael and making the Michael material available to interested segments of the population.

Author of the now-classic, refreshing take on human psychology and behavior, *The World According to Michael: An Old Soul's Guide to the Universe,* and a co-author of *The Michael Game,* Joya for several years also wrote the current event column for the quarterly, *The Michael Connection.* Her channeling work now appears in *Spirit Speaks* magazine.

For information about talks, workshops, or personal channeled readings (which can be done by telephone or through the mail), you may write her c/o New Sage Books, P.O.Box 969, Fayetteville, AR 72702.

MORE MICHAEL BOOKS

The World According to Michael
by Joya Pope $10.95
This is the starter book of choice and the one to share with friends.
Explains roles, soul ages, other personality elements,
task companions and essence twins.

Upcoming Changes:
Prophecy and Pragmatism For The Late 90s
by Joya Pope $13.95

Searching for the Light
By Carol Heideman $12.95
Overflowing with clear, practical information and specific
exercises to assist you during this time of transformation.

Tao to Earth
by Jose Stevens $12.95
This book covers the variety of human relationships, the laws
of karma and prosperity, and how a life is planned on the astral.

Earth to Tao
by Jose Stevens $12.95
Covers spiritual growth, the chakras, healing, and
the human relationship to nature.

Michael's Gemstone Dictionary
by Judithann H. David and JP Van Hulle $18.95
A most essential old-soul reference. Describes what happens
to your energy field with over 600 gems or minerals.

The Michael Game $7.95
A collection of articles by Michael students. Topics include
"101 Questions to Ask a Channel", "Confessions of a Walk-In"
and Joya Pope's, "Whales and Dolphins as Sentient Beings".

Parallel Universes
by Emily Baumbach $4.95
"Every time you make a momentous decision that changes your future
from that point on, you create a new parallel universe."
This booklet explains all.

The Michael Handbook
by Jose Stevens & Simon Warwick-Smith $11.95
Basic Michael, very thorough. Lots of tables, graphs
and comparisons. Scholarly types love it.

The Journey of Your Soul : A Channel Explores Channeling and the Michael Teachings
Shepherd Hoodwin $19.95
Intelligent. Highly readable, highly recommended. 448 pages

Loving from Your Soul: Creating Powerful Relationships
Shepherd Hoodwin $11.95
Topics include the nature of love, sexuality, anger, loneliness,
boundaries, listening, finding a mate, alternative lifestyles,
and body image.

Meditations for Self-Discovery
Shepherd Hoodwin $ 8.95
Guided journeys for communicating with your inner self.
Uplifting, imaginative guided meditations. Very special.

Transforming Your Dragons
by Jose Stevens $12.95
A delightful new book about taming your chief negative feature
so that your stubbornness, impatience, self-deprecation, etc.
are no longer blind spot/stumbling blocks.

Michael's Cast of Characters
by Emily Baumbach $ 8.95
Excellent descriptions of how each role, soul age and overleaf
looks on a person. Also contains tongue-in-cheek guide
to the overleaves of over 800 celebrities.

Michael: The Basic Teachings
by JP Van Hulle, Aaron Christeaan & M.C. Clark $11.95
Straightforward, with diagrams, illustrations and additional info
for your data banks. Good body-type illustrations.

Personality Puzzle
by Jose Stevens and JP Van Hulle $9.95
Designed to appeal to the mainstream reader, does not refer to
Michael or soul ages but has great photos and illustrations of roles
and overleaves and very interesting info on how your goals & modes
and attitudes and chief features work together.

ASK FOR MICHAEL BOOKS AT YOUR BOOKSTORE
OR ORDER DIRECT FROM:
NEW SAGE BOOKS   BOX 969   FAYETTEVILLE   AR   72702

⇔ <u>20% discount on 5 titles or more</u> ⇔

Send to:

Name_____

Street_____

State & Zip_____

Title	#Copies	Price	Total
The World According to Michael	_____	$10.95	_____
Upcoming Changes	_____	$13.95	_____
Searching for the Light	_____	$12.95	_____
Tao to Earth	_____	$12.95	_____
Earth to Tao	_____	$12.95	_____
Michael's Gemstone Dictionary	_____	$18.85	_____
The Michael Game	_____	$ 7.95	_____
Parallel Universes	_____	$ 4.95	_____
The Journey of Your Soul	_____	$19.95	_____
Loving From Your Soul	_____	$11.95	_____
Meditations for Self-Discovery	_____	$ 8.95	_____
Transforming Your Dragons	_____	$12.95	_____
Michael's Cast of Characters	_____	$ 8.95	_____
The Michael Handbook	_____	$11.95	_____
Michael: The Basic Teachings	_____	$11.95	_____
The Personality Puzzle	_____	$ 9.95	_____

	Subtotal: _____
20% off for 5 books or more ⇨	Discount amount: _____
	Subtotal: _____
P&H first title $2.00, additional $1.00 each	Postage: _____
AR residents add 7% sales tax	Tax: _____

★Total check or Money Order: _____

Bookstores: Order directly from Bookpeople, New Leaf, Moving Books or Baker and Taylor